Two Lives:

One Autobiography

Two Lives:
One Autobiography

Jim Potter

To order additional copies of this book, contact:
Xlibris Corporation
1-888-795-4274
www.Xlibris.com
Orders@Xlibris.com
20238

About This Book

"Jim, you should write a book." These comments came after I shared specific experiences with acquaintances and they realized my events may be worthy of sharing with more people. I guess the readers will be the judges of the concept.

In addition, due to the tremendous difference between my able-bodied life and my disabled life in terms of physical aspects, I felt a strong desire to expound on the experiences. My intent in describing the medical specifics regarding my disability is not to overwhelm anyone, but to hopefully stimulate AWARENESS of it and possibly some level of UNDERSTANDING. Except for some of the medical terms, which I have tried to describe in simple everyday language, I believe this book is written so that the reader seldom needs the dictionary. Someone once said, "Keep it simple, stupid," which implies that the real stupid one is the one who writes or speaks with words that few can understand.

It is my hope that in the reading of this material a variety of emotions will be triggered in you, the reader. Empathy is a word often tossed around, but true empathy comes only from having the exact experience while being in the same condition as the one with whom you wish to empathize. Maybe you can come close to empathy through the emotions you feel in reading my stories. For a person with a disability, pity and sympathy are of NO VALUE, and false hope that is often given freely generally is very DETRIMENTAL. Positive, realistic encouragement is VALUABLE.

I have included various people by name in this book, and I have left some out. It is not my intent to jilt anyone by omitting them nor to harm or embarrass any of those whom I have included. If I have upset anyone, I am deeply sorry.

Acknowledgments

I thank God for without the episodes of Him sparing my life I would not be here to write this story.

For my parents who brought me into this world, instilled in me a work ethic, taught me that nothing comes easily, encouraged me in athletics and educational ventures and, above all, helped me to learn patience in the face of adversity; I am deeply grateful.

For my teachers and coaches who directed me to be as good as possible in the classroom and in the sports arena, I am thankful.

For those who gave me hope and direction as well as opened new doors for me when the future looked bleak, I thank you.

For those relatives and acquaintances who cheered my accomplishments and tolerated my shortcomings, I thank you for helping me develop a positive attitude.

For those who held back from doing things "for me" and let me learn to do things for myself, I am most deeply appreciative.

For my former wives, Jo-Ann and Micki, who allowed me some experience in being a parent to their children, gave me many enjoyable experiences, challenged me and made me a stronger person and, above all, are still my friends; God bless you both.

For all who have done something to help remove barriers, both architectural as well as attitudinal, I owe you gratitude.

For my friends who encourage me with "How's that book coming?" thanks for keeping me on task.

7

For Jenni Potter whose computer skills made it possible for this manuscript to be in the necessary condition to go to the publishing company, I am very thankful.

For all the doctors, nurses and other health care personnel (especially those who kept me alive in 1966) who have helped me to be as healthy as possible throughout my life, I thank you.

For "Peach" Miller who reviewed a section of this material and gave her honest opinion of it as well as her encouragement during the writing of this book, Thanks.

For the sharing of her experiences of writing and publishing her book, *Shadow of the Mountain,* thanks to Julie Fricker Porter; and for his experience in electronics and photography from which the picture on the front cover was derived, thanks to Troy Porter.

For the inspiration to work through adversity, I wish to thank Lydia, a friend I met at the University of Illinois in 1968-69, who sent a Christmas gift to me in 1969. The gift was *The Family Book of Best Loved Poems* edited by David L. George which included three poems that I have found very valuable to me: "IF" by Rudyard Kipling (a poem that shows us some ways to become a better person), "IT COULDN'T BE DONE" by Edgar A. Guest (a poem that says that we should not say "No" until we try and that we can do it) and "OPPORTUNITY" by Walter Malone (a poem that keeps us mindful that opportunities are all around us and we need to be always open to take advantage of them).

Finally, Thank You to Betty Naimo Rich for the poem, "DON'T QUIT", Robert J. Burdette for the poem, "BROKEN DREAMS" and Charles Dedarich who is credited for the saying (and possibly the poem also) "TODAY IS THE FIRST DAY OF THE REST OF YOUR LIFE."

Chapter One

It was very early in the morning of August 9, 1943 when I entered this sometimes ugly, sometimes beautiful world. Charles W. and Ellen E. (Kahler) Potter were my proud parents who first saw me at St. Joseph's Hospital in Elgin, Illinois, where I was named James Herbert Potter—the "official" name to be with me the rest of my life. After a normal amount of time in the hospital, I joined my siblings, Donald Charles (11-18-37), Shirley Marie (3-4-36) and my parents at our rural home on Sanders Road between Wheeling and Northbrook, Illinois. Memories at an early age are nil probably until age three, but I know from then on for about five years they called me "Jimmy".

There was a huge wheat field across the road from our house which was probably a half mile long and a quarter mile wide to equal eighty acres. In the summer of 1947 I enjoyed watching huge combines harvest the wheat. Soy beans were grown by our landlord or some other farmer who rented the cropland beside and behind the house. A short distance behind the house was a small barn probably used for storage and a "taboo" silo pit. The pit looked so lonely without the stave walls above it or a large barn adjacent to it. The wooden silo walls had previously been blown down or removed manually leaving only a concrete pit wide open to collect water from rain and other things from the wind. The wall was only two feet or less above the ground and thus created a need to satisfy my curiosity. "Jimmy, you stay off that silo wall, you could fall in and drown—no one would find you," dad warned me when I was old enough to be left outside alone. I did lean on the side of the wall and peer over only to see yukky stagnant water darkened with old silage and other things that had blown into it. From that time on I stayed away from it.

WWII was over, but there was still a lot of activity at the Glenview Naval Air Station about six or eight miles to the southeast. It was exciting for me to be outside watching the multitude of planes in the air. There were the planes from Glenview as well as from two small airports in the vicinity. At times small planes flew over doing skywriting—a common one was Coca-Cola neatly scripted in the sky—as a way of advertising products. Another common thrill in the sky was the gradual appearance of a Goodyear Blimp overhead and nearby. I was somewhat hypnotized by it and stood like in a stupor watching it until it slipped over the horizon.

Sometimes in good weather on a Sunday afternoon the family went to a small airport where small planes came down just touching their wheels on the runway and then like a big bird swooped back up into the sky. It must have been some kind of airshow, but it seemed to happen every time we went to the Airport—maybe dad had a secret connection with the pilot! On the way home dad always stopped at a little store and bought Dixie Cup ice cream treats—the little glazed paper cup of vanilla ice cream and a wooden "spoon" for everyone. At five cents each, the whole family could enjoy the treat for a quarter. The same experience would probably cost at least three dollars today.

It was some time around my fourth birthday when I got a big thrill while standing in the front yard. Sanders Road was well known for trucks, cars, bicycles and people walking to get to their destination. But, fear came over me that day as a house was coming down the road from the North!! I instantly ran to the house. "Mom, there's a BIG house coming down the road," I said. "I gotta see this," she replied as we both rushed out to the front yard. Donald and Shirley soon joined us to observe the spectacle. It was my entertainment for a long time as I watched the huge object inch along and the electrical and phone company workers making sure the house didn't take out any of the lines.

Traumatic experiences are a part of most people's lives and I wasn't exempt even at an early age. I was barefooted playing on the north side of the house when suddenly—for some unknown reason—I ran into the orchard just north of the lawn. The direct route went right through the spot where the family trash was burned. You guessed it, stepped right in the ash pile. There was no smoke so there must me no fire. WRONG! A hot, sharp object drove into my foot dead center of the tender part and with terrific pain I hobbled to the house. Mom took me to the local hospital and with her at my side I lay crying on the examination table. There was no anesthesia used as the doctor cleaned the object and dirt out of the wound. THAT was probably the worst pain I ever experienced (at least while conscious). Hopped around on one leg for a few days until it healed and thus had my first experience with a minor "disability". Adversity strikes early in life.

It was about that same time that brother Don found out that traumatic experiences could happen to him too. Dad had brought home a wooden packing crate similar to the container in which a refrigerator or freezer would be transported today. However, it wasn't from an appliance he had purchased because all we had to keep things cold was an "icebox" (an appliance that kept things cold by the owner placing a large block of ice in the bottom of it). The icebox was not replaced until the early 1950's. Anyway, back to the crate, Don's curiosity prompted him to take the crate apart and salvage two of the corner posts. These posts were longer than he was tall, probably made of two inch by two inch pine wood and had wooden pieces attached about eighteen inches from one end. Wow, he thought, these would really make neat stilts and he could walk on them. He turned them so that the ledges were on the inside and stepped up on them. The nine year old walked a few steps smiling proud as a peacock. "I'm walking on stilts," he said and suddenly his smiles turned to tears as his nearly one hundred pound body was too much weight.

The left pole broke at slightly above his waist causing his body to surge left and downward on the left side jamming the jagged wood into his ribcage. The splintered wood was very sharp and went under the skin, glanced off his ribs, emerging from under the skin about two inches above the entry point. It then gave a slight puncture to an area above the exit point. He was most fortunate to not have broken his ribs and/or punctured his lung. He healed up in a fairly short time, but vowed to never try to build and walk on "stilts" again.

Change is inevitable in life and March of 1948 produced the first big one since my birth. Mom's parents, Albert and Hertha Kahler, owned a one hundred twenty acre farm about two miles south of Hillsboro, Wisconsin. This is the farm where my grandpa and grandma Kahler had homesteaded years before and had built the house and other buildings in 1915. My mom and aunt Ora were young at the time and aunt Vila, aunt Nina and uncle Herbert were born on that farm. They all grew up on the farm and in 1945 my grandparents moved to Hillsboro. Uncle Herbert and his wife, Sadie, ran the farm for three years until they moved to Hillsboro. It was then that our family moved to the farm where we lived for six years.

There was one unforgettable event during the trip from Illinois to Wisconsin. The generator on our 1936 Chevy had gone bad toward the end of the trip, so the last few miles were completed at night with no headlights working on the car. The only light was a flashlight mom held out the passenger side window so she could see the edge of the road and continually tell dad how close he was to the ditch. Everything was going fine, though at a very slow pace. Suddenly, mom yelled out, "Charlie, I can't see the ground." That startled me and I got scared. Dad stopped the car and got out to see why there was so much panic in mom's voice. He discovered we were on the bridge over the creek. There was nothing but about a four inch high concrete lip on the side of the bridge instead of a rail. Since we were running the car close to the side of the road, the only thing mom could see with her flashlight was the darkness of the water below the bridge.

Ironically, and unknown to me at the time, that bridge was about one hundred fifty yards from our new home. It was where our private driveway (off the town road) crossed the creek that ran through the lower pasture. Home at last, that "nightmare" was over!

Swinging in our back yard in Illinois

Chapter Two

At birth I was fairly large (over nine pounds) and had normal development of walking and talking at appropriate times. The only unusual thing was an apparently inherited gift of being "good with numbers" at an early age and throughout my grade school days in Arithmetic class. At age four, out of necessity due to my siblings being "too old to play with me", Sam, my imaginary playmate, was conveniently created. Sam and I played cards together—specifically 500 rummy where I dealt two hands, played both of them AND kept score. Somebody taught me that Aces were fifteen points, the ten, Jack, Queen, and King were ten points each and the two's through nine's were five points each. Somehow I knew how to add them and kept score for Sam and myself. Sometimes he won, sometimes I won! Consequently, self-entertainment was learned at an early age without any fancy or expensive toys.

Rummy games with Sam were few on the farm and soon were replaced with chores, fishing and other things for fun when time permitted. Growing older and bigger the chores increased and the fun time became more limited for me.

Shortly after moving to Wisconsin, I was baptized at St. Paul Lutheran church in Hillsboro. The church building was special due to the fact that my grandpa Albert Kahler was one who helped build the structure. With my mother's encouragement, I was nearly always in attendance at Sunday School classes and worship services throughout grade school and high school.

"You're getting to be a big boy now," mom told me on my fifth birthday, "soon you'll be going to kindergarten and meet lots of kids like you." The chill of September was there before we knew it and I soon found myself amid twenty-five or thirty other little, somewhat helpless, children who were totally oblivious to the fact they were beginning their quest for a High School Diploma. Kindergarten was only a half-day (morning) of school where Mrs. Mitchell taught us "Everything we needed to know in life!" The most prominent thing that I learned was that we had to obey the teacher when she told us to lay down on a three foot long and two foot wide piece of blue denim and take a nap—something that I hated!

It was a typical dairy farm where we lived at that period in time. The one hundred twenty acres included about sixty-five of cropland, fifty acres of woods and pasture land and about five acres where the buildings were located. The buildings included a four bedroom two-story house, approximately forty feet by eighty feet barn with stantions for milking cows on both sides of a center concrete driveway, two horse stalls and three calf pens on the bottom floor. The second floor was mostly hay mow with the granary taking up about twenty feet by twenty feet in the northeast corner. A milk house for storing milk and cleaning milking equipment was on the north end of the barn and a silo on the south end. Other buildings included a hog house and feeding area, a chicken coop and feeding area, a thirty foot by forty foot machine shed with machinery repair area and a corncrib off the south end of it. There was also a small eight foot wide garage, a smoke house and an "out" house. Neither of the latter two was used during the six years we were living there, except the outhouse when plumbing problems occurred. The water came from a well, sistern and windmill located some one hundred yards or so partway up the hill to the west of the house. The water pressure was good and was created simply by the gravitational pull that existed.

The "rent" for the farm was paid by us running the farm on "halves" with grandpa Kahler. Each paid half of the bills for the farm operations and each received half of the farm income. The major income came from the sale of milk supplemented by the occasional sale of cows, calves, pigs, chickens and eggs. Both families got their meat for dining from periodic butchering of a hog, a calf, a non-producing milk cow and chickens. When we butchered a hog grandma Kahler had some sort of special recipes that were used to make such things as blood sausage and liver sausage. Wow! Were they a delicious treat—wonder what ever happened to those recipes.

The normal operation on the farm was milking cows after supper, storing it in ten gallon milk cans and placing them in an open tank of cold water in the milk house overnight. The cows were milked early the next morning and then, after breakfast, both batches of milk were taken to either the condensery or creamery in Hillsboro. We did not own a pick-up truck so dad loaded the cans on a small trailer attached to the back of the car and hauled them to the condensery that way.

When school started that kindergarten year for me, I rode to school with dad but had to walk home those two and a quarter miles. One day in the "dead of winter" it was very cold and when school was over I *had* to walk home. (Sometimes someone came to get me if it was real cold). My wonderful teacher helped me get into my bulky snowsuit, boots, mittens and scarf so I wouldn't freeze on the way home. I walked, waddled like a well-wrapped mummy, proceeding with courage to make the trek. Just as I reached the mailbox out on the main road, the two mile mark, I knew there was only a short quarter mile to go. All of the sudden that ugly urge came upon me—in the gut area. "Oh No!" I said outloud. You guessed it—I had to go "poop", #2 if you prefer or have a BM (bowel movement). Even at the age five, I knew there was NO WAY I would ever get all those clothes off in time so I just let it happen! With some warmth in my crotch area and an even bigger waddle in my gait I headed for home scared of the punishment expected but ready "to take it like a man."

I entered the kitchen door and mom met me in the middle of the kitchen floor. "Mom, I pooped my pants," I said starting to cry either from fear or from embarrassment of what was ahead. "Well, let's get them off you," she said calmly as she stooped to unzip the bottom of the right leg of the snowpants. As she pulled the zipper up a small brown marble-like object fell out and rolled a few inches on the floor. At that moment she began to laugh out loud and I smiled suddenly realizing I wasn't going to get a lickin'!! The old saying "Don't make a mountain out of a molehill" can be learned at an early age, but we often forget what we have learned.

The advent of Spring on a farm usually means plowing, disking, dragging the ground and planting crops to be harvested later to feed the previously mentioned animals. This was part of "living off the land". The farm had three main crops—hay, oats and corn. The oats were planted first with alfalfa (hay) seed sown at the same time. The alfalfa grew only a few inches the first year allowing the oats to be harvested off the top of it leaving a full crop of alfalfa for the next year. The corn was planted in late April and in May each year. The alfalfa was the bulk of feed for the cattle in the winter supplemented with "ground feed" (a mixture of oats and corn ground together). The ground feed was also fed to the pigs and chickens along with whole corn and oats. Corn silage also was fed to the cows each night in winter about two hours before the evening milking. The pastureland fed the cattle in summertime along with some ground feed.

During grades one and two at school I rode the bus with Don and Shirley. I learned to read, but was a slow reader and this hampered me the rest of my school days. I excelled in arithmetic, enjoyed science and hated history. I worked hard in English and spelling classes and did well in both of them. As most kids did, I loved recess!!

Developed a hatred for drawing or anything "artistic" in first grade when my teacher jerked me out of my seat one day and swatted my butt with her hand as she looked with disgust at the drawing I had made of a house with a boy and a girl standing out in front of it—you figure it out. I never did. My second grade teacher was Miss Norton; she probably was a good teacher, but many of us "brats" referred to her behind her back as "Miss Snortin'". I continued to do well in arithmetic and loved those flashcards we used for speed in adding and subtraction. Some of us competed for speed as though the fastest one would get some great prize. Guess there was a hidden prize—Phillip Eastman and I were about equally the fastest ones in class. He now has a Bachelor's Degree, two Master's Degrees and a PhD in Mathematics; he is currently a Dean of a large College in a Major University. Where'd I go wrong?

Back at home I was busy feeding calves before and during milking time and sometimes cleaning the cows' teats prior to Don or dad putting the milking machines on them.

We raised a large garden each summer and when old enough to be a "helper" and not a "wrecker" of the plants, I helped with planting, hoeing and harvesting some of the delicious items. Mom did a lot of canning of vegetables, berries and jam. Whenever there was complaining about the work in the garden, mom always reminded us of the good food we would have canned and stored in the basement to enjoy during the wintertime.

The garden was really a great food source for the family. It was located only about forty yards east of the house. It covered nearly an acre and had some great perennials already in full stride. The back side (east side) had a wide strip of raspberry bushes full length of the garden and a wide strip of strawberry plants west of and adjacent to the raspberries. One corner had a large patch of asparagus and another side area had a good bunch of rhubarb plants. The remainder of the garden was planted with vegetables starting on the north end with early harvest ones such as leaf lettuce and early peas followed progressively by later peas, beets, green beans, carrots, bell peppers, tomatoes, sweet corn, cucumbers and finally cantaloupe, squash and watermelon. A large potato patch—usually about a quarter acre—was grown on part of a nearby cornfield.

In addition to this nice garden, there were many wild blackberry and blackcap bushes in the woods to the west. To top that, out near where the driveway came onto the property there was a very nice orchard with about twenty trees with a variety of kinds of apples in full production each year. Granted, the trees had to be sprayed and trimmed, etc., but it was real nice! And, it provided some really good eating during fall and winter. Apple pie, YUM, YUM!

During two or three summers the family raised a "cash" crop of cucumbers in a plot near the potato field. There was a "pickle" factory operating in Hillsboro and the cucumbers were grown, harvested and sold to the pickle factory. The smaller the cucumbers, the higher the price per pound that was paid to us. It was a lot of work for a little money—come to think of it, a lot of things were "a lot of work for little money" during those years—early 1950's.

Age eight and third grade was both challenging and rewarding. The major challenge was learning cursive writing—a skill that was difficult and quite sloppy for me for many years. On the bright side was the regular "start of the new year" height and weight check. One classmate and I were tied for the tallest in the class and I was proud to weigh in at a fairly muscular one hundred three pounds. The classmate weighed a slightly flabby one hundred five pounds and he cried because he thought he would be called a fatty. He had a poor self-image and mine was great. It was about that time in my life that others began to call me "Jim" and most people gave up the more childish "Jimmy" when addressing me. There are a few people who still call me Jimmy today but they are certain individuals who have had mutual respect with me for years.

The horse stalls in the barn were occupied by two "work" horses named Pet and Queen. Work horses were a necessity as we did not have a big tractor like farms have today. We did have an old Allis Chalmers tractor, but by today's standards it was a midget. Thus, the horses were valuable in the cold winters with deep snow. One night dad kept the car in the barn with the warm cows so it wouldn't freeze up. It was fifty-four degrees below zero that night.

The manure had to be cleaned out of the barn on a daily basis as the cows were kept in the barn about twenty-three hours a day in the cold weather. Normally the tractor pulled the manure spreader through the barn driveway; the manure was shoveled into it and then hauled out to be spread on the fields for fertilizer. When deep snow was on the ground, a wooden flat bed with side boards and sleigh-like runners instead of wheels replaced the spreader. The team of horses replaced the tractor. Once loaded with the manure, dad drove the team out to the field and the manure was unloaded and spread by hand with a manure fork, a five or six tine fork used for manure or silage or most anything except hay. The horses were also a "wrecker service" when the car or tractor got stuck in the snow or mud. At times the horses pulled the plow when fields were too wet for the tractor to function efficiently.

Pet and Queen were occasionally ridden for pleasure, mostly by Don in the summer. My experience in horse riding was limited. I rode Queen (the more docile of the two horses) one time with Don leading the horse by the bridle. I held the reins as the horse slowly walked around the farmyard. I didn't care for it and never asked to do it again. Don, on the other hand, would put the bridle on Pet (the wilder one) and ride the horse bareback down the lane (driveway) and around the lower pasture. He had a strange dismount from the horse. Just inside and above the barn door there was a ledge—probably a two inch by eight inch board—and Don discovered that as he and the horse entered the barn he could grab that ledge with both hands and pull up so the horse could run out from under him and on into its stall. One time he did not get a good grip on the ledge and subsequently hit the floor with a thud as the back of his head met the concrete. He doesn't know how long he lay there "out cold", but when he "came to" a massive headache gave him great discomfort. That was the last time he tried that trick! NOW we know why he has trouble remembering things today—or is it the "over fifty" syndrome!

There were two springs up the valley in the neighbor's woods that fed the creek, which ran full length of the lower pasture—a little over a quarter mile long. Toward the lower end was another spring with a wooden box (without a bottom) placed over it. This made a "container" to hold the water at about fifteen inches deep continuously and was excellent for keeping minnows alive in the summer. Just below the spring (in springtime and early summer) there was good-sized beautiful green bed of watercress, which was periodically harvested in small amounts and eaten with lettuce in a salad. Good stuff!

A love for fishing came naturally to me as both my parents and their families were active in this leisure pursuit. It started one Sunday afternoon when Don and I were goofing off down by the "big hole". The big hole was the largest body of water (probably ten feet wide and fifteen or twenty feet long) in the creek and it was formed at the upper end where the water ran from the neighbor's farm through a culvert (under a road to a field) to our farm. During heavy rains the volume of water coming through the culvert gouged out the soil to make the "big hole".

Near the "big hole" were some fairly big willow trees and the right branch made a perfect fishing pole for me. Don selected and cut the branch with his jackknife. It was about one and a quarter inch in diameter at the handgrip area and sloped neatly to about a quarter inch at the tip. It was about five feet long. Back at the house Don tied on a six foot piece of fish line with a small hook attached to the other end. If I had some bait, I was ready to go fishing in the big hole. Angle worms were not hard to find if we had rain recently—just go out and look under a board or plank laying on the ground by the shed or lift up some of the thin layer of straw around the straw stack and find worms. Sometimes we had to dig for them, but always found some.

The creek was not stocked with any fish but was mostly occupied by minnows, crayfish, frogs, leeches and a few suckers. My main focus was catching the minnows without harming them and take them alive to the minnow bucket at the spring. In the spring they stayed nice and lively until the family went on a Sunday afternoon fishing trip. We usually went to Bailey's on the

Lemonwier River just north of New Lisbon, Wisconsin—a twenty-five mile trip. By not having to buy minnows we could afford to pay Mr. Bailey for the right to fish on his property. Mr. Bailey was a fair man and rates were cheap. When dad drove into the yard, Bailey slowly came out to the car, looked at how many people were in the car and then usually said, "Well, five of you, I guess two dollars would be fine." Sometimes he said, "You know, they haven't been bitin' very good—why don't you go ahead and fish and if you catch anything you can stop on the way out."

There were three fishing areas at Bailey's and after driving down a lane you could go to the "left", in the middle called the "slough" or to the "right". Most of the time we went to the "right" where there was more open space up on the level, but the river bank was about four feet high and fairly steep. The area was less swampy and usually had less mosquitoes than the other two areas, but was inhabited by other fisherman more often. Sometimes we had to go through deep water holes in the "road" through pasture to get there. Generally the choice was determined by the number of other people there and we never liked to be crowded—takes all the fun out of fishing trips! The river held northern pike, walleye pike, bass, crappie, bullhead, dogfish, carp, and panfish. On a good day we could catch a few "keepers" and have a couple meals from the catch. Some days in the "dog days of summer" it was so hot the mosquitoes scored more bites than the fish by about a hundred to one! Thus, those times we were miserable and empty-handed on the way home. Sometimes we went to a place called Fish Lake slightly farther away—it was northeast of Bailey's and a backwater leg off the Wisconsin River. We had to pay a bit more there, but sometimes had nice catches of northern pike.

Chapter Three

Nestled in between a few Sunday fishing trips the summer offered a lot of hard work. Early in June was time to start the harvest of first crop hay with the hope that enough moisture was in the ground or would be added with future rains to produce a second crop of hay later in the summer.

The hay was cut with a hay mower pulled by the tractor. The mower had steel cleated wheels that, as they rolled, caused the five foot wide sickle bar to move side to side about three inches. The sickle bar was lined with many razor sharp triangular shaped blades called sections that cut the hay as it was guided between them by the sickle guards, as the mower moved through the standing hay. The guards helped keep larger rocks out of the blades, but smaller rocks (missed during spring rock picking sessions) sometimes got into the blades and broke them causing the mower to leave a narrow strip of uncut hay—lost hay and a mess in the field. "That's why we work hard picking rock from the fields before planting oats," dad told me one day after he had to come back to the shed to put a new section in the sickle bar. "I hit a small rock that should have been picked up," he said in a warning tone of voice. I understood. I had spent many Saturdays and time after school hours helping pick rock each spring and must have missed one! If only one was missed, it would be a miracle. I picked up hundreds of rocks each year, and it was hard work.

The best way to make a job easier is to make it fun; i.e., turn it into a game or contest. Thus, rather than carry them, I threw the rocks onto the wagon used to haul them away to be dumped in an area where erosion was beginning. When I was farther from the wagon or found a larger rock, I used the throwing motion similar to a discus thrower. At times I put in the spin move turning my body around like a top spinning and release the rock at the proper time so it landed in the wagon. It was early training for becoming a discus thrower in high school.

Once the hay was cut it was left to dry for at least twenty-four hours and sometimes longer if there was heavy dew or any rain since it was cut. When dry the hay was rolled into windrows by a hay rake pulled by the tractor. Then the loose hay was picked up by the hay loader pulled behind a hay wagon drawn by the tractor. When big enough I drove the tractor for this while dad was on the wagon building the load—necessary as the load usually went some six feet above the highest part of the hayrack. After loading was complete dad drove to take it to the barn.

Dad had to back the wagon into the center of the haymow (the hay was stored on both ends of the loft with an open space about twenty feet wide in-between for unloading the hay). This job took some real skill as there was a slight incline up to the doorway and it is not real easy to back a wagon like that on the level! It had to be backed in so he could get the tractor out to "pull up the hay"; thus, unloading the wagon. A fairly complicated series of pulleys, etc. that made it appear simple worked as described below.

A large hayrope (about one and a quarter inch diameter rope) was fastened to a clevis that was bolted to the tractor hitch. From the clevis the rope went through a pulley attached to the beam inside the barn door about two feet above the floor, then up and through a pulley on a large beam near the roof. From there it went full length of that mow to the end of the barn and through a pulley lined up with the track that went full length of the barn just under the summit of the roof. From the end pulley the rope hung loosely along the track until it went through a clasp-like piece of steel (called the carrier) and fastened to the fork (the fork was U-shaped with approximately twenty-four inch tines about fifteen inches apart with flip-out three inch barbs on each side to grasp into the hay). When not in use the fork was hooked up in the carrier that rolled along the track. There was also a long piece of half inch rope called a trip-rope attached at the top of the fork. The trip-rope had two functions; it was used to pull the empty fork back to the middle of the barn so it would release and come down to be "set" in the load, and when a full fork load of hay was over the haymow a jerk on the trip-rope flipped the barbs back in line with the tines thus releasing the hay from the fork.

With that background information, the wagon was unloaded like this: dad took hold of the loose end of the trip-rope and climbed up on the wagon load of hay while Don and I hooked up the clevis. Don got on the tractor to drive it while dad pulled the fork to the center of the barn where it released and came down— I slowed it some by holding onto the hay rope above the first pulley. If not careful, dad could get stabbed by the fork! Dad set the fork into the hay load and flipped two "arms" on top of the fork, which set the barbs. When ready, dad stepped off the load and Don slowly drove the tractor straight away from the barn pulling the fork load of hay up until it latched in the carrier and began rolling along the track until dad said, "Whoa." Because of the tractor noise, I relayed to Don, "Whoa," but he usually knew from past experience where to stop. After he stopped, dad jerked the trip-rope and dropped the hay to the mow. As dad pulled the fork back to the middle of the barn, Don backed up the tractor and I had a very important job. I had to pull the hay rope back to the barn so it wouldn't get caught under the tractor tires— especially the narrow front tires that were directly in line with the hitch and, of course, the rope. Usually it took four or five fork loads to empty the wagon. Then, it was back to the field for another load.

After the first crop of hay was in the barn from all the hay fields, it was usually time to begin to cut the oats. It was cut with a grain binder that had a sickle bar like the hay mower, but the grain lay straight on a conveyer belt that took it to a part of the machine where it was stood upright again and once the proper amount was together a twine wrapped around it and the machine tied a knot making a "bundle". The bundle was then released from the machine and fell to the ground. Dad ran the grain binder pulled by the tractor and the machine functions were propelled by the bull wheel—a large steel cleated wheel. Don and I worked to shock the oats bundles. A shock was made by standing up six bundles together, three on each side and putting one bundle over the top called a cap. The cap was to help the rain run off and keep the "heads" or grain part dry as much as possible. When the grain was all cut and shocked it was allowed to dry for a time and then was ready to be thrashed. Someone in the valley owned a thrashing machine and when our turn came up our grain was thrashed. Every farmer in the valley worked together to thrash everyone's grain. Mainly my job was pitching bundles onto wagons in the field or driving tractors for other farmers as they loaded their wagons. The only difference in our thrashing from that discussed other places is that our grain was put in sacks at the machine, carried to the nearby granary and emptied into the bins.

Cutting and putting up a second crop of hay followed thrashing oats. The second crop was usually shorter stalkes of alfalfa and somewhat more tender though I never ate any of it to see for sure!

Upon completion of harvesting second crop it was about time to cut the corn that was going to be silage. The corn was cut with a corn binder that functioned about the same as the grain binder and left the cut corn laying in the field in bundles tied with twine. These bundles were about ten to twelve inches in diameter at the point of the tied twine. The twine was tied around the corn stalks about three to four feet from the bottom of the stalks.

When everyone in the valley had their corn cut it was time to get the group together to do silo filling. The silo filler, as the machine was called, was powered by a belt drive from a tractor flywheel the same as a thrashing machine was powered. The silo filler had a flat "bed" with a chain type conveyer having steel cross pieces that carried the corn stalks to the cutting wheel/blower. The corn bundles were loaded on the wagons (same wagons used for hay without the side racks on them) and hauled to the silo filler with the butt ends toward the machine. They were unloaded onto the conveyer butt end first. The conveyer took the bundles to the cutting wheel/blower (similar to a rotary lawn mower blade but it had four knives instead of two and the knives had "wings" on the back side that propelled the chopped corn up an eight inch diameter galvanized steel pipe to the top of the silo—about fourty feet up). Once the chopped corn reached the silo it got the name of corn silage. Generally, the only job I did during silo filling was help load wagons in the field after school and possibly on Saturday if the group was working at our farm.

By this time it was late September or early October. The only crop in the field to be harvested was the standing corn left to dry in the fields to be picked as ear corn for feeding pigs or mixed with oats and ground at the local mill into "ground feed". Some well-off farmers may have had a corn picker machine, but we did not. We picked it by hand. The team of horses often helped with this task as they pulled a wagon with a box on it that measured about three feet high, three feet wide, and eight to ten feet long. To begin the horses pulled the wagon in a start and stop fashion along the side of the field as three or four of us picked the corn from two rows and threw it into the wagon. Picking the corn entailed getting it off the stalk with a jerking motion (often called snapping corn) and peeling the husks off it before throwing it into the wagon. When the first two rows were completed, the team of horses straddled the second row (already picked) as we picked rows three and four going back the opposite direction. For this job the horses usually wore "blinders" to decrease their peripheral vision and hopefully keep them from eating or knocking down the corn beside them. The blinders did not make the horses blind as they were shields attached to the bridle and located on the left side of the left eye and right side of the right eye.

We hauled the full load in to the corncrib where it was shoveled into the crib. The crib was made of wood with two inch by four inch board studs covered with one inch by two inch boards having a one-inch gap between them to allow air into the corn and not allow it to rot in the crib. When all the ear corn was in the crib, our harvest of crops was completed for the year.

Chapter Four

One time we loaded a big load of hay from a ten acre field up on the ridge. The trip down the "dugway" (a name for a roadway up through a wooded hillside to a ridge) was quite scary as water erosion often caused it to be quite rough. A brain storm hit me this day and I decided to ride down to the barn sitting on top of the hay load. About halfway down the dugway, the right side of the wagon went into a hole shifting the weight rapidly. About a third of the load and I landed in the ditch to the right of the wagon.

Another time on the ridge field I was simply walking along behind the hay loader when I apparently stepped on or kicked into a bubble bee nest. A bee flew up and stung me just under my right eye. Besides the initial pain, the swelling nearly closed off vision in that eye. Like most other things it healed with time.

For some reason dad decided to have the hay in a certain big field baled by a custom baler. It made "square" bales—some of the first square bales seen in the area at that time. Don and I were in the field with the tractor and wagon loading bales to haul them to the barn. I sat down on a bale of hay to rest a bit and stood up abruptly with a shrill squeal. A bumble bee had stung me in the butt. Revenge was on my mind and we located the bee's nest in an area where rain had carved a small ditch in the field. After dark that night, armed with a coffee can filled half full of gasoline and some matches, we went back to the field, located the nest again, doused it with gas and torched it. I slept much better that night even though I had a sore rear end.

One day in the late winter or early spring I was carrying a pail of feed to the pig pen. I had to go out the back barn door and around the silo to the area with great caution carrying the feed, but I made it safely. The caution was due to the footing—you see, the area had a concrete base with about two inches of ice on top of it and about half an inch of "liquid" on top of the ice. Due to excess snow in the winter the farmer sometimes cannot haul the manure out to the fields; thus, it gets piled behind the barn. Therefore, the "liquid" was a mixture of melted snow, liquid seepage from the pile of manure and cow urine frozen and then melted in the morning sun. On my return trip I did not need to be careful not to spill anything—slipped and fell flat on my belly and face in the yuk! I got to the door of the kitchen, but mom would not let me in—had to take my coat and pants off on the porch before she would let me in. What a stinky mess!

During a period of time I had a major responsibility in the egg business. My job was to daily gather the eggs from the hen house, wash them, check them on the egg scale for grading purposes and put them in the egg crate stored in the cool basement. I kept daily records of the production and thus began my first bookkeeping experience. It may have been seed for a later desire to be an accountant. We probably only got fifteen or twenty cents a dozen for the eggs, but the experience was good!

Every night in the months when the cows did not go out to pasture in the daytime they were fed hay after milking was completed. About midway through the milking time, dad sent Don and me up to the haymow to dig out the hay and throw it down to the center part of the haymow. When milking was completed it was thrown down the shoots to the areas in front of the cows' stantions. Playtime!!! King of the hay mound was common and Don chasing his "not-so-little" little brother around after some good provoking by me were the usual activities. One night Don was chasing me and I was laughing so hard I could hardly run. I got close to the edge of the hay and the floor was about twenty feet below. The bad news is that I fell off the mow. The good news is that we had already thrown a five foot high pile of hay down there. The bad news is the hay loader was stored just beyond the pile of hay with its large (about four foot diameter) steel wheel right in line. The good news is I hit the hay pile. The bad news is I bounded off it. The good news is I missed the wheel with my head as it wizzed by my ear within inches slightly bruising my shoulder. The Good Lord was with me then or I might not be here to tell about it.

Dad and Don had taken me hunting many times—I was good at toting the game, kicking brush piles and going around to the other side of the tree to make a squirrel visible to them. Don took me squirrel hunting with him on a warm fall day. We saw a squirrel go up a tree and sure enough I had to go around to the other side so the squirrel would go to Don's side of the tree. Pow, the sound of Don's .22 Cal. rifle followed, but he only wounded the animal. He watched it hobble down the limb to the trunk and crawl into a hole about eight feet off the ground. There was also a large hole in the trunk about four feet above the bottom of the tree. We rubbed branches along the side of the trunk and shoved one up the trunk from the bottom hole, but the squirrel didn't come out (unless it slipped out when we weren't looking). "Let's smoke him out," Don said with confidence in his voice. "Great idea," I said, "I'll get some leaves and twigs." We were not Boy Scouts! Don rubbed two sticks together until he was tired and then told me to go to the house and get some matches (I was also a gopher—go for this, go for that). Upon my return he lit a fire by the bottom hole, shielded it so the smoke went up the tree and out the top hole, but smoke was the only thing that came out. Then there was a slight panic when the tree caught on fire and we had no water with us. But Don got another brainstorm (he had some good ones). He found a large tree limb laying nearby, picked it up and leaned it against the tree. He then walked half-way up the limb, unzipped his pants and proceeded to put a good stream of urine on the fire. Mission accomplished!

Speaking of the woods, the Potter home was heated mostly

by a wood furnace and coal supplemented the wood some during the very bitter cold time. Dad, Don and I went to the back forty acres one day when crop work was light. We had to lay in some firewood for the next winter so we took the tractor and small trailer loaded with woodcutting tools. We had to go up the dugway, past the ridge field and down the back dugway through the back woods to get to our target. It was over a half mile and took over a half hour to get there with that transportation. It had rained the night before (possibly why we weren't doing crop work) and I wore my rubber galoshes. Everyone helped. Dad and Don were sawing off foot long sections of larger branches while I was working on trimming off smaller branches. I was only eight, but could handle a small single blade ax. "You be careful with that ax," dad told me before we started. I was trying to chop off a small branch that was on a limb that was laying across another limb a foot off the ground and very unstable. The task was nearly completed when my next swing (last swing) glanced off the front edge of the branch and went straight down through the top of my boot, through my sock and into my foot. Instantly, I remembered that I didn't' have my shoe on under the boot because my boots did not fit over the one pair of shoes that I had. "Dad, I cut my foot," I yelled after looking down to see blood shooting out of the slit in my boot. It reminded me of the old "bubbler" drinking fountains at the grade school—only this was bright red! Dad and Don came to the rescue. They took off the boot, wrapped the wound in the typical farmer's red handkerchief and helped me to the trailer. With Don holding the 'bandage' and applying pressure to the wound, dad drove the tractor on what was to me probably the longest ride of my life back to the house. Mom called Dr. Baker's office in Wonewoc, WI once she was aware of the crisis and found out that he was there seeing patients. When Dr. Baker told mom "Get here as soon as you can," it wasn't long before dad had the car out of the garage and Don helped me get into the back seat. "That's quite a gash," the doctor said as he probed the inch long and half inch deep hole in the top of my foot. "Probably won't need more than two stitches in it," he continued as he started to sew it up. When the Doc was done sewing, he gave me a tetanus shot and told his nurse to bandage my foot. "You be careful you don't bump that on anything for about two weeks and I'll see you back here in a week," Dr. Baker said as we started to leave. Adversity strikes again!

A week, much worse two weeks, of limited activity was extreme punishment to me, but it was my own fault. As a matter of fact, dad knew this quite well. When I did something bad, usually talking back to my mom, and dad was called or arrived on the scene, the perfect punishment was given. He said, "Now you sit quietly on that chair and don't move until I give you permission." Then he walked out the door and went to work in the barn. Didn't know if he would be back in fifteen minutes or three hours! As it turned out the first time it was a little more than an hour and I was careful after the second time that it never happened again. So I hate to be inactive. Anyway, after a week of healing mom took me back to Dr. Baker. "Looks good," he said, "but you continue to be careful and we will probably take the stitches out next week." I was careful, the next report was "nearly completely healed" and the stitches were removed. Free again I thought to myself as I could return to regular chores and activities. Then, about a week later I was in the barn doing something with some calves when one of them got past me and ran out the front barn door (the one I should have shut). Guilt came over me as I shut the barn door and saw the calf grazing by the garden fence. "I gotta catch that calf," I muttered to myself. "Sure don't want to cause more work for dad and Don." So I quietly got up close to the calf and grabbed its tail! What a stupid thing to do! Haste makes waste. Hasty decisions exacerbate problems. I held on tightly and the animal that weighed about the same as me, dragged me for a few yards before I let go. The "drag" had both my feet (you might have guessed—they were bare feet) topside down going through the dirt and gravel reopening the ax wound and filling it with dirt! Guess I wasn't too bright! Must be why four-wheel drive is so good. The calf and I were about the same weight, but it had four-footed drive and I only had two-footed drive! What did the Dr. say, you ask? Nothing. I didn't give him a chance!! I was too embarrassed to go back to him. We kept it clean and it healed with time.

When the calf was making its move away from the barn, where was Penny, the family collie and excellent cattle dog? Penny had gone to doggie Heaven only a few months earlier. He was a great dog. In the warm summer months when the cows spent the night down in the lower pasture, they had to be herded up the driveway to the barn for the morning milking. Without Penny, that would have been a time consuming task. But, all dad had to do was walk out in the front lawn and call, "Come boss!" Like a streak Penny went down the lane and circled around all the cows. Once the cows knew it was "that" time they began walking toward the lane and all Penny had to do was slowly walk behind them, which he did. Penny also helped get the cows in the evening, but it wasn't so easy as the cows were often in the back forty or worse yet over the hill in the back woods.

Penny had another interesting skill. Sometimes with me or Don in the pasture or down by the spring a bumble bee would buzz by Penny's head. "Snap, crunch, crunch, crunch" was the sound that was heard. The sound was Penny grabbing the bumble bee, chewing it up and then quietly letting the dead thing fall to the ground. Like in the song, *Ol' Shep*, Penny got old and sick. Toward the end of nearly fourteen years of life, Penny grew cataracts over his eyes and, nearly blind, spent all of his time lying under the straw stack. So it was time for another trip to the back forty where there was a nice spot for him to rest. With tractor and trailer we hauled him back there, dug a hole, placed him by the hole and dad instantly put him out of his misery with one blast of his twelve gauge shotgun. The force rolled him into the grave and dad covered him with dirt. Don and I couldn't look and were very sad even though we knew it was the best for Penny. He was gone, but his memory will last our lifetime.

Chapter Five

Two cousins came to visit for a week or two nearly every summer that we lived on the farm. They were Ona, close age to my sister Shirley, and Joe, close age to my brother Don. Although they spent nearly all of their time with my siblings, it always brought a pleasant change of pace to the usual routine tasks of farm work. I don't know if their presence made my work load lighter or if it just seemed lighter as I felt like while working I was showing off to, or maybe teaching, the older cousins (who lived in the Village of La Farge, Wisconsin) how to do farm work! Either way, it always seemed to be the highlight of the summer at home.

Another highlight of the summer for a few years after my eighth birthday was my first "job" for pay. My uncle Armen Wolf, husband of mom's sister Vila, had a farm up on the ridge about a mile or so to the east of our farm. He owned the thrashing machine that was used to thrash oats on his farm and six other farms in the "thrashing run" as it was called. The "run" always started at his farm where all the other farmers arrived around 10 a.m. or so (time depended on amount of overnight dew and them getting their morning milking chores done) with their tractors and hay wagons. Their job was to go to the designated field and, with a three-tine pitch-fork, pitch the oats bundles onto the wagon. Once the wagon was full, they hauled it into the thrashing machine, pitched the bundles steadily onto the conveyor belt that took them into the razor sharp thrashing teeth. When the wagon was empty they went for another load. The grain came out a spout into the bed of Armen's pick-up truck and the straw was blown out a spout to the straw stack. Arnold Wolf, Armen's brother, worked for Armen and lived with them. He was the man in charge of the grain and the straw. When Armen's truck was full, Arnold moved it away and backed his truck under the spout. Then he drove Armen's truck to the granary where my first job started. I shoveled the grain out of the truck into the hopper of the grain elevator that went into an open window high up the side of the granary. When unloaded, he took the truck back to the "machine" and I went to the granary where I shoveled the grain back away from the spout making room for more loads that followed.

My grain shoveling job only lasted a short half-day when Armen decided he needed me to help with the straw stack. Thus, I became the one to "tend the blower." Arnold was the straw stack builder and as the stack got up past two or three feet high a ladder was placed against the stack for Arnold to get on and off it every time he wanted straw blown to a different area of the stack. His stacks were beautiful—probably twenty feet wide and forty feet long, very rectangular with straight walls up fifteen to twenty feet and then tapered like a barn roof. I really had a cushy job; sit up on the machine by the base of the blower and turn the two cranks to move the blowers up and down or left to right. Arnold tapped his fork on the blower spout and motioned which way to move it. When his desires were met, he gave me the ok sign. The cushy job was yucky at times—when the wind blew from the stack toward me, I was showered nearly constantly with chaff and dust. This wouldn't be too bad, but I sweat profusely when it was anywhere from eighty to one hundred degrees. In early to mid August, it was always in that temperature range. Chaff and dust stuck to my face, neck and arms while some of it went down inside my shirt—really itched! But five dollars a day, pop and beer chilled in the milk house for drinking, delicious thrashing crew meals and working "with the men" was a big deal at ages eight, nine and ten for this farm boy. I found I could do a lot of itching for that! Only problem with that was it never took more than one and a half or two days to thrash all of uncle Armen's oats. So I could not get rich at that—though a little spending money was most welcome and appreciated. And, this led to other thrashing crew jobs in later years.

Periodically, during the winter months, we went to grandma and grandpa Kahler's for dinner after church on Sunday. After a nice meal the adults, my parents and grandparents, sat down at the card table for a couple games of sheepshead—a favorite old German card game often enjoyed by the family. While they played cards, Shirley, Don and I usually went to the local theatre to see a movie—a Dean Martin and Jerry Lewis comedy was always fun. The cost for me was twelve cents while both of the teenagers paid twenty-five cents. Popcorn was a nickel, coke was a dime, and candy was a nickel. Of course, after a big meal, we usually did not enjoy any snacks. Plus, if your mom only gave you fifteen cents to go to the movies, you only had three cents left for snacks. If the three cents "burned a hole in your pocket" (an old saying that meant that whenever you had some money you just had to spend it) you could get five pieces of bubble gum for it.

About a year after we left the farm and moved to town, new management took over the movie theatre and everyone feared huge price hikes. Well, prices did go up a little. Children's movie fare was up two cents to fourteen cents and teenagers had to pay a dime more with the new cost set at thirty-five cents.

Sometimes after the movie was over, I sat and watched the adults play sheepshead while they finished their last game before we had to go home to feed and milk the cows. Cows (our main source of income) really tied farmers to their farms—one farmer said, "too bad those cows can't learn to milk themselves!" Back to the card game, I asked questions and during the winter after reaching age eight learned how to play sheepshead. My early experience with playing 500 rummy indicated that I had a good "card sense" and once I learned the procedures and the scoring, sheepshead was fun for me. And, I could compete with the adults. So, during that winter my enthusiasm for the game was very high.

By that time, my brother had learned how to play and the four of us decided to have a tournament. My sister, Shirley, was not interested in card games and spent much of her leisure time reading or studying in her room. About three nights a week after milking was done, Mom, Dad, Don and I played one game of sheepshead a night in a twenty game tournament. To make a long story short, I won the tournament. After that my aunt Vila who was a good sheepshead player said to me, "You must have been born with a deck of cards in your hand." Other family members got a "kick" out of that.

Don't know whether I was eight or nine years old when it was time to learn how to ride a bicycle. I don't believe my sister ever had a girl's bicycle, but we had a boy's bicycle that my brother rode and that was what I was going to start on. Being a tall kid for my age helped me reach the pedals some of the time. We had a circle drive on the farm with the center grass area about twenty-five yards in diameter. The drive went a little above (west of) the barn, up a hill and a little below (east of) the machine shed and then down south of the house in a clockwise direction. At the top of the circle was a gas tank and pump as well as a water faucet. That is where I was to start my biking experience. The plan was for me to steer it down the hill by the house, gradually turn left and go on down the driveway toward the lane leading to the lower pasture. Dad held the bike while I got on, guided me a little as I pushed the pedal and then he let go of it as I started downhill. I gained speed swiftly down the forty-five degree grade and could not turn left when needed; instead, I gently turned right in a "go with the flow" fashion. The bike made a nice easy arc and headed straight for the wooden gate just below the front of the barn—the gate kept the cows in the barnyard when closed. The gate was open, but that didn't matter, as I never got that far. The surface the bike entered was what the cows left in late Spring after walking through, urinating on and defecating on a surface that was already five inches of mud. The bike and I eased into the slop and yuk until momentum was gone and stopped. Since I couldn't reach the ground with my feet, I just sat still and the bike and I went over to the left side like a huge tree being felled in the woods. Once again, I had to undress outside of the house!

The summer of my ninth birthday there was one special day for our neighbors who lived near the top of the hill named after them. Ernie and Elsie Berndt's daughter Pat got married to Wilmer Penshorn. Don and I did not go to the wedding, maybe we went to the reception but we surely went to the shivaree! There was lots of food and drink and noise. I drank some pop (that's coke to some people—the carbonated drink type) and may have been able to sneak a glass of beer, as there was plenty available. Don found some beer and drank plenty for sure. We shared a double bed in the north bedroom of our home. After we both were settled in that night all I heard was, "Oh, the room is going around— stop it Jim!" Again and again he repeated the same thing!

Later that summer I had a small money making business. My grandparent's neighbor (Mrs. Wopat) in Hillsboro liked to get blackberries, so she paid me a little bit for a quart of them now and then. One morning I went up to the woods where there were many nice ripe blackberries and picked a two quart pail full nearly to the top. I was on my way to the house and for some unknown reason I took a veer to the north and walked through a cornfield between rows. Suddenly, I saw an animal on the ground near the base of a cornstalk partially hidden from my view. I didn't recognize what it was and instinctively felt fear. So, I threw the pail of berries at it and scared it worse than I WAS SCARED. It whirled and let fly with the most foul juices known on the farm—it was a skunk and it had good aim. Fortunately it did not hit my face or eyes, but it sure got my clothes. I picked up the berry pail, still half full, and went home. Mom's keen nose detected me when I made it to the yard and she was out on the porch with specific instructions for me when I first saw her. "You get all those clothes off before you get near this house," she said. So I did! End of story!

Fourth grade was a good year at school as I continued to do well in the same subjects and fairly well in the others. We had a good teacher though she was quite strict which is what we needed.

The cords on her neck jumped out after she said, "There is something I want to stress." During recess in the fall we played tackle football quite a bit and never wore any uniforms or pads like kids do today. None of us got hurt very badly. Sometimes we played softball and did more of that in the Spring.

One day in the Spring I had the measles and they were supposed to be contagious, so I stayed home from school. Dad was planting oats that day so I did not have to be bored at all. I had a "job". I rode on the back of the grain drill and periodically lifted the lid to check if the hopper was nearing empty. When it was almost empty I yelled at dad so he would stop at the end of the field and refill it. Once in a while after the hopper was filled I watched closely for any rocks I might have missed in rock-picking time and when I saw one I would go and get it off the field.

During that school year (and possibly a year earlier also) my sister, Shirley, did babysitting for a woman with three children. The oldest child, Donna, was my classmate and somehow the two of us developed "puppy" love that year. My sister was a senior in high school and graduated that May. Soon after graduation she married Gordon Penshorn, brother of Wilmer. Thus, Donna and her family were invited to the wedding, reception held on the farm and the shivaree. That day I had fun with Donna, ate too much and drank too much pop. That night in bed I was sick to my stomach—ate too many brownies! At the shivaree twelve gauge shotguns blasted and hammers hit BIG saw blades and old kettles were banged together to get the bride and groom to come down from Shirley's room on the second story. Then the drinking began!

After they were married Shirley and Gordon lived in the upstairs half of his parent's home in Plum Valley and it was the last farm on my uncle Armen's thrashing run. After working on my "blower tender" job early in the thrashing run, I was hired by Gordon to work "running my own rig" while thrashing at Wilmer's place (next farm) and his place. The phrase running my own rig, meant using his tractor and wagon and having the responsibility of hauling loads of bundles to the machine and unloading them as any other farmer did. (I felt like a "man"). I could do that as I was tall enough to reach the brake and the small old John Deere B had a hand clutch that made it easy to control. Enjoyed that!

Gordon knew that I liked to do the work so he hired me other times over the next few years. One year I was running his rig while we were thrashing at the Bill Gale farm. This is a farm that even in 1960 did not have electricity. So I had hauled two or three loads the first day there and we all went to have a beer before the big noon thrashers dinner. Well, I was the last one going into the house and I knew later why they all hurried into the house. I got the last chair at the table and began to eat. It was about ninety degrees outside and the humidity at that farm nestled between two ridges well wooded was about ninety percent. As I began to sweat more, others quipped, "See that beer really coming out of you, Jim!" Right, I was sitting about eight inches from a wood cook stove that still had pies baking in it! It wasn't necessarily the beer, but it helped, as the temperature on my back was too hot!

Chapter Six

If a work ethic was not instilled in me by this time, it came to fruition during fifth grade. During some school board meeting in August, 1953 an edict was sent down to the rural families—specifically affecting me. The ruling was this: if you lived in a certain area, you had to attend a certain rural school. My assignment was to go to Staley School located about two to three miles out of Hillsboro off Hwy 80 toward Yuba, Wisconsin. Staley was an eight grade school with one teacher. There were probably two, three or four students in each grade for a total of about thirty students. NOTE: Some college Professors have one or two teaching "preparations" and complain about it! I wonder how they would do with about *fifty* teaching "preparations" like the late Miss Shore had as our teacher at Staley. My grades all dropped to C's and that was partly due to the workload I had at home. I did my fifth grade arithmetic and I did one sixth grader's arithmetic while trying to teach it to him. Why did I get C's in Arithmetic? Anyway, I was way ahead of the city classmates when I joined them the next year. During fourth and fifth grade I often tried to help others.

A typical school day went like this. Get up at 5:30 a.m., put on "barn" clothes and go to the barn, help with the chores until 7:00 a.m., go to the house to clean up and change clothes, make cold meat (if we had some) or peanut butter and jam sandwich for my lunch and get on the bus—a twelve passenger van—at 7:30 a.m. I rode the bus to Hillsboro and went within two blocks of the grade school I had attended the previous five years to go out of town to Stanley where school started at 8:00 a.m. The first month I was mad all over again going through Hillsboro! School let out at 3:30 p.m. and in order to get home to do chores, I took the early bus that went to my neighbor's farm on the ridge above us and got out there so I could run through the fields and woods to our house and get ready to do chores. If I had waited for the bus that went to my house, it would have been an hour or more later before I got home. Why did I try to be such a martyr? Maybe it was a necessity, read on.

That year Don was in his junior year of high school and was active on the football and basketball teams that had practice each day causing it to be nearly 6:00 p.m. before he got home. Due to poor milk prices and financial difficulties, both mom and dad had jobs in Hillsboro to supplement (or make up for losses) the income. Mom got home from work at about 5:00 p.m. or so and dad didn't get home until after 6:00 p.m.

My tasks to complete were to dig silage out of the silo and throw it down the shoot between the barn and silo, dig straw out of the straw stack and carry it to the barn and some days "clean the barn"—that phrase always meant driving the tractor with manure spreader attached through the barn (after letting the cows out to the barnyard) and shoveling the manure out of the gutters and into the spreader. If I couldn't "clean the barn" I at least let the cows out and, while they were out, hauled silage and ground feed to the feeding trough in front of the cows' stantions giving each cow the appropriate amount of feed. Then, when Don and dad got home they let the cows in so they could eat while we had our supper. That way the cows had time to eat before we started milking them. Note: I usually threw down a large pile of silage so it would be enough for the evening feed and the next morning's feeding. It was a lot of work, but on some Saturdays there was a little time for some fun.

On a Friday in February we invited my cousin Steve Kahler (oldest son of Herbert and Sadie—two years younger than I) to spend the weekend with us. There was about four inches of old snow on the ground and that Friday night the temperature went up to the low thirties followed by light rain before the thermometer went back down into the low twenties. We had a sled and a toboggan both of which were large enough for Steve and I to ride together. The sun glistened off the ice-covered snow on the hill out beside and above the windmill. The ice-covered snow was interspersed with patches of no ice on the snow; therefore, we surmised that the sled runners would dig in when we tried to cross areas without the ice cover and decided to take the toboggan up the hill and try it out.

It was mid-morning, the sun was bright coming back off the white snow and we could have used sunglasses as our slow ascent began. Even picking the most gradual slope of the hill to attempt to conquer it did not make it easy. Being some thirty pounds heavier than Steve, I led the way stomping the hard crusted snow to get footing with Steve pulling the toboggan and following in my exact steps. "Wish I had a hammer with us—sure would make this easier," I told Steve after a short distance and a slightly sore right foot from slamming it down on a solid surface repeatedly. "Yes, that would really help," he responded, "But we'll make it," he added optimistically. As the slope began to get less steep, we had it made! Now, after all that work, we had to make the best of it so we went to the left side of the woods where the hill was the VERY STEEPEST—so steep that partway down there was an area too steep to plant crops (so steep the tractor would tip over if driven there) as it was a drop-off. THIS was where we could have the most "fun", experience the most danger or maybe get killed! The grade was probably fifty yards long down to the flat area that covered about one hundred yards to the edge of the field. The field edge WAS the CREEK! The creek water level was about a five foot drop from the field.

"You ready, Steve?" I asked as he settled in behind me on the toboggan making me the "driver" of it, "Hang on tight!" We pulled in our feet thus releasing our emergency brakes and off we went. Wow! The drop-off acted just like a ski jump as we flew through the air and swiftly gained speed going down the steep grade. By the time we were on the "flat" we must have been going a cool fifty to sixty miles per hour—what a ride! Half way through the field I realized we would never get stopped before the creek, so I told Steve what we would do. "On my command, you roll off to your left and I will roll off to my right." Making the most of the ride, I waited until we were about fifteen yards from the creek 'til I said, "ROLL!" We both rolled off cleanly and slid on the ice/snow right up to the edge. Glad that we were not on "board", we watched the empty toboggan fly across the creek, just miss a couple of trees and skid until the front of it slammed into the bottom wire of the barb wire fence at the edge of the pasture.

"Let's do that again," suggested Steve, "That was fun!" "Are you kiddin' me?" I replied while grabbing the rope on the mildly damaged toboggan and heading for the house. "I don't care what you do, but the toboggan and I are not going to do that again."

On Saturday, a week or two later I took the sled by myself and went up above the windmill for a short ride down toward the house. As I got down near the buildings I was still going faster than I thought possible. My choices were to hit the wooden gate, hit some steel machinery, hit a building or try to let the old lime pile stop me. I braced myself gripping tightly on the steering bars of the sled and hit the lime pile. Instant brakes! Broke my right arm slightly above the wrist, but didn't know it was broken 'til I went to the doctor on Monday.

I had a pain in my arm after hitting the lime pile, but it was not severe enough to keep me from doing regular chores during milking. It did hurt quite badly when I put a heavy strain on it. X-rays showed a hairline fracture of the radius (the one of two forearm bones that connects with wrist bones on the thumb side of the hand) in my right arm. With a cast on down past the wrist I was forced to become a "lefty" for a while. If things weren't rough enough before, this magnified the situation. About the only good thing that came out of the deal was that I dribbled a basketball around the house with my left hand—really made mom happy! Of course, I'm being sarcastic. It helped me be more ambidextrous playing basketball in years to come.

Joy, Joy, Joy! That was the feeling I had one day in late March when mom called me to her side and told me, "Grandpa sold the farm." I hugged her and cried tears of happiness as I felt like the "weight of the world" had been lifted from my shoulders! During the next month or so my parents found a decent house in Hillsboro and we moved into it May first. Dad got a new job—he was patrolman for the Greenwood Township, but it had nothing to do with police work. His job was road maintenance; grading roads, trimming brush and plowing snow or anything else that was needed. Reminds me of that old saying, "The bark (or was it nuts) doesn't fall far from the tree". You see, my grandpa Potter was a Township patrolman for many years and dad's brother, Stanley, worked in a similar job for Vernon County much of his working life.

With a month of school left and Staley had a fairly good softball team with games scheduled to play against DeBello School and Greenwood School, I quickly decided to finish the year at Staley. I only had to walk less than a block down Pine Avenue to Highway 80 where I could catch the bus that I had ridden all year. So I put off becoming a city boy for another month.

Chapter Seven

Living in a small town differs drastically from the farm. The workload in summer is nil comparatively speaking; mow the lawn (a job I did some on the farm) and work in the garden were the main jobs to do at home. Quickly I learned that many city kids had spending money in their pockets much of the time. Many of them had fairly wealthy (by my standards) parents and got nice allowances for doing very little or nothing—two to five dollars a week seemed to be common. However, I was pleased with the one dollar that I got for doing some work in the yard. More money seemed more satisfying so I looked for ways to earn some. I mowed Uncle Armen's mother's yard and made fifty cents usually every week. Then I helped my grandpa Kahler, who was custodian of the church, by mowing the church lawn some of the time—it was a fifty cent job by the going rate for the size of the lawn. As I developed friendships with some guys in the area of town, I was given opportunity to make a little money assisting with paper routes at times. When the chips were down there usually was a little money to be made by scrounging for pop bottles, at times at the dump ground, for the resale of two cents each. One time a friend and I got enough pop bottle money to buy a dozen skinless wieners for a nice wiener roast for our supper that day. At times we found some other things of "value" at the dump! Another friend and I had the job of "shagging" foul balls at the home games of the city baseball team and bringing them back to the bench for reuse. We got free admission to the games and twenty-five cents a game for the job. Thus, with my allowance and other money earned, I had enough money to pay for a movie or pop or candy bar or ice cream cone occasionally.

My first experience in money management

There were a few more recreational activities available in town such as playing games with friends, fishing in the pond or creek feeding the pond, swimming lessons and "free" swimming plus little league baseball in the organized summer recreation program, going to movies and the afore mentioned city team baseball games. Did I forget about television? No, but we did not have one in our home until 1957 or 1958. Occasionally on Sunday nights we drove about seven blocks to my grandparent's house to watch "I Love Lucy", "To Tell The Truth", and "I've Got a Secret".

Of course, we still did go on some fishing trips for the bigger fish. Sometimes we went bullhead fishing at night late and got home at 2 a.m. or so. Getting home that late, we usually put the bullheads in an old style wash tub with a little water that kept them alive until they were cleaned the next day. The tub was often full with fifty or sixty fish, eleven to thirteen inches long.

The Hillsboro Fireman's Labor Day Celebration marked the end of summer and school always started on the Tuesday after Labor Day. Sixth grade set the stage for many good things to come in the future years. The school building was a new one located on the west edge of town about ten blocks or so from our house. K thru 12 had outgrown the old school building and it now housed grades 7 thru 12. I joined my old classmates from kindergarten through 4th grade and a few new ones that had entered the group in fifth grade or in sixth grade. One of those stood out in the group (literally) as he was three or four inches taller than me; however, he was thin and probably weighed less than I did then. His name was Lewis and later got the nickname "Boob" from a classmate. Our teacher was Mr. Urban who was a real disciplinarian as well as a good teacher. He had apparently gotten his degree, possible taught some, and then was called into the Korean War where he served his Country and returned to teach us a thing or two. He was strict!

Mr. Urban had fought some battles and overcome diseases in Korea, but he ran into a case of the mumps during the spring of that school year. Some of us kids had heard that the mumps were very serious when you caught them after becoming an adult. That was sure right as Mr. Urban was very ill for about two weeks and then seemed weak when he first came back to teach. We all were sure glad he lived through that illness and came back to us—most of the students liked him.

The highlight of the year for me was the basketball season. Though I was only in sixth grade, I, along with Lewis "Boob" Patterson and Phil Eastman, tried-out for the grade school basketball team. We all made the team, but I was especially thrilled as I was named as a "starter" on the team and played most of the time in each game we had. I played guard and mostly passed the ball to others who scored a lot—I think I scored eight points all year. Learned a lot about playing by having a chance to do it against and with older more experienced players. Thus, my athletic career began at age 11.

The following summer found me alone at home with my parents. Don had graduated from High School in May of 1955 and went into the Air Force on the buddy plan with nine or ten of his classmates. I missed him but did not envy him as he was in basic training in San Antonio, Texas that summer going through military conditioning in many days of one hundred to one hundred fifteen degrees and fairly high humidity. My summer was filled with some regular lawn mowing jobs, some work at thrashing time, swimming lessons at the Elroy, WI pool (only pool in the area at that time), practicing baseball with the Little League team and other activities previously mentioned on these pages.

By the end of the summer of 1955, my dad had gotten a new job as a custodian at the old school. I had developed friendships with neighbors who lived less than a block away; i.e., Dennis Degner who was a year older and regular attendee of the same church as me, Steve Subera, two years older and a skilled basketball player from whom I learned a considerable amount and Francis Blaha who was a few years older and taught me how to play crochet and pick up night crawlers to sell to the late Al Jelinek for the big price of twenty five cents for a pound coffee can full of solid worms with very little grass. There were probably five or six dozen night crawlers per can. The summer ended with the Labor Day Celebration held in downtown Hillsboro where I got a job with one of the booth owners. I worked where you had to break three records (78 rpm) with three tosses of a softball to win a teddy bear. My job was to retrieve the balls and replace the broken records with whole ones. I believe pay was fifty cents per hour. The work ended at about six p.m. on Labor Day and school started the next morning.

Chapter Eight

Seventh grade brought the class together at the old school in a room on the second floor. The difference from sixth to seventh grade was like day and night due to the teachers being as different as day and night. Unlike Mr. Urban, Mr. Cooper was a nice guy, but way too easy in the discipline area. Can't give the teacher all the blame for the situation as our class was not easy to manage. First of all, the class size was thirty to thirty-five kids and in retrospect could be broken down somewhat like this: twenty-five percent were good students who studied hard and got good grades no matter who was teaching, twenty-five percent struggled to get B's and C's with a good teacher so suffered in this situation, twenty-five percent had great difficulty learning with the best teacher on Earth and struggled to pass the subjects, AND, last but not least, the other twenty-five percent thrived on causing trouble and some form of disruption of the learning process—basically acted like they didn't give a damn! If a teacher was not firm from the start, THEY HAD YOU! This last group got more attention from the teacher and other students than the course work received. They had an assumed "leader" who was called "Doc" and he had nicknames for many others who were "Swampy", "Fungi", "Fat Boy", and "Boob". There were others who were more like second team players in this organization geared to upset the normal process of learning.

Now Mr. Cooper (Coop, as he was called) was fed up with the

lack of respect he was receiving, so he came to school one day with what later became "the infamous hickory stick". He showed it to us in a warning manner and put it in his lower right desk drawer. When the morning was over, we all went to lunch. After lunch we entered the classroom again at about 1 p.m. and after most of us were seated we observed "Fat Boy" entering the room with his right pant leg rolled up about eight inches and about half of the hickory stick showing out the top of the extra large cuff. Rumor had it that "Fungi" had stolen it during noon hour and "Fat Boy" had the right to brandish it in front of the class! Needless to say, the hickory stick didn't scare those guys a bit!

Not all the trouble makers were in our class. Tradition was to play softball some before school and during recess times during the school hours. One morning I arrived at the playground on the side of the building to observe some of my classmates playing softball with some high school freshmen. But the "game" was different . . . the pitcher had his back to the building and the freshmen batter was facing directly toward the Principal's office window located on the second floor. The window was made with eight panes (measuring eight inches by twelve inches) separated with wooden strips on the top half and the same on the bottom half. Unlike the story in the poem "Casey at the Bat" the pitcher floated a nice easy pitch and the batter lofted a real blast that went through the upper right corner pane with a loud CRASH of glass. Within seconds the playground was vacant as though a tornado had just passed through. Fear of getting "caught in the act" swept instantly through the large group of students that had gathered to watch as the batter had earlier hit three or four that had missed the window (target) and bounced off the wall. There was an obvious dislike for the Principal of HHS at that time. The Principal and our seventh grade teacher were both released of their duties at the end of the year. We also learned later that the softball went through the window and bounced off the Principal's desk just missing the High School Leader.

Speaking of excitement at school, we often had the foul rotten egg odor coming from the chemistry lab as students did one of the more famous experiments in the curriculum. Another time we initially thought of the chemistry lab as the source of the odor, but such was not the case. An upperclassman, male student, thought he was going to be "cute" and he smeared Limburger cheese on some or one of the radiators or heating units. It was in cold weather and windows were not often opened so the result was a very stinky school building. The student responsible for the act was later identified and some form of punishment was given to him. I think he had to clean it up!

The two stories just told did not please my dad one bit. He let me know in "no uncertain terms" that if I was ever a part of any such pranks, I would have trouble sitting on my fanny for a long time! He also let me know that it made much extra work for him replacing the windowpane and having to provide some good cleaning fluids for the student to remove the cheese. Dad liked most of the students and was cordial to them when he saw them or met them in the halls, but he had little time for any who were destructive of school property.

The grade school basketball season was the highlight of the year for me as we won most of the games including the annual grade school tournament in Wonewoc. We played an offensive set with a point guard and two players on the wings. Big Lewis (Boob) was our center and I played forward as a shuffler who started under the basket and went to either corner as the ball was passed to that side of the court. Often the ball was passed to me in the corner where I had a good shot, or with a little faking, made myself open for one. My shot was a set-shot as I had not developed a good jump-shot yet. I scored a career high number of points in a game at La Farge that year—31 points and about 20 of them were from a very high arched corner set-shot. Counting eighth grade, Jr. Varsity my freshman year of high school, and three years of Varsity basketball there were about 90 games in which I was a "starting" player and NEVER did I come close to that 31 point total in seventh grade!

Chapter Nine

The summer of 1956 was an interesting time in my life. Previous to that we had gotten a new Minister at church, Rev. M.J. Nommensen. He and his wife had a daughter, Betsy, who was in my class. There was a lot of encouragement for good students to work toward going into the ministry as a Lutheran teacher in parochial Schools or as an ordained Minister. My good friend, Dennis Degner, and a third cousin, David Kahler, were both planning to work toward that end and started by planning to attend Northwestern Lutheran High School in Watertown, Wisconsin the next fall. Betsy Nommensen had already started in that direction as she went to the Lutheran Grade School in Wonewoc in seventh grade, she planned to do the same in eighth grade and then go on to Watertown. Many people in church thought that I would be a good one to work toward becoming a minister. I was interested and decided to start by going to Wonewoc parochial school in eighth grade. Besides all this planning going on that summer, I was a first base player in Little League baseball, attended swimming lessons (I was a poor swimmer) and recreational swimming, worked for Wilmer Penshorn putting up first crop hay for a dollar-a-day and a very good dinner as well as all the other things in which I was involved during the previous summer.

Next, I had to have a little fun. Dennis, David and I planned a little camping/fishing trip toward the end of summer. It would not happen without the help of Dennis' dad, Art Degner, who agreed to take us to the spot we planned to pitch the tent. With fishing poles, bait and tent gear loaded we headed out north to Buckhorn Bridge, went across it on County Highway G and followed that until we got within a quarter mile or so from the railroad crossing. At that point we turned right and went about a quarter mile until we turned left and went north where we were just below the railroad tracks. There was a nice small hill there, mostly rock, and it gave us a shield from any north winds as well as the fact it "looked" like a good camping spot.

The day was passing fast when we got there, so we pitched the tent and prepared to get a good night's sleep so we could catch some fish the next day. As typical teenagers do in camping situations, we started telling scary stories. One of the scare tactics used by the two older boys on me was, "Did you hear that rattlesnake?" or "I think a snake just crawled over my leg". I think we were all a little scared, but soon we were all sleeping and suddenly it was morning. We got up, went fishing and had some luck and were ready to go home when Art came to get us that evening.

I wonder if we had some premonitions about the rattlesnakes. The next year that area was condemned for camping due to an excessive amount of timber rattlers found in the area!! The area has since been somewhat more developed and there is a business located by the rock known as Ken's Marina and a few other people have camper trailers there in the area.

Before I could get over being nervous about going to a new school and big changes in my life plans, it was Labor Day and I was selling chances to throw balls at records to win a teddy bear! Summer was over and school starts TOMORROW!

Mrs. Nommensen was a teacher at Wonewoc Lutheran Parochial School so it was logical that her daughter and I rode to school and home with her. I studied and began to learn the names of other kids in the short time I was there. You see, I was only there three weeks. Do you think there is too much emphasis put on winning and losing in high school athletics today? Even in Little League or children's soccer leagues there is a lot of parental pressure to WIN today. What about the 1950's? Why did I only go three weeks to school in Wonewoc?

Dennis Degner and David Kahler were attending high school at Northwestern Lutheran in Watertown. Apparently the rumor chain around town propelled the idea that I was going to follow in their tracks the next year. One particular school board member, now deceased and shall remain nameless here, was threatening that he would make sure my dad was fired from his job if I did not return to school in Hillsboro. After much discussion and prayer we decided to give in to the blackmail. I guess I haven't regretted the way it turned out, but you often wonder, "what if . . .", regarding many of the forks in the road of life. Sometimes we just resign to the idea that, "maybe that's the way it was supposed to work out." As some comedians have said, "When did God die and put you in charge?" Anyway, the only logical reason for the school board member wanting to have me attend school in Hillsboro is because of my potential athletic ability.

After rejoining my former classmates in the Hillsboro Jr. High, I was very pleased to meet my new teacher, Mr. Bernard Braithwaite. He came to us with about 30 years of teaching experience and was, without a doubt, the best teacher I ever had before or since!

Mr. Braithwaite was firm and received our respect as he commanded it and did not demand it with threats as seen previously. He knew the subjects inside and out so he could focus on encouraging us to learn. Consequently, we learned all we missed in seventh grade plus what was involved in eighth grade. One thing I thank him for is the fact that he introduced me to the greatest secular poem—"IF" by Rudyard Kipling. I did not appreciate it much then and did not care for having to learn (memorize) part of it, but years later I became reacquainted with it and used it many times in classes I taught. If a person can come close to doing all of the things involved in that poem, he or she would be a special person.

In basketball that year I played center and big Lewis played forward, where he was closer to the basket for rebounds. By that

56

time, with much practice in the summer at the outdoor court, I had developed a good jump shot and a good hook shot to be used from the new position I was playing. Mr. Braithwaite was our leader, but he was not a coach so most of the coaching came from some of us on the team as we had learned from watching the high school teams the past few years. You might say we were self-coached that year. Our team lost one game that year by five points on a day when I was home sick with the flu. The loss was to Wonewoc Public Grade School, but we made up for it by beating them for the championship in their annual tournament. Even more important was a game that probably has never happened again; i.e., on a night when the opposing H.S. team did not have a JV team there was no preliminary game before the varsity game, so we challenged the H.S. JV team who were all freshmen and sophomores. We won the game by three or four points!

Mr. Cooper went into business and opened Coop's Cue and Coffee Center downtown. It became a major hangout for many of the kids in high school and junior high. Those same guys who gave him the most grief in seventh grade became good friends and best customers at his establishment. He did short order cooking, served soft drinks, had four or five pool tables he rented out by the hour or by the game and a good juke box as well as a couple pinball machines to catch our coins. He found a good way to mend all the ills from his teaching days and nearly everyone liked him.

During junior high and part of high school my mom was working as the City Clerk. It was then when I learned how to wash and dry dishes regularly (didn't say I liked it) and fix my own chicken noodle soup (warm it up from a can) to go with a cold meat sandwich for my lunch in the summertime.

Speaking of washing and drying dishes, it was in connection with that job that I received my only "laying on of hands" from my father—but he only used one hand! You see, mom and I were having a disagreement over my unwillingness to dry the dishes one evening. Dad was in the living room watching Red Skelton on TV with one eye and reading the evening paper with the other eye when the noise from the kitchen distracted him enough that he came in to see what was the matter. He already knew what was wrong. I was being disrespectful (downright ugly) toward my mother and he was not pleased. One rapid swing of his right arm caused his hand to hit the left side of my face. I was apologizing to mom as I rose to a standing position from the floor about seven feet from the spot where I expressed my unpleasantness about the dishes. Dad was 6'1", 170 pounds and I was about the same size then.

Hillsboro had a mill pond; that's right, a mill pond! A pond of water held by a dam and released as necessary to provide the power to run the mill that ground the corn and oats in the early years of my life. The "pond" really made a nice little lake that was "Y" shaped. The bottom and the left branch of the lake was about an eighth mile wide and went about a quarter mile southwest to the creek, one source that fed the "pond". In the middle it was merged with the right branch, which was also about an eighth mile wide and a quarter mile long to the point where it met the other feeder creek. Below the dam was the west branch of the Baraboo River that started as a bay with a diameter of about fifty feet and the river below it that varied from eight to twenty feet wide and maybe two to five feet deep.

There was one particular activity that some classmates and other kids in town enjoyed during every spring thaw. A considerable amount of ice formed on the lake, the bay below and the river each winter with thicknesses ranging from four inches in areas with more water flow to eight or ten inches in other places. During the thaw large chunks of ice broke away and floated freely amid the other ice chunks and as time passed went down stream. The "fun" activity was called "iceberging". After school each day the kids went straight home and then straight to the river to "go iceberging". They "rode" the icebergs and jumped from berg to berg and propelled their berg with poles or tree branches. They nearly always went home wet and very cold. I did not swim well in warm water—I didn't go!! Chicken?? Ok, I'll admit it wasn't my cup-o-tea, but I wanted to live to see another summer!

Iceberging was too dangerous for my athletic ability, but many of the guys thought it was good fun. There was another activity that was thought up by someone looking for a different than "normal" kind of baseball or softball. I think the game was called "rockball" but would more aptly be named "gravel ball". It was played in the alley approximately behind Coops Cue and Coffee Center. I never played the game so I don't recall the exact rules, etc. as related to the scoring.

There was a pitcher, who used small pieces of rock (half-inch to one-inch gravel) for the ball, and a batter who used a piece of snow fence lath for his bat. The batter stood near the buildings and the pitcher stood out past the alley as far away as he could get without falling over the edge of the hill there that went down to the old coal building at the Farmer's Coop. Success was measured by how far the batter hit the rock; i.e., past a certain tree was a single, hitting the side of the coal building was a double, hitting the roof of the coal building was a triple and over the coal building was a home run? One "strike" and you were out or anything hit short of the "single" line and you were out.

I think they scored as follows: if you hit a double, a triple and a single in that order before making an out, you scored two runs; the triple would send home the imaginary man from "second" and the single would score the imaginary man from "third" leaving a man on "first". It was challenging, required good hand eye coordination and lots of fun until . . .

The pitcher threw the gravel and the batter hit a line drive straight into the pitcher's eye causing him to live the rest of his life with an artificial eye. After that day, to my knowledge, no "rockball" was ever played again!

In 1949 two new physical education teachers joined the faculty at Hillsboro Public Schools. They were Claude and Millie Kaczmarek who were graduates of La Crosse State College, La Crosse, WI. They lived in town in the upstairs half of my grandparents house for a few years and I knew of them, but first met Claude ("Kaz" as he was called) when he taught our junior high physical education class in seventh grade.

Kaz was a solid man of about six foot—one inch and two hundred ten pounds of all muscle. He was firm and generally fair as a teacher and a coach of football and baseball. He was preceded by stories of the way he did pre-season training and conditioning of his players. Every potential football player with this advance warning did some conditioning on their own before that dreaded day in the heat of late August when the first day of football practice came. I had listened intently when my big brother told me what to expect those first few days. He was speaking from experience. During my three years in the city I had become good buddies with Phil Eastman. Sometimes I went with him and his folks to games out of town as his older brother, Class of 1956, and my brother were both players. Sometime during those years Phil's folks bought the house next door to us and moved in. Thus, during that summer when I wasn't out thrashing or mowing lawns, Phil and I didn't have far to go to get together to play catch with a football. His brother had been a fullback and Phil had sights on becoming a quarterback. My brother played end and I had watched some other ends, Don Hora, Class of 1956, to name one that I desired to emulate. So there were a lot of passes from Eastman to Potter before we got into high school. It was also easy for us to plan and practice a lot of basketball that summer at the courts outside behind the gymnasium of the old school.

In the Lutheran church as in some other denominations, students in seventh and eighth grade participate in study of the Catechism in preparation for Confirmation at the end of the second year. I had already completed the first year and was attending as an eighth grader in the fall of 1956. We were in the basement of the old church building and in early September it is often hot outside even in the morning. It was 11:30 a.m. and we had just completed our study and were "closing" with the Lord's Prayer.

The humidity was high and it was very warm in the room— no air conditioning. Shortly after the start of the prayer I noticed the gal standing in front of me start to weave a bit as though she was ill. Suddenly, she just keeled over toward me and I instinctively caught her with my hands in her armpits. She had fainted and only later did I realize that I had saved her from serious injury she could have received had she fallen to the floor and banged her head. Her name was Diane and she was a nice and attractive young lady in the seventh grade.

In April or May I was Confirmed at church and was active in that church throughout high school serving as an usher whenever I was needed and singing in the choir some of the time.

Chapter Ten

As usual the opening of the school year was the Tuesday after Labor Day and being the start of high school it was a confusing day at first. The change of going to different classrooms to see different teachers for each class took a little adjustment. The curriculum was set up that each student must take four classes plus physical education each year. The classes I took were required four years of English, Algebra and Advanced Algebra plus one semester of Geometry by correspondence, four years of Industrial Arts, Science, Biology, Chemistry and Physics in the Sciences area, World History, American History, the required Physical Education and I was in Chorus for fun. The day went from 8:30 a.m. to 3:30 p.m. with a forty-five minute lunch break. Classes were seventy minute periods with each class meeting four times a week as there was a "floating period" that allowed an extra class per day or a period of study hall.

Like my days in grade school, I had no love for history, did poorly, but passed. I enjoyed most of the English and liked the science classes as well as the mathematics classes. Sometimes it doesn't take much to amuse students in advanced algebra, especially when you are working hard at learning and have a teacher who helps you. The late Mrs. Joyce Schroeder was our teacher and a good one. After a while five of the students, (Phil Eastman, Lewis Patterson, Stuart Pacl, Paul Tatter and I) noticed that our teacher wore clip-on multicolored earrings. White, Red,

Yellow, Green, and Blue were the choices. We started a pool everyday where we each put a dime in a pot and from someone's hand drew out a piece of paper with a color on it. The person with the correct color matching the earrings she is wearing the next day wins the pot. Big time High School gamblers!

One of the more interesting and enjoyable classes was Industrial Arts. My first thought of it was "a lot of woodworking", but we did a variety of things over the years including drafting, woodwork with hand tools, leather craft, woodwork with power tools including the lathe, plastic crafts and others. Mr. Deiter was our teacher the first year and Mr. Schauf was instructor for the last three years.

Though the first year was quite basic and not so enjoyable, the last ones were challenging and rewarding. The basic drafting skills gave me tools that I've used off and on all my life. In leather craft I made some small coin purses and billfolds, but the highlight was making a nice-sized shoulder bag for my mother. It was lined with a soft lining and the outside was hand-carved with a flower pattern of which I was very proud. The most enjoyment for me came from the wood lathe. Mom and dad had recently gotten a new lamp for the living room. It was some form of painted glass and stood about eighteen inches from the base to the socket with varying diameters throughout. I liked the design and drew a pattern of it to remind me as I worked on making one from wood. I glued together five, one-inch by five-inch, two-foot long boards. When dry and ready I squared off the ends with the table saw and marked the centers for putting on the lathe. The lathe work was loads of fun, once I got past the rough outer part. When the diameters were right in all the places, I sanded the wood to a smooth finish that was later varnished to seal it. With the aid of a drill press, I drilled holes in both ends, which met in the middle. An eight-inch long quarter inch pipe was put in the top to which the socket was fastened. Then I took a six foot piece of electric cord, attached it to the socket, ran it through the lamp to the base, cut a groove in the base where the cord ran to the edge after it was stapled in tight, wired it to a plug and the lamp was complete. Now all that was needed was a bulb and shade that clips over the bulb.

That same lamp was in my parents' home for about ten years and has been in my home for the last thirty years. Due to my interest in bowling at that time I made two small lamps in the shape of bowling pins out of ash wood and put walnut wood round bases on them. The bases of all three lamps were also turned out on the lathe.

At the end of four years of high school I was no high honor student, mostly a B-C student who barely made the top twenty per cent of his class—thirteenth out of sixty-eight to be exact. However, my grades and SAT scores were good enough to make me college eligible. Since neither my sister nor brother went to college it was obvious that my parents desired for me to go and I wanted to go to become a physical education teacher and a mathematics teacher. So, with high school diploma in hand I was ready for college. However, when I enrolled in college the next year I discovered only one semester of high school geometry was not sufficient for me to start toward my degree with a double major in math and P.E.

Small town athletics is a big part of the total community level of activity. It played a tremendous role in my life and the part it played in development of self-esteem was obvious to me. My insecurity in the classroom was offset by my success on the court or field in athletics. I could "walk tall" so to speak in spite of my weakness of not being one of the top scholastic students. When a student is involved in many sports teams he or she (there were no 'she' teams back then) learns self-discipline, has a lot of fun and puts in long hours with a lot of work. About ninety-five per cent of my school days started at 8:15 a.m. when I left home and ended at about 6:00 p.m. when I returned home . . . then there was homework. But, it was all worth it!

Football season started with conditioning and preseason practices two weeks before Labor Day and the first of an eight game schedule (there was no tournament back then and schools were not divided into classes then except for Track and Field which had Classes A, B and C with the small schools like Hillsboro in class C) started the Friday after Labor Day and usually ended the last Friday in October.

There were usually only about thirty boys "trying out" for the football team so it was apparent that all would "make" the team unless they had some physical problem preventing them from being active on it. Conversely, one of our major conference opponents was a larger school and a noted "football power" that usually had one hundred or more boys trying to make their team. That was Westby High School in Westby, Wisconsin—a school that is now in a conference with large schools in their Class.

At that time I was about 5 foot, 8 inches and 150 pounds with interest in playing the "end" position, which would now be called "tight end". Though I wasn't very fast, I also was trying to play defensive end and speed was not a problem as the outside linebacker generally had responsibility outside of me where speed was needed.

Coach Kaz had put us in condition and prepared us for the first game. I was a second team offensive end and a second team defensive end. Kaz had told us defensively we needed to make good tackles and that was done by hitting the ball carrier at the waist with our shoulders, wrap arms around the guy's thighs, lift him up and plant him back on his "duff". "Anyone making a tackle that way will be rewarded with a malted milk," said Kaz, "and I'll buy," he said. Our first game was at Desoto, Wisconsin some sixty miles to the west. After a tiring bus ride we soon were playing the game. In the third quarter I was asked to play defensive end for a series of "downs" and did all right. Then it happened- the tailback on their team received a pitch-out and was headed around the end toward me—all 6foot, 4 inches and 220 pounds of him. When fear was gone from my mind, I put my head in his gut, picked him up and set him on his "duff". It had been third down, so they now had to punt. When I got to the sideline, a strong hand was firmly placed on my shoulder and the coach exclaimed, "YOU just earned a MALT." It was forty-five years ago, but I remember it as if it happened yesterday.

Homecoming game was always the third Friday in October.

Coaches are sometimes difficult to figure out. I had played some as an offensive end (very little) and a fair amount as a defensive end prior to homecoming game. I don't have the foggiest idea why, but for some reason the senior that normally played defensive nose tackle (over the offensive center) was replaced by me for the homecoming game—My first "starting" assignment in my high school career. TAKE NOTE: History will repeat itself later!

We had a winning season that year and did not win the conference championship. Unfortunately, Kaz's previous teams were good, but usually ended in second place as we did the next two years. Kaz's saying was, "Always a bridesmaid, never a bride!"

Basketball season always started about the middle of November with a non-conference game or an alumni game; so the first practice was often three to five days after the last football game. Didn't matter much to some of us anyway as we were out on the court the first Monday after football was over whether it was a "regular" practice with the coach or just our desire to play. The "farm" boys couldn't do that due to there being no "late bus" for them to ride home afterward as there was during the official season.

Larry Marshall was our coach when the "real" practices started. He was the varsity coach and a few freshmen tried out for the varsity team. Phil Eastman and I made the team as substitutes and since we were either freshmen or sophomores we were still allowed to participate in the "B" team (JV) games as long as we were not "starting" on the varsity team. There were also two sophomores, Harry Nemec and Cy Hotek, who were on the varsity and eligible to be on the "B" team. So, the four of us plus big Lewis Patterson (now about 6 foot 4inches) made up the "starting" five of the "B" team. We had a great season winning all or nearly all of our games. The varsity also had a good season and won some games by a fairly big score allowing me to get a chance to play some times later in the games. On the "B" team I average about fifteen points and twelve rebounds a game. The varsity finished the year with a 17-5 record after losing the second game of the sub-district tournament. It could have been a great year, but a couple losses like 75-73 and 66-64 shot us out of a conference championship during the latter part of the season.

Coach Marshall was a former star (all-Conference) at Platteville State (now UW-Platteville) and one day in practice someone was complaining about shooting so many free throws for practice. Coach got upset and he promptly showed us what he would like us to be able to do. In succession he shot 100 free throws. He missed number 54! He made 53 in a row, missed, and made 46 in a row!

Volleyball season started on Monday after our last basketball game. YES, we had a men's volleyball team back then and a good one. Of the six starting players that year, five were seniors. They were Wendall Shore, Sherlin Durkee, John Dooley, Bill Kouba and Gene Levy. The sixth starter was Steve Subera, a junior. We had a great coach, Bill Voelz, a man who stressed good serving; i.e., "Get the ball over the net so it lands inbounds on the other side, how hard is that?", he said in practice. He did not believe in the "power" serve we often see today and his philosophy was sound, "You work so hard to get the serve away from your opponents and then waste all that by serving it into the net or out of bounds—that's stupid and a big letdown for the team—just make the serve good and count on your good defense and offense to score." (paraphrasing his message) Larry Shear and I were freshmen that made the team as subs. We got to play a lot of the time, as our first team would be leading by 11-2 or 12-0 many times. I don't remember ever losing even a game during the season and the district tourney. We may have lost one in the sectionals, but regardless, we were the best team from the region and went on to State—what a thrill for me! We rode in cars or a couple station wagons and went to Milwaukee where we stayed at the YMCA on Friday night before a full day of games on Saturday. We all went out for a relaxing evening by going to a movie—*The Bridge on the River Kwei*. There were six teams in the tourney and we played round robin style—two games with each team. Waukesha H.S. was a perennial power and won the event, *Hillsboro H. S.* came in second! We even ended above

South Milwaukee H. S. Both Waukesha and South Milwaukee were schools with enrollment about ten times the size of HHS.

The following Monday it was time to join either the baseball team or the track team as both of them had already been practicing some. The choice was easy for me, as I did not feel baseball was my strong sport and wanted to throw the discus— use those skills I practiced picking rock years before. I was throwing around a hundred feet that year (not too bad for a freshman) and won First in some of the dual meets. My best throw was one hundred eight feet and I "placed" in the conference meet. Much of the fun that year (and the next two years) was watching my buddy Phil run the mile in very good time, winning the conference meet, placing high in the sectionals and doing well at the State Class C meet.

Most of my social life during this year was relegated to going to local movies and attending dances called "mixers" that were held after each home football or basketball game. Many times players did not feel much like dancing after a game, but it seemed like most of us would get our "second wind" about an hour after the game was over. A good long shower and about a half hour of rest was usually enough to make me ready to dance. Fox trot, jitterbug, and the twist were popular dances and due to the ethnicity of the area, many of us had learned how to polka and waltz. The latter two were more commonly exhibited at wedding dances and lots of freelance fun. I love to dance and was active doing that all through high school and later. I did have a "girlfriend", but most of our communication was by mail or phone as she lived about ten miles away outside of Wonewoc, Wisconsin and went to that school. I did see her on occasion after a game vs. Wonewoc or on a rare occasion when I got one of my older friends (with driver's license) to take me over to see her for a short time. At Hillsboro H.S., Elaine B. and I were good friends during school and as freshmen we were voted King and Queen of the spring Sweetheart Dance.

Chapter Eleven

In the fall of my sophomore year I had the starting position as offensive end and defensive end on the football team. We had another good season and did not win the conference championship. I caught a few passes in the games and played fair defense. I was about 6foot 1 inch and 170 pounds—possibly a little weaker due to being near the end of my "growth spurt". However, being continually involved in sports helped me maintain coordination skill.

The most memorable event of that football season was the first game when DeSoto H.S. came to Hillsboro to play in what I later called the "mud bowl". The local field was the outfield of the baseball field and was located about a quarter mile downstream (west branch of Baraboo River) from the dam by the mill. A dike separated the river from the field, so no problem with flooding. However, it rained all day long prior to the game and the totally flat (with a few low spots) field looked like a series of lakes that night at 8 p.m. kickoff time. Every step was another "slosh" sound and if you got onto a high spot you could see the water ooze out the top of your shoes by the laces. DeSoto was not the perennial power that they became in the 1990's. Our strong line pushed them around in the mud and it was fun for us—We won 38-0! However, we lost two conference games and tied with Cashton HS at Cashton, Wisconsin in late October. That was named the "ice game", but there was no ice—just icy cold 40 mph winds. My duties had expanded throughout the year and by that time I was punting and kicking some extra points (made one that night at Cashton—with the wind) and I had a punt (into the wind) go for a net yardage of eight yards. It was not a good night for a nice high spiral punt. Later, I got a net punt distance of over twenty yards when I kept it low into the wind.

A new friend moved into town the summer before that year and lived a block away from me. Dave Schell was a junior and played end in football, and he was a very good shot with a basketball. He had come from Westby where he was active in sports and as the basketball season developed he joined seniors Frank Sinkule and Steve Subera with freshmen Phil Eastman and me on the "starting five". We got off to a great start and were riding an 8-0 record in December when on a Monday I arrived at practice with a sore, swollen right elbow. "Why didn't you bang your left arm instead of your shooting arm?" coach Marshall yelled at me as if I were his own son. "How'd you do that, anyway?" he went on. "Well, I was ice skating and when my feet both went out in front of me, I landed on my back and instinctively tried to cushion the fall with the normal first defense—the dominate arm," I responded. "OK, you all hear this—No One on this team is EVER allowed to put on ice skates while I'm your coach," he screamed. "Yes, Sir," we said in unison. My arm was not as bad as coach thought, but my "follow through" was somewhat limited when I shot the ball. Adversity strikes again. I compensated and did not lose my position on the team.

We were playing good basketball and had amassed a 14-0 record. Most players at all levels have some form of ritual—coaches too! I ate chicken noodle soup and a cold meat sandwich at least two hours before a game—sometimes longer if we had a long bus ride. Coaches wear the same sweater, etc. I had another ritual (or habit) and that was a simple prayer that I said during the playing/singing of the National Anthem at the basketball games. Why the superstition discussion, you ask? It was game number 15 at Mauston Madonna, a Catholic H.S. in Mauston, Wisconsin that did not have a pep band, ergo no National Anthem was played, ergo no prayer was said by me! Result, we lost 50-48 in a hard fought game!

Regarding superstition, they (whoever "they" are) say that religion and superstition don't go together. If you are really religious, you are not superstitious. Can't you be religiously superstitious especially when the ritual involves prayer? Think about that a while . . .

We finished the regular season with five more wins, won both games in the sub-district tourney and won our first District tourney game. Then we went up against a real good Trempealeau H.S. team that beat us soundly in the District final. So we completed the year with a 22-2 record. Steve Subera led our team in scoring with nearly twenty points per game as an average and the rest of us were somewhere in the eight to twelve point range. Obviously, the second team members scored plenty as some of the games were blowouts—82-35 was one score.

Volleyball season was somewhat of a letdown from the previous year. Second in the State is a hard act to follow. However, it was a good year for me as I made the starting team as a spiker and played regularly. We won most of our games/matches during the short season and won the first level of the tournament only to lose at the level just prior to going to State.

Rules were changed by the start of spring sports and a student was allowed to participate in both baseball and track if they could work it into the practice times. Since my track events were all individual; i.e., discus, shot put and sometimes high jump, they could be practiced after the baseball team practice was over. So I played first base on the baseball team along with my track events. I was not a good hitter, but a fairly good fielder and first baseman. My batting average was usually under the famous Mendoza Line—.200.

In track I placed a few times in the shot put and high jump while I continued to improve distances with the discuss. My best for the year was 122 feet and I broke the old school record with it. I also won first place in the conference meet with the discus.

At the same time my good buddy Phil Eastman was busy

setting records of his own. He told me often, "No guts, no glory?" This was usually after he had completed running fifteen or twenty miles and I innocently asked him why he worked so hard. That year he won every mile event that he ran! That means he won all regular meets, the conference meet, the sectional meet and the State Meet. He set the school record and conference record with times between four minutes forty-four and four minutes fifty seconds. He won the State Meet with a time of four minutes and forty-one seconds. Unfortunately, that was his last State Meet in the mile run; will tell you why later.

Summer arrived and it was time for me to go to work. Matching my skill with opportunity I was hired by my mother's cousin, Ray Kahler. I lived and worked with him and his family on their farm that lay only a quarter mile from the farm where I had previously lived. My schedule worked out to actually twelve and a half days of work per two weeks. Every other week I was off from after milking cows on Saturday night until milking cows on Monday morning. The opposite weeks I was off from after the Sunday morning milking until the start of the Sunday evening milking. When I started I was only 15 years old and a job with board and room plus twenty dollars a week clear cash was a good job—if you don't think so, you should have seen how much I ate back then!!

I learned a lot about farming that summer and worked with all phases of crop growing from plowing the ground to harvesting the products. I did not like milking cows especially at night when it was so hot in between the cows in the barn and the squatting under them was not good for my knees. Some days we baled hay until dark and that really pleased me—any job to stay out from between those cows. I was also pleased one morning when he had me cut a few acres of hay while he and the others did the morning milking.

The most boring job on the farm is raking hay. A poorly trained chimp could probably do it. Set the tractor in a fairly slow gear and steer so you drive over the mower swath of hay and the rake does the rest. Some mornings after spending the night before at

Wisconsin Dells with my friend Tom Lindemann and getting home at two or three in the morning, staying awake while raking hay was a real chore around 11 a.m. Wow, the night seemed short when Ray called me at 5:30 a.m. with his usual, "Jim, up and at 'em"! I'd vow that I'll never do that again, referring to the staying out so late, and say, "I'm going to bed right after chores tonight, honest," but when night arrived somehow there was a renewed energy to "play" that was not there early in the day? And, if Tom did suggest going out by way of a phone call around 8:30 p.m., I'd probably be rarin' to go!

Rainy days on the farm usually meant one of three or four jobs for me to do. Some were kind of tedious—cleaning and straightening things up in a machine shed for example. Some were challenging and required thought, figuring and skill with a saw and hammer—making a four-foot high sixteen-foot gate out of five sixteen foot, one inch by five inch, oak boards. Some were dang hard work—tugging my guts out with a three tine hay fork trying to peel off layers of straw bedding and manure trampled down in a calf pen for a few months; i.e., cleaning a calf pen. Some were dusty and dirty—cleaning and preparing the granary for the new oats to be stored in August. But . . . they all had to be done!

The summer ended when school started, but the job did not stop totally. Many Saturdays during the next two school years Ray hired me to work on specific jobs for him usually starting around 9 a.m. and working until 6 p.m.—gave me a little spending money.

Speaking of money, one leisure interest that I developed during my freshman year (as if I needed another one) was bowling. Aunt Nina was an avid bowler and she loved the sport so much that she thought I would enjoy it also. She likes to share things and give things to her nephews and nieces. She took me bowling a few times and said I could get to be good at it with practice. After my first three or four sessions of three games I averaged 138 per game, which wasn't bad for my age at the time. With the development of that interest in bowling, I was somewhat prepared for things to come in the years ahead. More later . . .

Casual summer dress in high school years

Chapter Twelve

School started in the fall of 1959 and I was again active in football playing offensive end, defensive end, punting, kicking extra points and kicking off. When you add that up I was playing every time the ball was snapped or kicked—rest time was halftime! Of course, when you think about it, there is about fifteen to twenty seconds between each play for rest if you call standing in the huddle a way of resting. Our season was not that good—lost two non-conference games and had a 3-2-1 (won, loss, tie) record in conference play. The bad news is that was Kaz's last year as football coach—the next year he became the Principal of the High School. The good news is that my efforts were recognized by the other coaches in the conference and I was awarded a position on the All-Conference Second Team.

We rarely had serious injuries due to good conditioning, but did have some ankle strain and sprain injuries to both our quarterbacks. Then on a weird play Dave Schell had his left shoulder dislocated. Fortunately, it happened in the next to last game of football, but unfortunately he was a starter on the basketball team and the first game was three weeks after his injury occurred. How will he play with that bad injury?

Basketball started the next week after the end of football and poor Dave Schell had to wear a type of harness that prohibited him from raising his afflicted arm above his head. Any rapid movement of his arm above his head would have resulted in a repeat dislocation of the shoulder joint. He could throw passes, shoot the ball with his right hand, dribble the ball, catch passes (high ones with right hand only) and was limited to about seventy-five percent of full function. With specific exercises he was able to strengthen his shoulder and in time could play without the harness.

After a fine previous year, this team had some standards to "live up to". However, we had some injury obstacles—guards Phil Eastman (ankle) and Harry Nemec (ankle), Dave Schell (shoulder) and me (some knee problems as a carryover from football). Dennis Degner had returned to Hillsboro to finish his last two years and at 6 foot, 2 inches he was a valuable forward and a senior. We were joined by senior Cy Hotek and junior Lewis Patterson (now six feet seven inches and about 175 pounds) to make the seven players who carried most of the load that year. Starting line-ups varied and were unimportant.

Some schools had new gymnasiums, measuring eighty-four by fifty feet. Our gym was sixty-six by thirty-six feet with bleachers lining both sides with the front row so that the fans' feet were usually on the out-of-bounds line. The only openings in the bleachers were one about four feet wide on the east side to get to the locker room and the remainder of the school and one on the south end of the west side to get to the stage and a side exit. The small gym gave us an advantage at home but we were at a disadvantage when at schools with large gyms. The fans were really noisy and when we won an important conference game by a close score, they just poured onto the floor with hugs and pats on the back.

We lost game number 4 to Cashton by 63-58 and beat them later 63-57. We beat Wonewoc 52-34 early in the season only to lose game number 18 to them 63-58. Ironic that both our losses were the same score during regular season play. We won the sub-district tourney, but lost to Gale-Ettrick in the District tourney. Gale-Ettrick had a strong team and they won the La Crosse Sectional to go to State. We were proud of them, as they were a small school competing against giants. Thus, we finished our season with a 21-3 record, nearly as good as the preceding year.

Some interesting events occurred on the court that year. First, there was an elderly lady who lived in town and I had met her through Steve Subera and helping him deliver papers on his paper route. She did have a name, but Steve always called her "Gramma" when we saw her at the Post Office. She never missed a home basketball game unless ill and always sat in the second row of the bleachers about center of the court. One Friday night at the game I was going for an errant pass out-of-bounds. I leaped in the air, hit the ball back in-bounds and landed in Gramma's lap. I hadn't seen her in the Post Office for quite some time, but ironically the morning after that incident I saw her there and said, "Hi, Gramma." She paused for a minute, looked closely at me and then said, "Oh, It's you, Jim, I didn't recognize you with your clothes on." I wonder what those who overheard that, thought!

Secondly, we were playing a game at Ontario one night and during a time-out there was some problem at the scorer's table. The Official Scorer (scorer for the home team) made a comment to (or about) Phil Eastman that upset Phil tremendously. Phil did have a temper and he used it. He jumped up as though he were going to punch the scorer (he could do it too as he very often practiced releasing energy on his punching bag in his room at home). As a team leader I could not allow him to be ejected from the game so I got behind him quickly and grabbed him around the waist. I picked him up off the floor so his feet dangled and his arms were flailing at the air. He was upset with me, but I knew he would get over it.

Third, we were playing Cashton at Hillsboro and they had a guard by the name of Mike Schroeder, a Junior who was named to the All-Conference First Team with me at the end of the year. He was a great shooter and ball handler who also at 5 foot, 9inches got a fair amount of rebounds. After the game and all the hugs and pats on the back from the fans, I was just about to open the locker room door when I received a tap on my right shoulder. I turned to see Mike and heard him say, "Shanks sha lot, Potter." It sounded weird as he was saying it while showing me his front teeth of which ONE was missing. He then went on, "I DID have PERFECT teeth." I asked, "Did I do that?" "Look at your arm," he responded. I looked and there was a stream of blood from the middle of my forearm down to my wrist and gouged out tissue at the source (exactly in the shape of a tooth). I felt sick and apologized profusely, but that didn't change it or put back his tooth. Then I remembered getting a rebound, pivoting around with my elbows out to protect the ball and someone running into my arm. It sounds better to say, "someone running into my arm" than to say, "my forearm hit someone in the mouth." No Matter how you say it, he and I will never forget it! The strange thing about it was that I did not know anything had happened until he pointed it out after the game. I guess the intensity of competition masks pain and other things. If it had been today, the referee would have seen the blood and stopped the game due to the AIDS scare.

Fourth, thinking of that junior year brings back memories of my weakness on the court. It was in that Cashton game at Cashton where we lost early in the season. They were a team that used the "press" about as good as any. Both our guard, Harry Nemec and Phil Eastman, had suffered ankle injuries when they both played quarterback in football that year. Both of them reinjured their ankles in that Cashton game and I was assigned to help "bring up the ball" with reserve guard Butch Pacl in the latter parts of the game. We weren't pretty, but we got the job done and THAT was not what beat us. Dribbling full length of the court against a press was not my forte!

Speaking of team leader I always felt that the captain needed to have a cool head and use tact especially when dealing with officials or our coach. Coach Marshall had a bit of a tendency of becoming a little "unglued" at certain calls by the officials. One night during his last year at HHS we were in a strong tussle with a very close score up on the scoreboard and less than two minutes left. Some form of violation or foul was called against us and coach literally jumped in the air—the same jump he would make at the final buzzer when we won by one or two points! When he came down he was looking, pointing and talking loudly toward the official. Fortunately, I was only a short distance from him and went up to him face to face—well not really—actually at 6 foot, 2 inches and he was only 5 foot, 8 inches (if you stretched him) I looked down at him. I gently put my right hand on his chest and pushed him down so he was back in his normal coaching position sitting on the bench and as I did that told him, "We do not want a technical now!" We did win that game and even though he never said anything to me, I'm sure (in his heart) he was appreciative of me keeping my cool in the heat of battle.

As usual, then it was volleyball season. We had a good team, won most of our matches, but had limited competition until getting to the Sectional Level where we found the competition too tough. Our loss negated a trip to the State tourney—something I was eager to do once more before graduating.

The baseball and track & field seasons were fairly successful with one major exception, which I'll discuss later. I had one very interesting and productive day. I traveled nine miles with the baseball team and played first base for five innings of a game against Elroy. Then the track team stopped and picked me up to take me with them for a duel meet against/at New Lisbon. In the meet I placed first in the discus, shot put, and the high jump helping the team to easily defeat the opponents. In baseball my batting average was still probably below the proverbial Mendoza Line, but I enjoyed first base, though it still was a little too inactive for me. In the discus that year I managed to have another personal best of 130' setting a new school record.

Phil Eastman had the record time in the mile at the Conference meet the previous year and was out to beat that mark this year. We were at Sparta for the Conf. Meet and I was standing with a teammate who held an unofficial stop watch so he could tell Phil his times after each lap. At the half-mile mark I heard the timer yell "2:01"as Phil ran by. I immediately said, "That's too fast. Do you realize that if he were in the half-mile race he would have just set a new Conference Record in that event—and he still has another half-mile to go!!??" Well, sad to say, I was right. As Phil came around the last corner to head down the home stretch where I had many times seen him "kick" to finish strong, he appeared to be slowing and when he got to about thirty yards from the finish he was walking and stumbling. He stumbled over the finish line (the kid did not know quit) and fell to the cinders with a time around 4:40 or 4:41, but nobody cared about the time as they tended to him and then rushed him to the Sparta Hospital for treatment. He spent the night in the Hospital and was released the next day. He had suffered "lack of oxygen to the brain" we were told later. He was told to never run a race longer than the "220"—that's 220 yards and now is call the 200 meter race. Consequently, he had no chance to repeat as State Champ in the mile run.

You've all heard of the term, "Glutton for punishment". Well, I must be one. After some experiences with substitute work for various paper routes in town, the opportunity came for me to have my own route. Only there was one problem, it wasn't much of a route and I sure didn't have time to expand it. I bought an old clunker of a bike from my neighbor for ten dollars and it took me half a year to pay for it with my route. I delivered the Milwaukee Journal—how many people in little Hillsboro wanted a paper from a big city over a hundred miles away? Not many, but fourteen did want it on a daily basis and twenty-one took it on Sunday. The big problem with that is that I covered the whole town delivering fourteen papers just like I had previously done as a sub delivering eighty or ninety papers for Steve Subera—different paper. My huge paper bag was a quarter full with the daily papers, but on Sunday the paper often had over three hundred pages and twenty-one of them was more than the bag would hold. Of course, remember this is Wisconsin and many days during the winter there is too much snow for using a bike, so you walk.

One Saturday morning after a ten-inch snowfall I trudged to my fourteen customers faithfully. I did not own sunglasses and really did not like wearing them anyway. The sun was very bright that day and after over two hours walking on/in deep bright snow, I finally got done. About an hour or so after I got home I began to get a headache and my eyes hurt badly—snow blindness was mom's diagnosis and I agreed with her. I spent the remainder of that day lying on the couch with severe head pain.

When the school year was over I quit the paper route as I had that other job to do. Ray Kahler wanted me back to work for him for another summer with a five dollar per week raise I couldn't pass up.

The summer of 1960 was filled with a lot of hard work and some fun at the races at Wisconsin Dells. It wasn't much different than the previous summer, except maybe Tom Lindemann and I went to the Dells more often and I was very tired raking hay some mornings—have fun while you are young—you won't always have the energy to do that!

Throughout the years since Aunt Nina introduced me to bowling I had done some leisurely and occasionally with a date or other friends. My game had improved some and. I was probably averaging around 150 or so. Since I didn't have a paper route anymore, I needed to get some kind of job for a little spending money during my senior year of high school. I had done some dating in the past and of course needed money to go to dances and other things. Now that I was a senior and had been driving the family car for a year plus driving Ray's truck on the farm, I felt that maybe dad would let me use the family car a little more that year. And, I was right, so I also needed money for gas.

Speaking of money for gas, let me digress for a short time and tell a good true story. During my junior year I had developed a good friendship with Billy Richardson—probably the best high school musician I've seen or ever will see. He could play at least a half dozen instruments—no wonder he went to college to study music and played in the U.S. Marines Band—but I think his main instrument (the one he played in the H.S. Band and the group called the Ferraris) was the trombone. He could make it cackle just like the sounds of some of the glass pack mufflers on hotrod cars when they let off the gas going down a hill. I was impressed! Anyway, at times he and I would take girls out to a movie and double date as it was called. Sometimes we would just drive to the neighboring towns to see who we might see. Bill seemed to be able to "get the car" more often than I did. His dad didn't care as long as Bill put gas in it and not leave him empty. His dad was an insurance salesman who drove the 1957 Ford Fairlane with stick shift and overdrive all day. When Bill got the car it was always near empty and if he/we were going very far we had to put in gas.

One night Bill "got the car" and called me to see if I wanted to go "cruising"(looking for girls). I said yes and we took off. The car had its usual little amount of gas in it and Bill was not about to put in gas *again* so his dad could drive free all the next day. So we drove to Wonewoc (eight miles) and up and down main street a couple times. Then we drove to Elroy (another eight miles) and up and down main street a couple times. Finally, we headed for home (about nine miles) and went about three miles before we ran out of gas. He steered, pushed a little, and I got behind the car and pushed it—thank God it was all level—about a mile to the little gas station on the north end of the Village of Union Center. The service man came out and said the usual, "Fill 'er up?" Bill replied, "No, I want twenty-five cents worth of regular." The price of regular gas was between thirty and thirty-three cents a gallon depending on where you got it, so we were probably getting about three-fourths of a gallon. We drove to Hillsboro (five miles) and sat in front of my home with the engine running while we talked for about fifteen minutes and then he drove home. The next morning his dad got in the car, started it and drove about one block where he ran out of gas—mission accomplished, we got him!! Not so fast—how did we get him—did we inconvenience him any? No! From the spot where he ran out of gas it was one and a half blocks downhill to Ernie's Mobil Station where his dad usually got his gas!! That's one day we didn't pay for his transportation.

Chapter Thirteen

Back to the subject of bowling . . . The Township Bowl was owned by Jack and Pat Dempsey and Jim and Virginia MacDougal. Aunt Nina bowled with Virginia in the women's league and had a friendly relationship with Jim and Virginia. Somehow word got to me that Jim and Jack were looking for a person to work cleaning the bowling area (not the bar) at Township Bowl. (If I was going to have any kind of social life during my senior year, I better have some income). So, every morning for the next nine months I was at the bowling lanes before 6 a.m. on weekdays and before 8 a.m. on weekends to do my two-hour job.

The job consisted of cleaning up all the empty bottles, glasses and the spills in the seatee area; throwing out all the trash including bathroom wastebaskets; cleaning the bathrooms; dusting the benches in the seatee area; dusting the floor and mopping it in the seatee area; dusting the approaches; dusting the six lanes with the linoduster and every other day treating the wood of the lanes with "dressing" sprayed from a spray can. Then, after turning the cloth of the linoduster to a new clean spot, I pushed it down each lane and pulled it back smoothing the oil dressing evenly over the lanes to hopefully make the lanes respond equally for bowlers throwing a curve ball, hook ball, or even a back-up ball. I never really got the full impact of lane consistency until I bowled in the Petersen Classic in Chicago years later. More on that later . . .

The job was good for me. It got me going early in the morning, paid me fifteen dollars a week and a fringe benefit was the privilege to bowl at "open" bowling times for only fifteen cents a game instead of the usual thirty-five cents a game. As time passed, I was involved in cleaning the Brunswick Automatic Pin Setting machines and learned about their functions as well as how to "troubleshoot" minor problems. I often helped Jim or Jack when I was bowling by going down and taking care of minor problems for them—either for my machine or any other one.

When bowling leagues started in September, Aunt Nina and I joined another couple to form a four-person team to bowl in the Couples' League on Wednesday nights. I had a good year and improved with help (some coaching from Jim MacDougal) and with the inexpensive practice games finished the season with a 173 average. Some experienced bowlers said, "That's pretty good, especially since you only use a 'conventional grip' and not a 'finger-tip grip' as many good bowlers use." And, as years went by, I never did get a new ball with it drilled for the finger-tip grip.

Eugene Finley joined the staff at HHS and replaced Kaz as our football coach. Some people thought "just when Kaz might have a chance for a Conference Championship, he leaves the position to become Principal." Why? Because of the "starting" eleven on the offensive team, ten were seniors! The other starter was a gifted athlete—sophomore Ron Benish at left end. Yes, we did win a share of the Conference Championship that season, but it wasn't easy. And, as a matter of fact, HHS has not won a football championship since then—1960.

DeSoto came to town for another mud-bowl game and we managed to slosh our way to a 6-0 victory. Then we squeaked past Wonewoc 6-0 followed by a 12-0 loss to Royall H. S. (combined Kendall and Elroy high schools). The three powers in the conference seemed to be Royall, Westby (perennially) and us. So to prove that, we had to beat Westby, at Westby, the next week. We were down by a 13-6 score when defensive tackle Bill

Henthorne burst through the line and nailed the back in the end zone for a safety, 13-8. We had a chance, but it was getting late in the fourth quarter when we HAD to SCORE. There was no scoreboard as high schools have today so the back judge official kept the time on his stopwatch. We were down to our last series of plays—"twenty-three seconds," the back judge said as we huddled with first down on the Westby twenty-six yard line. "I'm calling three plays," Phil Eastman our quarterback said, "Left formation, flat pass—the first and third time (if needed) the end goes long and the wingback cuts off short, the second time you two guys (Kenny Janousek and me) switch." The fans were screaming but we didn't even hear them. The first time Phil threw to Kenny high and out of bounds over his head. The second time he threw to Kenny high and over his head. The third time he threw to me, even though I was well covered due to my history of catching quite a few passes. I had a defender behind me and in front of me. The defender behind me (between me and the quarterback) got turned around and the ball came down bouncing off his shoulder pad and up in the air.

Where are my rebounding skills when I need them? It was an easy rebound for me as the defender stumbled and fell down. So I grabbed the ball, spun around and with a stiff arm got rid of the defender who was out ahead of me. Then it was off to the goal line about ten yards away and a halfback or safety defender waiting at the two or three yard line. As I approached the defender I simply lowered my head and let my 185 pounds overpower the 140 pound guy in my way. I bowled over him and into the end zone for the winning touchdown. Then, for good measure, I kicked the extra point for a final score of 15-13. That was my single greatest thrill in high school sports.

We had a little letdown after that and we lost (for the fourth year in a row) to our non-conference nemesis, Mauston Madonna. However, we then regrouped and finished the year with wins over Cashton and New Lisbon to secure a share of the title.

Jim Potter

"I'll punt in the snow, if you have a camera"

Homecoming was usually something special in the school year. Part of the thrill was winning the football game, but many students put more emphasis on the dance and the crowning of the King and Queen. The King was always chosen by the football team and was a senior player on the team. The Queen was a senior girl chosen by the classmates. The only bad thing about that system is that it may make the King being crowned with the Queen while his steady girlfriend looks on. Kenny Janousek, wingback and defensive halfback on the team, was King and Linda Linton (not his steady girlfriend) was the Queen. I had dated Linda once or twice in our early high school days so I asked her to go with me to the Big dance.

I was normally a good dancer (that's what they told me) and she was also good so I really looked forward to a good time—she was also pretty. However, during the game that afternoon I received a cross-body block (nearly a clip) on the side/back of my right knee that sidelined me for a few plays in the second quarter. Unfortunately in a small school an injured "regular" player is usually better than many of the substitutes, so I played with the injury the entire second half of the game. Then we went to the dance that night and I sat on the side of the gym most of the night watching Linda dance with other guys (why should she have a lousy time due to me). I probably danced two dances with her and they were VERY slow ones—slow ones were nice. Adversity strikes again.

The next morning I checked into St. Joseph Memorial Hospital with a huge amount of fluid on my knee and spent the weekend in the hospital. Torn cartilage was the diagnosis and the torn piece of cartilage moves around in the joint thus giving it the name trainers call a "mouse". Periodically the piece gets caught in the joint sends a big man down to the floor in a split second. Such was the case for me when the fluid had gone down and I started the basketball season. "Doc" Tatter to the rescue! Paul Tatter was a junior and was on the basketball team. He also was very intelligent and liked to serve as the trainer unofficially.

"Doc" taped ankles for some of the guys and he/we developed a way to prevent my knee from hyper extending which would cause the "mouse" to get caught in the joint. It was inexpensive and unique. He took two pieces of one-inch wide adhesive tape, the kind used for taping ankles, that were about ten inches long. Leaving flat ends about two inches long each; he twisted the tape so it made it strong like a rope in the center. Then, with my knee slightly bent, he put one end of each strip on the lateral (outside) side of my leg just below the knee and the other end just above the knee. He repeated this on the medial side (inside). He then wrapped tape around my leg securing the flat ends to my leg below the knee and above the knee. Consequently, I could play as hard as possible and never totally straighten my leg. This prevented the "mouse" from getting caught in the joint between bones and prevented any pain all year long. "Doc" taped my knee before every practice and every game for the entire senior year season.

No knee brace needed for a photo

Larry Marshall had coached HHS to a combined record of sixty wins and ten losses during the past three years and had the opportunity to coach at a bigger school in Stoughton, Wisconsin. There was a man originally from Elroy who was coaching at La Farge H.S., named Bill Moran. He became the next HHS basketball coach and some townspeople commented, "He knows which side his bread is buttered on" referring to the fact that he was coming to a talent laden team and, if he was a good coach, he should have a good year which would be great for his career. He hadn't been a star player, to my knowledge, but he "ate, drank and slept basketball"—the old saying that referred to people who were extremely knowledgeable about the game of basketball. He was a good, ah, great coach who inherited three senior starters from last year, developed junior, 6 foot, 3 inch Don Sterba and sophomore 5 foot 10 inch Ron Benish to join Lewis Patterson, Phil Eastman and me. He had three quality seniors (Richard Housner, Joe Levy and Butch Pacl) as his front line reserves as well as Pete Nelson, Paul "Doc" Tatter, Larry Holak and Dave Braithwaite "pushing" the regular players to be better.

Based on the successes of the past three years—two conference championships—the local fans were excited about the prospects of three-in-a-row and, needless to say, fan support was at an all-time high. On top of that there was a history making event in Hillsboro that year. Mr. Kubarski had previously put up an antenna on the high hill by the water tower and had developed the Community Antenna System for city folks to hook-on for MUCH improved television reception. From that he expanded to the FIRST EVER closed-circuit televising of high school basketball games. It was a good thing—most nights the gym was filled to where all the "standing room only" spots were filled with a body. The foyer area by the entry was about ten feet by twenty feet and often it was filled with people standing—only those in front of the group could see the game, but they still were there in support of us. The closed-circuit TV was good as many elderly people could see us play as they sat at home.

Some may say that when you have a good team and don't win the State Title or don't go to State you had a bad year. We did not do either of the afore mentioned things, but we had a GREAT year in my mind. We started with a victory over a good alumni team and went on to an undefeated eighteen game regular season. We breezed through sub-district and district tourneys unscathed. We met our "Waterloo" when we faced Reedsburg, a school about four times our size, in the first game of the sectional tournament.

We played them 'toe to toe' for the first thirty-one plus minutes and were leading by two points. With about a half-minute or so to go we had the ball taking it out of bounds on our half of the floor. Phil threw it in to me and I was guarded with a man between me and the basket plus one man on each side. I dribbled the ball toward the one open side (away from the basket) and the nearest defender stepped in to steal the ball throwing his left knee into my left thigh. The whistle blew and I walked toward the free throw line when I saw the referee put his hand behind his head— the signal for offensive foul!

I was numb, I guess, but I still had faith that the player would not make both free throws (was a bonus situation) and we still could win. I was also sick, knowing full well that it was my fifth foul and I would no longer have any say in the outcome of the game. He DID make both free throws and tied it at 60-60. Our team came down with the ball, but could not score before time ran out sending the game into overtime. In overtime Phil fouled out with one and a half minutes left and I felt like we lost our quarterback and were behind by a touchdown! Reedsburg won and then beat La Crosse Central High the next night for a trip to State; a trip all of our fans thought we should be making. All we could say was, "We got beat in overtime by the team that went to State". Fans and most people (including me at times) thought that had we beaten Reedsburg we would have "automatically" beaten La Crosse Central the next night! NO ONE in their right mind could guarantee that. La Crosse Central had handled Sauk City High with a fair margin of victory Friday night, so they may have done the same to us on Saturday night. How many points does the letdown of losing cost you in your next game—especially when it is your last game of the high school career? We were able to regroup and did win the consolation game against Sauk City by only 57-55! I don't care what others say, it was a great year— 23-1 record, the best HHS has ever had.

Regarding the "call" for my fifth foul, there was a loyal fan in the stands that night who had been a very good athlete back around the late 1940's at HHS. He had a little trouble with referees and umpires who did not make the correct call as he saw it and often as others saw it . . . the story I got later was that he "went through the roof" after that call and after the game he let the official know exactly how he felt. I was captain of the team and could have spoken to the ref at the time, but it was not my style; and, it might have gotten me a technical foul giving them another free throw and the ball, which would cause us to lose in regulation time with it all my fault.

One week after the sectional tourney was the State Tourney at Madison, in the Field House. As was the case with many other schools, our traveling team for tournament play was rewarded at the end of the season with a trip to watch the "best" play in the State Tournament. Since it was less than a two-hour drive we traveled by car with a coach driving us back and forth each day—two cars, two coaches did the job and we really enjoyed it. Unfortunately, Reedsburg did not do well at State. I think Milwaukee North or Milwaukee Lincoln won that year. They were both powerhouses during my high school years. They were both large schools, and remember, there were no classes of schools for basketball then.

Before we knew it we were active in volleyball with basketball only a distant memory. We had a good team and our great coach, Bill Voelz, was not at HHS anymore. The replacement volleyball coach was our football mentor, Eugene Finley. The irony is we could have coached ourselves that year due to the fact that of the ten on the team, eight were seniors who were well trained in sound fundamentals of the game. We waltzed through our regular season games—there was no conference in volleyball—with many wins of 15-1, 15-2. Competition got a little tougher in tournament but we were determined to make it to State in this sport, and we did.

The State Tourney was held at Wisconsin Dells High School that year and not at Waukesha as in the past. Since it was only about forty miles away and coach Finley was not rigid, we were allowed to go "on our own" so to speak. True, the sophomores (all two of them) and maybe some others rode with the coach. Some of us went in private cars and took our girlfriends with us.

Kenny Janousek drove and Mary, Diane and I rode with him. Ah! Young Love! Wasn't it something else? In the games—two against each of the five other teams—we lost to the powers, Waukesha and South Milwaukee, split with Montello, and took two from Butternut and Prescott. Thus a 5-5 record was ours. Waukesha and South Milwaukee split and beat everyone else twice. The tie caused a best-of-three games playoff and the Waukesha H. S. team won the title for the sixth straight year, after beating South Milwaukee two games straight. We finished third in the State!

As volleyball season was finishing up that year, the baseball team was already having indoor practices with their new coach, Bill Moran, our basketball mentor. Since Kaz, former coach, was Principal it was time for some new leadership. I had my plans to throw the discus in track & field, but I wanted to have a new challenge and be more active in baseball. So I went up to coach Moran the first day and said, "Coach, I want to learn how to catch." "OK," he replied. "But I can't guarantee how much you will play, you know Pat is a pretty good catcher even though he is just a sophomore." "I know," I said, "I'd just like to give it a try." It wasn't easy, but I tried and I liked it even though it was not very good for my right knee.

I played only part of the time—Pat was a better catcher—and I only hit three for sixteen (.187) but I had one fun day at New Lisbon. The pitcher gave me a slow "fat" pitch and I hit it way over the left fielder's head—due to my excessive speed (ha-ha) I had to scamper back to second base, after rounding it, to get a double. There was no fence there as a home run barrier, but many of the players said that at home the hit would have been over the scoreboard in left field. For once I felt like I did something in baseball.

In track & field I had a good year. I practiced hard with the discus and at the Prairie du Chien Relays I did my best yet—136 feet and the "Relays" record—but the way I did it made me proud. The wind was blowing in from the thrower's left and most of the guys were throwing straight out toward the center of the throwing arc. The wind did catch their discus and turn it up on edge causing it to head for the ground and give them a very short throw. I decided to take a chance. (I love the line from the movie *Grumpy old Men* or *Grumpier old Men* that says, "The only regrets you'll have are the chances you didn't take." The chance I took was to throw the discus right into the wind. It was remarkable, the "plate" went out, was caught by the wind, leveled out and continued to sail onward. That was using my head and using the wind to my advantage.

Not long after my good fortune at the PDC Relays, we were at Elroy in a triangular meet. It was there that I reset the school record in the discus at 141 feet, 5 ½ inches. The record was 122 feet when I started as a freshman so I improved it by nearly 20'. Many teammates said, "That record will stand a long time." They were correct as it stood for forty years. The person who broke my record was 6 foot 6 inches, 265 pound solid muscles, State Heavyweight Wrestling Champion and a good kid, so I'm proud for him. His record (about six feet past mine) will last a long time.

Flipping the discus

The track team got home late one night near the end of the

school year from either the conference or the sectional meet. Phil Eastman and I had gone home to grab a bite of supper before we were to go to Yuba to play in a softball game (summer league had already started). We still lived next door to each other and he had a car he had bought after having a good job at the local mink ranch in the summer. We met at his house and he said, "I gotta go up to school and see if I can get my baseball shoes before we go." So we piled into the old Chevy and took off for school. The gym doors were locked and all the track people, coaches too, were gone. We went around to the physics classroom where the window was only about seven feet from the ground and, being late May, the windows were usually open for much of the day. "Maybe they're unlocked," Phil said, "I'll crawl up and see." Just as he opened the window we heard a woman holler, "Hey," from across Mill St. and we responded, "We'll be right back." We went in the window, ran through the school to get to the locker room, and got his shoes. We were late already for our game, so we went out the gym door to where Phil's car was parted and on to Yuba. We knew who the woman was, but we did not know what she would do!! God Forbid.

The softball game went well and we went home to bed never thinking about the school again. The next day at school it was weird. There were these County Sheriff's deputies walking around and the local police too. "What's going on?" Phil and I asked different people. "Somebody broke into school and they're taking inventory of everything in the chemistry/physics lab as well as the offices," was the general response. Phil and I remained quiet and the investigation continued.

Phil and I didn't have many classes together, so we didn't have to give our guilty looks to each other all day long, but occasionally we met to discuss our position. There was about a week to go before Graduation—wouldn't it be ugly if both of us were not allowed to graduate, what should we do? These questions ran through both of our heads. Finally, about 3:30 p.m. we decided to get excused from Study Hall and go to the office to see Mr. Shold, the Superintendent. With solemn attentiveness we relayed our tale of woe. "You DUMB FOOLS," he hollered as though we were a hundred yards away! Then he calmly let us know how irresponsible our behavior was the night before AND during the day while all the investigation was going on. "Do you have any idea how much your stupidity cost the school today?" "No," we replied squirming in our chairs. Whew! Boy, were we glad to get out of there.

Wait a minute! Did I not tell you earlier that my dad was custodian at school—yup, still there! What do you think happened when I got home that night? Well, he didn't hit me, but I sure got an ass chewin' verbally. Actually, I was much more relaxed talking with Mr. Shold than I was with my dad. I stated earlier that he did not have much tolerance for that type of behavior around the school, and coming from me, God, I ought to know better! If I don't graduate soon, I may not live to do it.

Graduation day arrived and with our robes we went to get the coveted diploma and other awards, scholarships and the like. No scholarships for me, no academic achievement awards, but I did get the Class of 1961 Athletic Award. I was proud of that after earning a letter four years in football, basketball and track as well as three years in volleyball and baseball. Somehow that all seemed fitting as I had desires to go to college and become a physical education teacher. Shortly after graduation, Kaz told me that he had heard from Dartmouth where they might give me a scholarship to play football. I felt honored, but not excited because Dartmouth sounded "scary" to this small-town boy.

Our high school intramural sports included basketball, volleyball, ping-pong and tennis. Being a varsity player I was ineligible for basketball and volleyball, but could do the others if desired. Through the teaching by Kaz many of us had learned how to officiate basketball and volleyball, so we usually did that for the intramural games. I played some ping-pong, but was generally slower than the better players and did not last long in the tournaments. In tennis I was just a "country boy" compared to at least four guys in the tourney, but I decided to try my junior year anyway. There were two seniors; a junior and a sophomore that I knew could beat me any given day. To make a long story short, I won the tournament that year! Must have "psyched them out"!

Officiating intramural sports provided me with a truly fun experience in high school. There was a team that was coming to town for a game as a fundraiser for some group. A team made up of faculty and other interested adult players was scheduled to play this all female team—the Texas Cowgirls AND, I was assigned to be one of the referees! What fun. Those Texas Cowgirls toyed with the refs in a similar fashion as the Harlem Globetrotters do. On top of it all, they were very good with the basketball. I enjoyed the job! The post high school rewards were good. My experiences officiating basketball led me to "working" some high school games for a little income while I was in college.

Chapter Fourteen

It was about mid-May of 1961 when Jim MacDougal asked me if I was interested in going on a trip to help him out. I said, "Sure," and he picked me up at 5:30 a.m. Saturday morning. He had just closed the bowling alley bar at 2 a.m., slept three hours and he and his wife were ready to go. She drove to Madison while he slept and I rode quietly. She left us at Hertz truck rental and went back home to Hillsboro. We got into a movers truck, cab-over with just one rear axle, and Jim started it up. Note: Neither Jim or I had ever driven any truck bigger than a half-ton pick-up, so hold on to your hat.

Jim let out the clutch as you would with a pick-up and it lurched forward in a jerky fashion, and then stopped as he had put the clutch in again and was laughing from the experience. He let it out again and same result, again, again, again, he let out the clutch as we both are laughing so hard tears are in our eyes. We are jerking back and forth in the seat with my head nearly hitting the dash. Finally, he stops, looks at the gearshift and says, "Oh, this must be a four-speed transmission, I bet I have this empty truck in dual low." "Good deduction, Jim," I said. "You want me to drive?" "No, I'll get it," he said while shifting into second gear to start out. Prior to that we jerked about eight times and went about forty feet! Now with it in the right gear we had no trouble and were on our way. After about a hundred miles he asked me if I wanted to drive so he could get a nap. I said I could and got behind the wheel. My hands were wet with sweat as I was as nervous as the proverbial "cat in a room full of rockers". I kept drying my hands on my pants (thighs) and then back on the wheel. Jim laughed! Then he went to sleep. We were headed for Indianapolis, Indiana and then on down to Louisville, Kentucky where we were going after a house full of furniture left there by his in-laws when his father-in-law became ill and went to the treatment facility. His mother-in-law had gone on to Hillsboro and neither of them had been in the house since. So, I drove three or four hours and then gave the reins back to Jim. He drove on to Louisville and stopped to look at his directions. We went a few blocks, turned right and went on looking for a specific number on a house. After about two or three miles and upon entering a neighborhood that did not look like it was too safe, Jim finally stopped at a gas station. "Fill 'er up?" said the coal-black man who was the operator of the station. "No," said Jim sheepishly, "ah, we're looking for 708 East York Street," (not real address). "Whale, yall done come too fer, yats bout twenty-six block tother way" and he motioned back the direction we had just come from. Feeling some obligation to the man, Jim said, "Do you take credit cards for gas purchases?" "Sho do," the man answered. "Then pump me ten dollars worth of regular, please," said Jim. The man responded and took care of us just fine. We headed back where we had come from.

Finally, as it was beginning to get dark, we found the house. Jim went up to the door and discovered that his key would not open the lock. He then found a note—"Locks have been changed, please go to see Mr. Smith at *504* Glory St," (not his real name or address). "Where the heck is Glory St., can you find it on that map, Jim?" Jim asked me. We looked together and found the address, got our bearings as to where we were in this big city and Jim pointed the truck in the right direction to see the man. We got to his house and he let us in, but that is about as far as his hospitality went. "Yall's last munt rent chek no good," he said with a Kentucky drawl that you could cut with a sharp knife." "How can that be?" Jim answered. "Jus did," the man said. After much discourse between the two the upshot was that the renters had closed out their checking account before the last month's rent check cleared causing it to bounce and the man wanted his eighty dollars! Jim tried to pay him with a check from his bowling alley business account and the man would have no part of that. "How do I know that check won't bounce too?" was his response to that idea. Finally, the man agreed to take a twenty-dollar check on Jim's business account and sixty dollars cash from Jim's pocket—extra money Jim brought for food, etc. Whoopee! Jim was broke and I had eight dollars in my pocket—money I brought for food, etc. Thank God Jim had credit cards for gas. NOW, we get the key to the house. NOW, it's after 10 p.m. and very dark! NOW, we go back to the house.

The key does open the door and we go into the house. Thank God the electricity was still hooked up so we could see what we were up against. Have you ever seen two grown men cry? Well, we could have, but we didn't have time. I forgot to tell you, incidentally just like Jim forgot to tell me, that he wanted to get this furniture loaded so he could get back to Hillsboro in time to work at his business the next evening. "Rots o' ruck", as some would say, meaning there is no way in the world that will happen. And, realistically I initially thought we would have time to take in a show of some kind in the big city. We might have if everything had not "gone to the dogs" since we entered Louisville.

Imagine for a moment that you have in-laws who live in a distant city, a place you have never visited as they've only lived in that house a short time. One morning after you finish your breakfast you get a call saying, "We just finished our breakfast and he is very ill, I've called the ambulance and we are going to the hospital." Weeks later you walk into that house to find dirty breakfast dishes in the sink and on the dining table in the kitchen. NOTHING has been touched since they left.

That is the scene Jim and I walked into about 10:30 p.m. that Saturday night. Jim's first thought was to wash the dishes. "No, that food is so stuck on them we'll never get them clean . . . there aren't very many so lets just throw them in the trash can with the other things we don't want to move such as this spoiled stuff in the refrigerator," I said as I stared into the 'fridge. "Good idea," he responded, "I'll go out and see if I can find a trash can, you just pile the junk in the sink for now." So I piled up the junk, salvaged some silverware and was ready to fill the trash can when he returned. What next, I thought looking around the living room. "Look at all those houseplants, are we going to move all them?" I asked. "No, they look dead, maybe we should dump out the dirt and dead flowers, and keep the pots," he said. "OK!"

Next it was time to do things "on top". We took all things on top of dressers and the bureau and put them in the drawers . . . that led us to lamps that would not fit into drawers so we went around and took shades off lamps and bulbs out, unplugging them as we went. Back in the bedrooms we stripped the beds and used the linens to wrap around dressers, etc to protect them from scratches. Once we had things in some semblance of order in the house, we started to move them out to the truck. "Refrigerator and stove go first so they are tight against the front of the truck," I said. He agreed. Did we have the muscle??

I was my same 6 feet, 2 inches, 185 pounds since last fall. Jim, on the other hand, was a real heavyweight (pun) as he was about 5 feet, 11 inches and 135 pounds if weighed wearing a sweat suit after being out in a heavy rainstorm. He did have some strength, but I don't know where it came from.

"I'll open the truck doors, Jim, while you get that dolly under the fridge," I said going out the door. Outside I was met with another unwanted surprise. It was raining a nice easy steady shower—the kind that could last for hours! To shorten an already long story, we loaded furniture and appliances and dishes and lamps and clothes—all of it . . . in the steady rain. About 5:15 a.m. we put the last box of something into the back of the truck and swung the heavy doors to shut them. Three inch gap? Won't go shut? What else? "Push on that," Jim said. I did as hard as I could. "We'll have to rearrange things," Jim replied seeing that both of us pushing on it was not getting the job done. "Wait a minute, I have an idea," I said, "We've got it narrowed to only

two more inches and you will be able to drop the latch." I walked
back about ten yards from the truck and told Jim to drop the
latch when I hit the truck with my shoulder. It was like hitting the
blocking dummy back in football; only this one was made of
steel. I ran and hit the door full force—Jim dropped the latch.
"That's it," I said with jubilee in my tired voice. "One more thing,"
said Jim. "We have to tie this old gas pump onto this back ledge"
(about an eight inch steel ledge was outside the back door). It
was an awkward six or seven foot long steel gas pump (like they
once used on farms) that probably weighed one hundred fifty to
two hundred pounds. But, we got it tied on.

Jim locked the house door and we piled into the truck. I
realized that I had just been up (out of bed) for exactly 24 hours,
working hard with loading a truck for seven hours, had driven a
fairly large truck for about four hours and I was soaking wet!
God. was I tired!! Jim started the truck and the heater felt so
good on my cold and wet skin. He said he was feeling pretty
good and would drive for a while, so I could get some sleep, then
I could drive later while he slept. Within minutes the warmth and
my tired body put me sound asleep.

I woke up in daylight (was almost daylight when we left the
house) and looked at my watch, 8:30 a.m., and I was hungry.
Why were we not moving? Jim WAS going to drive for a WHILE!
How long is a while? Not very long. I woke Jim up and asked
where we were. "Just outside of Louisville," he answered.

"We probably went ten miles and I got so sleepy I had to pull
over," he went on. "Glad you did, I'm hungry," I said without
hesitation. "What are we going to do for money?" he asked. "I
still got the eight dollars I brought for spending money," I said,
"Maybe we can get pancakes cheap in this little restaurant you
conveniently stopped beside," I suggested. "Maybe," he said
getting out of the truck. Jim was more of a ham and eggs man
with little desire for carbohydrates as indicated by his slight frame.
But, he had a short stack and I had a large stack of pancakes
costing us less than three dollars total, not bad. That fit our budget
(what budget?) and our bellies. I felt good and told Jim I was

ready to drive and he could continue his nap. "First," he said, "we better get some gas. You keep your eyes pealed for a (brand name) station 'cause that's the only place my gas credit card will work for us," (no ATM's back then). Within about ten miles or so I said, "There's one," referring to our next stop for gas. Jim took care of it and NOW he could get his nap as I drove on toward Indianapolis. Once on the edge of the city there were three or four lanes going toward the center of Indianapolis and three or four lanes going out with a buffer in between. There were some main streets that crossed the highway, but they were marked with stoplights. I moved with the flow of traffic, about the speed limit or slightly below it, and the stoplights were green, green, green, green, yellow as I hit the intersection, yellow just before I hit the intersection, yellow a while before I hit the intersection, red while I was in the intersection and red as I approached the intersection . . . "Oh shucks"(possibly not an exact quote), I said as I slammed on the brakes! Screech . . . finally stopped, looked down the cab-over nose of the truck to see cars flying by within inches of my front bumper. "What happened?" Jim asked as he peered out from under the glove box where his sleeping body landed during the sudden stop. "You sleepy, you want me to drive?" he queried with an 'I don't trust you' tone in his voice. I don't think he messed his britches, but he could have based on the fear in his voice. I guess that would be truly a "rude awakening." "No I'm fine," I said and explained to him how I was timing the lights and they 'got me'.

I drove on through Indiana and across northern Illinois while Jim got a good nap. He took over in Wisconsin and we stopped someplace near Madison to get a couple burgers and fries for our "supper". Still had money left from my eight dollars! Jim drove on to Hillsboro and let me off at my place. Somewhere, maybe by Madison, he called Virginia to have her get someone to work for him that night. After leaving my place he drove out to the in-laws' farm and they unloaded the truck. *Not one thing broken!* he exclaimed to me the next time I saw him. "We must be professional movers, don't ya think?" I said facetiously.

During the first three years of high school I had dated many different girls from Hillsboro, Wonewoc and Elroy. They were casual, no commitment, generally less than five dates with any one girl and included going to movies, dances and other social events. Many of my friends had "gone steady" and I wondered what it would be like not to have to make five or six phone calls before I got a date. As a senior, I felt it was time that I pursue the "going steady" experience and I had a girl in mind that might be interested. She was a junior and, believe it or not, the same girl that I had caught when she fainted at church that day four years earlier. She was attractive, full of energy, athletic (unfortunately a girl's athleticism was restricted to intramural sports and/or cheerleading back then) and a joy to be around. We came from the same socio-economic background, attended the same church and generally had some things of common interest. BUT FIRST, I had to get at least one date with her before thinking about "going steady". So, around the start of basketball season, I asked her for a date and we were seen together often for the next ten months. It ended with her feeling anger and hurt after I had wrecked my dad's car while hurrying to help with thrashing at my sister's farm in August. When I saw her after the wreck, I vividly remember her words, "What are you trying to do, kill yourself?" Surely it was for the best as I was about to enter college (someplace) and she had an exciting senior year of high school to finish. Maybe it was love, maybe it was infatuation, maybe it was fitting in, maybe it was puppy love or maybe it was just two people having fun together. But, it was dating security for both of us.

Summer was upon us and college was only three months away so it was time to make some money to help or pay most of the expenses incurred there. Brother Don had gone into the service (Air Force) and after basic training was stationed at Chanute Air Base in Rantoul, Illinois. It was in 1956 or 57 when he was coming home on leave with some other men that they were hit by a drunk driver down near Janesville, Wisconsin. The two in the other car were both killed and one in the car with Don was killed. Don was fortunately in the back seat, but he still suffered a major broken leg (thigh area) and a back injury. The leg required an eighteen-inch long pin down the center of the bone and he was in traction for a long time. Somehow everything did not heal right after extended treatment at an Air Force Base in East St. Louis, Illinois and he was discharged from the Air Force with partial disability. In 1958 he married Mary Wood and they lived in Madison for a while until they moved to Poynette, Wisconsin. They lived there in 1961 and they must have been the ones that told me about the canning factory at Arlington, Wisconsin just five miles south of Poynette. California Packing Corp. canned peas and other things during the summer and hired people from all around to work for them. Their major label was Del Monte, but, as I found out my second year with them, they also labeled canned peas with twenty-five to thirty other labels. I went down there when I heard they had started the pea-packing season and applied for a job. One dollar and five cents (minimum wage then) per hour and time-and-a-half after ten hours a day was my starting salary. After completing the paperwork, they showed me where I would work/live for the next six weeks or so.

They took me south on US 51 (road actually runs east and west there) until we were about a half-mile from the intersection with State Hwy 60. I could see a large pea viner spitting out pea vines on the right just before we turned left into a driveway leading to the bunkhouse and cook shack. It was almost noontime and while we were there some of the workers had finished lunch and gone into the bunkhouse next door to rest on their cot a few minutes before going back to work. A farmhouse was off to the east where the people lived who owned the farm.

They showed me the bunk that was "mine" for the duration, told me how the meal ticket was punched and how that system worked, showed me the showers and place to wash clothes and introduced me to the few guys in the bunkhouse. I could hardly understand the guys (southern drawl). I found out later that I was living with and working with fifteen guys ranging in age from fifteen (he lied about his age) to twenty from an area northwest of St. Louis, Missouri. "The South will rise again!!" If I heard it once, I heard it a hundred times in the next six weeks. Education? I thought I had one, huh, I was just getting started down that road!

At 1:00 p.m. my indoctrinator from the office took me down to the viner to meet the viner "boss" as he was called. The boss gave a brief set of rules and instructions along with a three-tine pitchfork and said, "You're ready to go to work." So I did. Some of you who were farm kids remember tugging on the pitchfork trying to remove the layers of straw mixed with feces packed down in a calf pen that you had to clean out. The same pain hit my back as I tugged at the pea vines with the fork on this job. The peas were cut like we cut hay on the farm, rolled into windrows and picked up with a loader into a huge dump truck. The truck hauled the vines to the viner, back up to the front of the feeder part of the viner and dumped them all matted and clung together. Do you know how sticky they are? VERY! There were usually two guys at each viner pitching peas into it—one on the left side, one on the right. Sometimes I felt like I had pitched two-thirds of the load into the viner—I don't think those other boys were brought up with regular use of a pitchfork as I was. Plus, I was much bigger than most of them as they averaged around 150 pounds per "man." "Man", I use that word loosely referring to them. "Boys", would be a more exact term!! At 6:00 p.m. we broke for supper and returned at 7:00 p.m. to complete the day. The end of the day came any time between 9:30 p.m. and midnight usually. But remember, THAT WAS OVERTIME! Whoopee! One dollar and sixty-two and a half cents per hour!!

It wasn't overtime for me—not that first day—because I had not worked in the morning. Our typical day was as follows: Up before 6 a.m., breakfast (and you better eat it) at 6-7 a.m., work from 7 to noon, lunch noon to 1 p.m., work 1 p.m. to 6 p.m., supper 6-7 p.m., work from 7 p.m. until quitting. Then shower, do laundry or whatever and sleep fast before getting up at 5:30 a.m. This went on seven days a week unless it rained so much the cutters and big trucks could not get into the fields—that was our only time off. If you missed a block of work; i.e., morning, afternoon or evening—you were done!! It was a great way to teach people to be responsible in the "real" world. We probably averaged thirteen and a half hours a day. That's $10.50 regular pay and about $5.65 overtime pay for a gross daily pay of $16.15! After Social Security was withheld and we paid fifty cents each for our meals (bunkhouse was free) we probably cleared $13.50—ironically equal to a dollar an hour net pay! Now, believe me, it was all profit, there was absolutely no way you could spend any of that money unless you quit!! In 40 days that added up to a nice $520, which was about half of the total cost for me to attend La Crosse State College for two semesters, fall and spring.

Someone quit and we had a new guy join us at the viner station. Talk about a different dialect of the English language!! I had already gotten so I was talking a lot like those guys from Missouri, but this was another new experience. "What is your name?" I asked the new kid. (This is what MY ears heard) "Do Rat," the guy said. "What?" I asked with a confused voice. "Do Rat," he repeated. "Man, ain't you ever heard of the Rat Brothers?" he went on. After further queries and by association, I figured out that his name was Dewey Wright! "Where you from?" then I asked without hesitation, then almost wishing I could retract the question for fear of more confusion. "Corbin, Kentucky," he said so fast I had to have him slow down and repeat it several times to understand!

The steady summer job ended about the end of July and with my full red beard—didn't shave at all during my six weeks in "prison" at the viner station—and a southern drawl I went home to get back to catching with the City Baseball team (I did some before going to Arlington) and preparing to go to college someplace. Many people did not know it back then, but we had two local men who pitched in the minor leagues of professional baseball—they were Bill Stenerson and the late Rudy Rott. I had the opportunity of catching Bill Stenerson and now I know what baseball commentators on TV are talking about when they say a pitcher throws a "heavy" fastball and a fastball that moves. Bill did both and I had the sore hand to prove it. I also had the privilege of catching my former HS coach, Bill Moran. His fastball wasn't heavy and not too fast, but he had a great "drop" ball. I guess they would call it a curve ball today since what we used to call the curve is now called a "slider" by the announcers. Anyway, Bill Moran was pitching one night in Hillsboro against a pretty good team from Camp Douglas and I had the most fun ever as a catcher. I really was not a good catcher I have learned as I watch more baseball on TV, but at the level we were playing I didn't have to be. The pitchers were experienced and knew what they wanted to throw on each pitch, so I simply went through the signs like I knew what I was doing, with them shaking them off until they saw one they liked, nodded OK and threw the pitch to me. The signs just kept me from getting something that I didn't expect!

Camp Douglas had one player who was a good/great hitter. Bill Moran and I had managed to get him out each time with much use of his "drop" pitch and it was a good one especially that night. It came in waist high and dropped a foot or more causing even the best batter to hit nothing but air. We were ahead 7-0 in the seventh inning and that good/great batter was coming to the plate. I called for the fastball and Bill didn't shake it off, he just threw it. I thought, well, maybe his arm is tired from throwing so many "drops" that he just doesn't have many more of those left! Anyway, the pitch came in and the pitch went out just as fast. There was a tree about twenty feet tall just beyond the dike that was just beyond the center field home run fence; the ball left the batter's bat and flew like a bird over the top of that tree. I went out to the mound and Bill was laughing, "Guess that's why you never wanted to throw him any thing very good," I quipped in jest. We went on to win the game 7-1.

It was near the middle of August and it was Sunday. Normally one thinks of Sunday as a sort of "laid-back" day, but I had a schedule I wanted to keep. My folks and I had gone to church and it was nearly noon so I grabbed a bite to eat and then had an argument with my parents about my plans—they thought it was too much to do, but I (now 18 years old) KNEW BETTER! My plan was to go to Shirley and Gordon Penshorns to help with thrashing for a while, then go to Hillsboro to play a City Baseball

JIM POTTER

team game and then back to help more with the thrashing. If I would have had my own car it may have been different. So, I rushed out of the house, jumped in dad's car (a pretty blue '55 Chevy—would love to have one today) and took off fast for the farm. I was going fast down the gravel road toward the farm and it was noon hour so I expected all the tractors and wagons to be parked while the men ate dinner. I went around a fairly sharp and blind curve only to be confronted with a tractor and wagon taking up the entire narrow roadway. I steered toward the ditch on my right and hit it, but the ditch was narrow with a bank of dirt/rock wall behind it. At the point where I hit there was sand rock that protruded into the ditch. It lifted the right front of the car some and spun the rear of the car around. As the rear end spun it swung out into the roadway and sheared off the left rear wheel of the empty wagon sending the wheel and tire intact out through the adjacent pasture. The rock lifting the front right of the car caused it to turn up and stop resting on the left side of the car. The left door apparently was jarred open some and I was somewhat stuck in between the seat and the door. My biggest wound was a bruise where the lever for moving the seat forward and back was poking into the meat on the right side of my buttocks. I shut off the engine and soon men were working to tip the car back on its wheels. They did and I was able to exit the right side door. All I could think of was, what a dumb thing to do! And, how angry will dad be? I felt sick, not physically, but emotionally. The tractor driver was Gordon's dad, a person who ate light and worked hard. Thank God he was not injured. After that the baseball game lost all importance!

About that Dartmouth scholarship to play football there and go to school in the Ivy League, it sounded nice as it would pay three-fourths of the year's expenses which at that time was about two thousand eight hundred dollars. But, I wasn't ready for the "big time" so I turned it down and planned to attend La Crosse State College, one of the top ten schools for Physical Education in the Country.

Chapter Fifteen

It was then late August and I was busy getting some clothes lined up to take to college and I was scheduled to live in Reuter Hall, the first Men's Dormitory on campus. Dad was working at school and mom was working at City Hall as City Clerk leaving me home alone to get ready for school when the phone rang. "Hi, Jim, this is Dick Sweeney, did you get a letter from Vickroy?" "What, what, what?" I said confused at his question. Dick Sweeney grew up in Hillsboro and co-owned, co-operated Hillsboro Sweater Company with his dad. He played shortstop on the City Baseball team and was a sports enthusiast. He also knew many coaches around the state as he traveled so much on his job selling letter-sweaters and jackets to schools. He also had graduated from La Crosse State and was Captain of the baseball team that was coached by Mr. Bill Vickroy; Vickroy also coached football.

Anyway, after some discussion I knew that there was a letter from Mr. Vickroy in the mail (got it the next day) that invited me to come up to La Crosse to practice football with the Varsity Team— an honor given to only a handful of freshmen students. "They want to try you out as a tight end," Dick told me as he drove and I rode with him in his car going to La Crosse the day after I got the letter. "You know, with your good pass catching record from high school, they think you might make a good one," he continued after rounding another one of the many curves on Hwy 33 between Cashton and La Crosse. "Well, I'll sure give it my best try," I answered modestly feeling a little unsure of myself and having some pre-college academic anxiety.

As Dick drove up to Reuter Hall, we saw the football team practicing out behind the dormitory on the large open practice area; the area would hold at least two regulation football fields. "We better hurry so you can make it to the practice," Dick said as he stopped the car in front of the dorm. We ran into the dorm with Dick carrying most of my baggage and fortunately the housemother was there. Mrs. Davis was a very nice lady in the over-sixty (I imagined) age bracket. We explained our haste and she gave me the key to room 408. "We'll talk more later," I told her as we headed for the stairway on the end of the building. Once in the room we "dumped" my belongings on the bed, hung up a sport jacket and locked the door. We rushed out of the building to the car and Dick drove to Whitich Hall—the physical education building and locker room for team sports. Luckily we found someone who could get me a uniform and in ten minutes I had it on and was on my way to the field for my first college football practice. Dick drove me to the open spot in the chain link fence, parked the car and went with me to report to Head Coach Bill Vickroy. Later I met back coach Bob Kime and line coach Bob Batchelder.

The practice was no different than it was in high school that first day. Since I was an hour late or so, I went though a series of conditioning exercises mostly on my own to get loosened up and did a few wind sprints that were timed. I knew then that they were probably thinking "he's kinda slow", so I had to really show off my pass catching ability to impress them enough for me to stick around and make the team. Fortunately, my pitching peas for six solid weeks made me in good physical condition at least strength-wise. The team had been practicing for a few days already so I was a little behind the others, catch up time. After the practice was over I was measured and weighed—6 foot 2 inches and 191 pounds was the tally. Dick stayed around (almost like an expectant father) to make sure that I was comfortable in the new environment. He encouraged me and I thanked him for all his help as we parted and he headed back to

Hillsboro while I went to my empty room to get it organized a little and put my clothes away.

For the first week or so in La Crosse I practiced football, oriented myself to the campus, visited my aunts and uncles in the city. Then I waited for new student orientation day, registration for classes, and school to start after Labor Day. During registration for classes I learned that my one semester of geometry in high school was not sufficient to start out with a Mathematics major to go with my Physical Education major. So, I opted to get a minor degree in the chemistry-teaching field. In high school I had some visions of becoming a good accountant, but all that went by the wayside when I enrolled at La Crosse State College (as it was called then). The classes were good; world history was very hard (only thing I remember is when the professor told us about some very young woman who married Peter the Great when he was in his sixties and then he said "But she divorced him when she discovered he 'couldn't hit the long ball anymore'"). My English teacher was strict and put the fear of God in me but I did OK. My chemistry teacher was good (he was Chancellor years later) and I enjoyed my physical education classes.

My strong desires to be part of this college football team went sour and it was time for a reality check when we prepared to play the first game at St. Norbert College. Reality was that I found myself listed as #7 on the depth chart as a tight end. From my past you see that I was rarely on the second team much less way down the list. There was first team, second team, a few names on third team and then the long list of tight ends that went way down to me. Obviously, I did not travel with the team for the first game. I was somewhat "down" the next week in practice and then it happened—I was walking past the linemen's work out area when one of the defensive tackles, Big Joe, a freshman at 6 foot 7 inches and 280 pounds, suffered an ankle injury. Coach Batchelder yelled out, "Hey, do we have any defensive linemen around here?" I walked over to coach and said, "Batch, can I give it a try?" "Sure, Jimmy, get in there." (Batch was one of the few who had the respect and was allowed to call me Jimmy). If I

am allowed to call coach Batchelder, Batch, he sure can call me
Jimmy!!

So I went into the defensive line at left tackle and worked
there the rest of the week practicing our defense against the
freshman team (later known as the "hamburger squad") that was
running the offensive plays of the next opponent. On Thursday
the coach posted the depth chart for the Stout State College game
that Saturday; I was listed as second team defensive tackle
behind Mike Rose. Mike was what I then called an "iron man".
He was about 6 foot 3 inches and 210 pounds—all muscle. He
was an all-conference football player and swimmer; he had a
work ethic that would put most to shame.

All I wanted to do was work hard and maybe, just maybe, the
coach would give Mike a "breather" allowing me to get into the
game for a few plays. Three times I was on the field for a series of
plays and each time it was three plays and punt for the opponent.
Having lost to St. Norbert a week earlier, 14-3 we wanted to avenge
the loss and we did, 3-0 in a great defensive struggle, winning
our first conference game in the process. I finally felt like I was a
part of the team.

Our next foe was Whitewater State College (Conference game)
at Whitewater. I was able to maintain my same position on the
team and made that trip with them. Some things take a little time
to sink in and what was slowly sinking into my mind was the bare
fact that all, yes ALL linemen playing college football were bigger
than I was—in high school I was always one of the biggest, but
not here in college. So, I had to work a little harder and be a little
tougher, if possible. Anyway, I got into the game on three or four
series of plays and had one of my highlights in all the football I
played. It was third down and nine yards to go when I broke
through the line rushing the passer. Just as the quarterback threw
the pass with his arm coming forward, I hit his arm and the ball
went toward our secondary at a forty-five degree angle. Dick,
one of our defensive backs, saw what had happened and was
able to intercept it and ran it back for a touchdown for us. NOW,

I felt like I was a contributing part of the team and helped us win 21-13. I was thrilled!

A Conference game with River Falls State College was next in line and it left no specific memories except that I played a fair amount of time and we had the "game in hand" most of the time with it ending 33-7 in our favor. But, going to Eau Claire State College the next Saturday did leave memories—bad ones! First, we lost that Conference game 20-13, secondly, I did NOT play for one single play, and third, my right knee was "acting up" from kneeling on the sidelines all night. Even "Big Joe" with his ailing ankle got to play—why didn't I get to play? Needless to say, the bus ride home was a long one that night. I felt sick!

The next day, Sunday, I don't think I went to church; I think I slept until noon, went to lunch at the cafeteria and then went downtown to John's Bar. The Green Bay Packers were playing on TV at 1:15 p.m. and I usually watched at the dorm, but I did not want to be around my fellow students. Besides, I needed to drown my sorrows, so to speak. At six o'clock, after enjoying the Packer game, arm wrestling with a couple local tough guys, and having my fill of glasses of beer, I walked back to the dormitory. The cafeteria did not serve supper on Sunday so my roommate, Steve, suggested we order a pizza. "No thanks, I'm full," I said.

On Monday and Tuesday I limped some but tried my best to hide it during the practices. When Wednesday's practice time arrived I learned something that will always make me question— What makes coaches tick? At the previous game I could have been invisible, it wouldn't have made any difference. In the first two practices this week I was somewhat less than one hundred percent. Now, as we prepare for Superior State College, Conference game and our Homecoming, I find my name on the depth chart— First Team nose tackle. Sound familiar? Same position as I played in the Homecoming game in high school my freshman year!! My spirits went from zero to sixty in about three seconds! Instantly my knee felt much better and I was ready to give them all I could. I was excited as my parents and brother were coming to see the game. I played most of the time on defense and we won the game by a huge margin, 40-13. I was a "happy camper!"

Oshkosh State College was on our schedule (next, I think) but we did not play the game due to rain. Memorial Field in La Crosse was nearly flooded as it rained most of Thursday and Friday that week. Somehow it could not be relocated or rescheduled thus leaving LSC one game short on the Conference schedule. That became important because Oshkosh was one of the weaker teams in the conference, winless or nearly winless in conference play. Stevens Point State College was our next opponent who had a 6-0 conference record having beaten Oshkosh while we had a 4-1 record so, even if we beat them, we still could not tie for the championship.

We prepared as though we DID have a chance to be champs and I was again at the nose tackle position. It was a night game and quite a spectacle greeted us after we ran from the locker room to the field. From the opening in the fence to the other end of the field (over one hundred yards) we ran between two human chains—two lines of cheering fans standing side by side. I was pumped and so were my teammates. We warmed up and just before the game we went to the sideline for our final instructions from coach Vickroy. (Mr. Vickroy was NOT known for enthusiasm, generally very stoic, businesslike) We huddled. Coach said, "You know, these guys (opponents) want to go to the Cigar Bowl" pause . . ."But the only bowl they're going to is the TOILET BOWL." Laughter and cheering roared from the breaking huddle and we were indeed "fired-up" for the game.

The game was a tough one and our offense seemed to have trouble moving the ball so our defense had to come to the front and do its best. We did ok and aided the offense with a turnover or two. Then, in the fourth quarter leading 22-14, the final gun seemed to take forever to sound. Three times we came off the field after forcing them to punt when the middle linebacker (Bear, his nickname) said to me, "I wonder how many more times we will have to hold them?" "Probably once more," I said looking at the clock. Our offense punted and once more we went to the field to stop them.

Incomplete passes the first two downs and a six yard gain on the third down left them with fourth down and four. "Watch for the draw play," Bear said to me just before they came to the line. "OK," I responded lining up in the called defensive formation. The ball was snapped and I went nearly untouched into their backfield (Bear was right) and followed the quarterback going back to the fullback. Bear was right behind me. About one second after the fullback received the handoff, I hit him low and Bear hit him high—crunch—we did it! Our conference season was over and with our 5-1 record we were finishing second to the team we just beat as they had a 6-1 record.

I guess the last game of the year was scheduled in case we had a great season and needed a lesson in humility. It was at SIU, aka, Southern Illinois University in Carbondale. The most positive thing about it was a day off from classes that Friday—most people of sound mind would gladly go to their three or four classes on Friday rather than ride in a team bus all day to some foreign territory. To make a long story short, they beat us 47-13. Their highlight was having Amos Bullock, the leading ground gainer in the country, run for way-too-many yards. After they scored a touchdown (often) they lined up to kick the extra point. I was eager to bust through the line (hadn't done it while they were running over us, but maybe) when the center, 6 foot 3 inches, 235 pounds came up over the ball and his right guard, 6 foot 4 inches, 245 pounds, beside him shoulder to shoulder. So I'm looking a 480 pounds of muscle across from me when the center says to the guard, "Why don't we cream this guy this time??" It was indeed a long afternoon for me at SIU. If school size means anything, La Crosse State was about two thousand students and SIU was probably four or five times that size. But, there's next year . . .

The fall semester progressed along and I was able to be the B-C student that I was in high school. Had a 2.8 GPA on the 4.0 scale. Spring semester I had many of the same classes and did fine with a 2.6 GPA at the end. One highlight was a speech class that I enjoyed. I never was in forensics in high school, but by being involved and in front of people often through athletics, I did have fairly good self-confidence. The instructor was "cool" as he said, "I don't want you to read a bunch of magazine articles and think you know all there is about the subject and deliver a speech on it. We can all read the magazines. Make your speech on something that you definitely know more about than anyone in the class." I spoke about defensive football strategy and why it sometimes doesn't stop the runner. It was a great success; "A" in the class.

Part of the general Physical Education Curriculum for all freshmen was a class that covered four sports areas with the last nine weeks being volleyball. I had played a lot of successful volleyball in high school and I had just recently completed playing on an intramural team that won the championship with a good rhythm of pass, set and "kill" being used repeatedly. So, what is this 60-year-old instructor going to teach me about volleyball? I didn't know, but I was going to go with the flow and do the best I could to impress him with demonstration of good skills. During the process I came down crooked on my right foot after a spike; a fairly strong ankle and weak knee resulted in a twisted knee. That was my last volleyball game for that semester as I went to see Dr. Phillips, orthopedic surgeon, in La Crosse. Thank God there were only a couple weeks of school left and I could ambulate on crutches until final exams were over and surgery could be done on my torn medial meniscus cartilage. The day of surgery I took my last final exam with crutches beside me and, when done with the exam, I hobbled my way some eight blocks or more to the hospital for surgery. Adversity strikes again.

It was St. Francis Hospital, a well-noted treatment center run by the La Crosse Diocese of the Catholic Church (I think). What gives me that idea is the fact that there were many nuns working in various nursing positions and there was an adjacent convent (OK, nuns' quarters if not a convent). The upshot of this is that the Nurse Anesthetist was a nun in full black dress and she hooked up the IV to put the "juice" to me. The LAST thing I remember was the Doc telling her, "Don't turn that on until I return." I think she "knocked me out" before he even got very far away and NOT after he returned. The good thing is that I woke up a few hours later patched up.

Either a physician's assistant or a physical therapist was beside me as I gained total consciousness. "We don't want you to lay there too long before we start re-strengthening that leg," he said. "How can I help?" He went on, "Just do what I say and we will see if you can stand beside the bed." He helped ease my leg over the side of the bed as I raised my upper body from the flat of the bed. It is amazing how soon your equilibrium gets messed up when you are lying flat. As my leg was gently lowered, the blood rushed into it and it began to hurt and feel like it weighed about a hundred pounds! Once standing, the whole room began to turn black as my unbalanced equilibrium left me very lightheaded. The therapist put a chair behind me so I could sit down and put my head between my legs until I could get the blood back into my brain. After that I got up periodically and went to the bathroom by dragging the chair behind me incase I needed to sit down in a hurry. The next day I was discharged with the crutches and instructed to do certain leg-raiser exercises to strengthen the quadriceps muscle. I really had a scare the second day at home when I couldn't lift my leg with the quadriceps muscle—I thought "Oh my God, I haven't done enough exercise and it has lost all its strength." I thought about paralysis and wondered if it was "setting in". How dumb that was, but panic can bring out weird thoughts. Soon the leg strength was back, the crutches were gone and I was getting ready to go to my summer job.

Chapter Sixteen

That job was back at the canning factory and I thought I would be pitching peas again. Upon settling in there for the pea packing season, I was assigned a bed in one of the bunk houses near the factory and right next door to the diner house. My job was working at the section of the canning process right after the crates of canned peas came out of the cooling tank. We received these crates holding five hundred pounds as they came up the track out of the water. There we pushed them along either a track to the right or a track to the left leading to a scrambler. The scrambler was a machine that unloaded the crates. The track took the crate so it was directly above a hydraulic hoist (like a jack for a car) with a surface diameter smaller than the crate's diameter. The crates had open centers in the bottom and the cans were layered in the crate separated by steel "holy" sheets (thin sheets of steel with many half-inch diameter holes in them) for drainage. The other part of the scrambler was an arm with an arc on the end of it. With the crate in proper position, the operator pushed a lever to move the arm and arc out past the top of the crate. Pushing another lever he then raised the layers of cans up so that the bottom part of the top layer was level with the flat surface of the scrambler bed. He carefully moved the arm forward pushing the cans onto the bed where a conveyor took them to a track that carried each can into the next room and into a label machine.

We started at 8:30 a.m. one day (the day really doesn't matter as every day is "workday" at the cannery) and worked until noon, broke for lunch and returned at 1:00 p.m., worked until 6:00 p.m., broke for supper and returned to work at 7:00 p.m., worked until midnight when we took a fifteen minute break, then worked until 5:30 a.m. Wow! Are you tired yet? If you were hungry you could grab a little breakfast at the 24 hour diner, but most of us went to the cot to grab a little sleep before the beginning of day TWO at 8:30 a.m. Day TWO, THREE, and FOUR were all carbon copies of Day ONE! The last two days, especially during the night hours, we tried to cover for each other and allow the more tired ones to lie down for a half hour of rest. I did lie down once for about fifteen minutes, but I woke up and went right back to it. We were all walking zombies, but somehow we did the job. On day FIVE I went to work at 8:30 a.m. and after having my lunch at noon I took a short nap hoping to get woke up to go back at 1:00 p.m. Nope! Slept all afternoon and went back to work at 7:00 p.m. I really didn't lose anything by sleeping as the boss put us on "shift" starting that night. I had already had my "off-shift" so I was ready to work. The "shift" system was very simple—work as scheduled for 24 hours and be "off" the next time period. Since I was off from 1:00 p.m. to 6:00 p.m., my 24 hours ran from 7:00 p.m. that night until 6:00 p.m. of Day SIX. Then I was off the next period (7:00 p.m.-5:30 a.m.) and expected back at work at 8:30 a.m. on Day SEVEN. Then I worked all day and night until 5:30 a.m. of Day EIGHT and had "off" the work time from 8:30 a.m.-noon.

This shift scheduling was wonderful for those of us who had just completed a cool seventy-four hours work in the first FOUR days. Most of us got about three hours sleep a day for each of those first four days. BE POSITIVE, think of all the money we were making at $1.15 per hour for the first ten hours a day and $1.72 per hour after ten. BIG BUCKS!! *$11.50 plus 8.5 times $1.72 ($14.62) equals $26.12 a day for four days.* That's the closest I ever came to killing myself for one hundred dollars! With the shifts we got one full night of sleep every three days, one good sleep (5:30-noon) and one good nap (1:00 p.m.-6:00 p.m.) so the mood and quality of work done was much improved. I think the first four days was a test to cut out the lazy ones.

After two or three weeks on schedule and with the same crew of workers things were running quite smoothly when one of the guys quit and a "new" fellow joined the crew. He was a bit of a smart aleck and seemed to be a little "Wet behind the ears", to coin an old saying. Immature, is what I called it and I was not happy one day when he was sloppy as he pushed a crate of canned peas and swung it on the track causing the bottom of the crate to strike my knee—the one that recently was cut open!! We had steel toe covers that we wore in case a crate came off a track (it did happen a couple times in six weeks) and landed on someone's foot, but we did not have any knee guards to protect against what happened to me. From that time on I had some fluid on my knee and it hurt some of the time. I had to make money to go back to school, so I had to work the remainder of the canning season—there was no time to find another job, so I just had to tough it out.

When the pea packing season was over, I had cleared five or six hundred dollars toward next year's school expenses. The last month of the summer I did some odd jobs and was able to work some on the thrashing crew to earn a little money. Labor Day came and went. I did not report to La Crosse State for early football practice due to still having excess fluid on my right knee and my career of football was over. Coach Vickroy knew that I had had surgery in June, so he probably had not expected me to be ready to play football in the fall of 1962. As the season went on I learned that my "old" position of nose-tackle was being filled by a freshman who was about 6 foot and 220 pounds and quite good. In retrospect I say, "He probably would have beat me out for the starting position anyway as he was bigger and maybe tougher than I was." Maybe things are just going the way they are supposed to go. In hindsight I can honestly say, "One roadblock in life can lead to many opportunities otherwise missed."

I concentrated on my classes that fall semester and while

attending a dance class that was part of the sophomore curriculum in the physical education major I learned of a dance group on campus called the L-Bar-X Dancers. A classmate of the opposite sex was a member of the L-Bar-X Dancers and after she danced with me in class she told me that I should "try-out" for the dance group. The class was a square dance class and it was the first time that I had ever done any square dancing. I had always had good rhythm in dancing in high school and thought I would enjoy doing square dancing, and I did enjoy it. But, the L-Bar-X Dancers was a somewhat elite group with not everyone making it. The group was limited to usually thirty-six members. That made it possible to have four "squares" dancing at a time with two men and two women extra in case someone was ill on the day of the show. Each "square" required four couples (eight dancers) and our leader and teacher, Miss Bernadine Kunkel, liked symmetry and always wanted to have four squares dancing at a time. We did a "show 'n' share" program when we went out "on tour" for a weekend of dancing. "Show 'n' share" meant that we started the program with us showing a dance to the audience and then our leader would say, "Ok, kids, each one get one," and that was our cue to go out into the audience and get our next partner. After that we would teach a dance to that partner as a group and then dance it with them as a finished product. Thus, as prospective future teachers, we were involved in teaching during this extra-curricular program. Then we would 'show' another number or two before going back out to get another partner.

I was part of this group the last three years of my college life at La Crosse. One very productive and fun event was the weekend trip we took to the Rice Lake, Wisconsin area. The Dancers (group) included students from three different communities in that area and, with the help of people in their hometown, they arranged for places for all of us to stay in homes of friends for Friday and Saturday nights. We were scheduled for four performances; i.e., Friday night, Saturday afternoon, Saturday night and Sunday afternoon and headed straight back to La Crosse after the last show. The shows were held in school gymnasiums in three different towns and the Saturday night show was at the Elks Club.

The most enjoyable part of that trip was during a show in a school gym. In the 'share' part of the show I went up into the bleachers to get my partner and selected an attractive lady who appeared to be past sixty years young. She enthusiastically took my hand as I reached out to her indicating that she was my choice among the ladies with whom she was seated, young and old. Once we were on the same level we soon discovered that there was about a foot difference in our height (maybe fourteen inches) and her weight was probably about half of mine. If you know a little about dancing a waltz and if you know what is contained in Gustov's Skoal you are now laughing as your mind visualizes this lady and I dancing this dance. For the majority of you, here's the scoop: 1) Gustov's Skoal is a *very deep knee bend* waltz, 2) I hold my partner in the skater's position (she is on my right side and my right arm is behind her back grasping her right hip area, she has her left hand on my right shoulder), 3) we join with another couple by facing opposite directions and the men hook left elbows together, 4) once the dance starts, the ladies have to travel about three or four times as far as the men (as each of us dances forward the four of us go around in a circle). So, after DEEP, two, three; DEEP, two, three; DEEP, two, three; DEEP, two, three my five foot tall partner doesn't even have her feet touching the floor—her legs are just flying as I hold her with my right arm!! AND the smile on her face was worth a hundred dollars (a hundred dollars was a lot of money back then). When it was over and I took her back to her seat, she thanked me nicely and planted a little peck of appreciation on my cheek. She was sweet.

The Saturday night show at the Elks Club was educational as I learned that college kids weren't the only ones who liked to drink a little or a lot. Teaching square dance is not real easy but it gets to be a real challenge and in fact quite fun when your students are all having a "wonderful" time enhanced by some spirits, fermented variety. They had a good time and we had a good time, enough said.

In addition to the dancing, my sophomore year was different in a few other ways and they were major. First, I was selected to be an assistant counselor in the new White Hall dormitory on the third floor and the Head Counselor (unfortunately, my roommate) was a real nerd—senior, English major, damn near 4.0 GPA who acted like he would fit in well with a women's homemaking group. I MUST HAVE got some kind of compensation for it—I know the Head Counselors got free room and board—or I wouldn't have put up with the crap. Maybe all I got was the experience so I later could become a Head Counselor. In a nutshell, my roommate was a pain in the ass.

Secondly, this was academically the toughest year of all four. I had anatomy—physiology as well as organic chemistry both semesters. On top of that I had an English Literature class that I hated, taught by an instructor that used a lousy method of testing—bottom line . . . I flunked it! Year-end cumulative GPA was 2.04! All my freshman year good grades were blown away with one bad semester. 1.99 GPA was the dropout point!

Thirdly, I discovered a group called the La Crosse State Bowling Team, tried out for the team by bowling about a 182 average and made the team. I was usually the fourth or fifth from the top as there were three of us usually in the 180 to 185 range. Two of our teammates were usually above that range. Bob Beran, Director of Intramural Athletics, was our coach/advisor/car driver and I knew him from being in intramural basketball and volleyball activities. We were like a little family, and that's what made it a lot of fun especially when traveling to the matches in the tri-state traveling league of Wisconsin, Minnesota and North Dakota. Bob, five bowlers and a trunk full of bowling balls took off on Friday afternoon to go to Fargo, North Dakota. We stayed in a motel that night, bowled all day Saturday in a meet involving all the teams in the league and then drove home Saturday night—we were on a VERY low budget. I'm not sure, but we might have each had to pay for our own meals. I was a part of the bowling team for three years and in the tri-state league we bowled four-man teams, scratch (no handicap) bowling. Occasionally we bowled great—one game was an 834 total.

We also bowled in a "postal" league, which included the teams in the Wisconsin State College conference. This was five—man teams and we bowled scratch with the scores being sent in to a designated conference secretary. Talk about being on the honor system!! I don't think the NCAA could cope with something like that, but that's what we had—obviously, there was no big prize or award for the winner or someone would have cheated. You wouldn't get much satisfaction if you knew that you won and you knew that you cheated to do it and nobody else even cared!!

Back to traveling, we did make one trip that I will never forget. John Johnson was about a 190 average bowler and our anchor man. He came to La Crosse from Milwaukee and he and his parents opened their home to us late one Saturday night so we could get some sleep. Our trip was to bowl in Whitewater vs. Whitewater State on Saturday night, stay in Milwaukee and bowl in Chicago vs. the University of Chicago on Sunday afternoon before going back to La Crosse. We were bowling our second game against Whitewater State (five—man teams) when the fun started. John Mattson was our leadoff bowler and he was a real "card". I was in the number two slot and in the first frame I bowled getting nine pins and picked up the spare. CLUNK was the sound as the ball hit the pin. The buzz during the first game was about how heavy the pins appeared to be. Most lanes were using three pound three ounce, three pound four ounce, or three pound five ounce weight pins. These sounded like they were three pound ten ounce at least. The second frame I threw a perfect strike. The third frame produced another strike, as did the fourth. After throwing three strikes in a row, John Mattson came over to me and put my bowling towel (the one I used to wipe oil/dirt off my ball) over my right forearm saying, "We got to keep that arm warm!" As John came off the approach from bowling in the fifth frame he gently lifted the towel off my arm, I rolled a strike for four-in-a-row and came back to John with my arm extended for him to put the towel on as before. John rolled frame number six and returned to me to get the now famous towel. Frame six ended with strike number five-in-a-row and John promptly put the towel on my arm so as to not lose any of the heat—when you are hot, you want to stay hot—until the next frame. These antics were starting to irritate the Whitewater bowlers, but that was their problem. Six-in-a-row was followed with seven, eight and. nine with each one following the same pattern of using the towel to keep that arm warm between frames. Naturally, I was thinking, "just two more strikes for a 290 game". As I released the ball for my second shot in the tenth frame I "pushed" it a little causing it to land one board (three-fourths inch) to the right of my usual spot resulting in being right of the "pocket" leaving the 1-2-4-7 railroad for a spare which I converted with the last ball for a 276 game. That was the best game I ever bowled and it helped us have a five man three game total scratch pins of over 3000. Unfortunately, my other two games were only about 170 each giving me a series of only 615. Since my average was only about 185 during my college days, a 600 series did not come too often, so I was happy with 615!

Chapter Seventeen

In the summer of 1962 (the previous year) while I was getting banged around at the cannery my good buddy Phil Eastman had gotten a job from my old boss, Jim Mac Dougal. Jim was working as a supervisor/trainer with the Vernon County ASCS (Agricultural Stabilization and Conservation Service) and Phil worked measuring land for compliance of farmers in the Feed Grain Program and those with Tobacco Allotments.

After some discussions with Jim and Phil during the year, Jim felt that I would also be good at the job and I could make a little more money than doing canning factory work. So, in the summer of 1963 I worked with the help of my dad's car (mom's car too—we only had one) traveling from farm to farm in various townships on the eastern side of Vernon County. That year was the start of the use of aerial photography scaled to a planimeter as a means of measuring acreage. Some fields showed up really good on the photograph and the only real problem areas were some edges of fields that were in the shade of the woods due to sun angles. All the photos had some easily identifiable reference point from which we could measure to verify field boundaries so we could plot them on the photograph.

Part of our job entailed the use of a little psychology and/or some good sound reasonable explaining. You see, farmers reacted to the aerial photos in many different ways, from "We've gotten the same measurement on that field for the last five years when

126

my neighbor Joe was doing this job, why do we have to use those pictures?" to "Every year they measure that field they come up with a different number of acres, maybe with this photo it will be the same each year from now on". Our job was to explain it to them so they understood it, not necessarily to make them happy. But, ninety-five per cent of them were fine with this new thing once they understood it and overcame their feeling that the Government was out to "screw them out of some more money". The photos did cut down on the number of measurements that had to be taken; thus, it cut down on the amount of time the surveyor was at the farm and the amount of time that the farmer was with the surveyor helping him measure.

Measurement was done with a "chain" that was divided into one hundred "links" with a total length of sixty-six feet; i.e., four rods. This "chain" automatically converted the feet and inches into decimal numbers that could easily be used to calculate acres. It was called a chain with links but it really was a steel tape of sixty-six feet evenly divided into one hundred sections. Since one acre is said to be four rods by forty rods, then something measuring one "chain length" by ten "chain lengths" would be an acre, two chain lengths by ten chain lengths would be two acres. Thus our formula was *length times width* equals acres. So, you could measure a field to be two chains, twenty links by six chains, fifty links and easily do the math for acres. 2.2 times 6.5 equals 1.43 acres, after dividing by ten. With the new photographs we didn't need to calculate the acres, but many farmers would ask, "How big is that field?" So, I would lay my scale (a small steel ruler scaled to coincide with chains and links) on the length and width of the field in question and with some quick math work in my head, give the farmer a very close, if not exact, acreage.

It was about thirty-five miles to Reedstown, Wisconsin and many days I went eight to ten miles past that town; nearly one hundred miles a day was common. I think I had the oil changed four times that summer in dad's 1955 Chevy—you know, the blue one I wrecked two years earlier and it was now painted black. It was almost like I owned the car without having to make payments or pay the insurance. Fortunately, I earned enough money to pay all the car expenses and put away a few hundred dollars for my next year's school costs.

Fall arrived too soon and I went back to La Crosse State with great intent to get my grade point average up from the lousy 2.04 where it ended after two years. I had played a little summer City team baseball with my old friend Steve Subera and learned that he was going to go to La Crosse State that fall—he had attended Platteville State previously. We shared a room in a rooming house in the thirteen hundred block of Main Street, a location about five blocks from Main Hall where most of the classes were held. To increase my GPA I cut my credit load down from seventeen to thirteen and included the repeat of English Literature (one I flunked) in that total. My English Literature teacher was Mrs. Lord, the same teacher I had in freshman English Comp. In English Comp. she always looked at me like I didn't know the answer to her question and then she would ask me the question, and usually she was right—I didn't know the answer. I was paranoid to the point that, if I saw her coming my way down the hall, I'd turn and go the opposite direction. "Oh, Great," I thought, "Now she will kill me for sure." But I didn't quit. She made English Literature very interesting and I actually learned to like to read due to *having* to read various books. Her final exam was one question, "What have you learned from this class?" I got a "B" in the class and it wiped out the previous "F". After doing fairly well in my other classes, I nearly got a 3.0 GPA that semester, and my cumulative GPA was up some. I learned to like Mrs. Lord and got over paranoia.

Steve and I went home to Hillsboro fairly often on weekends that fall and we were on our way home (about ten miles west of Cashton, Wisconsin) for Thanksgiving Day break. It was about 3:30 p.m., November 22, 1963 when Steve turned on the radio in his car, "President Kennedy has been shot" came over the airwaves. Everyone knows where they were that day.

In the Spring Semester, the College needed a person for the

job of head counselor on one of the floors of Reuter Hall. The pay was board and room so I could not turn it down unless I felt I could not keep my grades up with the extra responsibilities of the job. I did the job satisfactorily, kept my grades up with about a 2.6 GPA and managed to continue my previous involvement in L-Bar-X Dancers and the Bowling Team. When weather warmed up some I had a part-time (Saturday) job doing yard work for a nice lady on the eastern edge of La Crosse. I worked in her lawn, garden, compost heap, and anywhere else I could be of help. I started at 8:15 a.m. after she came to the dormitory and got me at 8:00 a.m. About 10:30 a.m. she called me to go into the house for lunch (snack) that could have made a full meal. Then at noon I wasn't hungry so I just kept on working until about 2:30 p.m. when she called me in for another snack—sandwiches and cookies and milk. Somewhere around five o'clock she took me back to the college and usually paid me twenty dollars for the day's work— best per hour pay I got all year. Turned out that I got about two dollars per hour plus all that food plus transportation to and from the job. I was thrilled with the pay! She liked a neat yard and I liked making her yard neat.

Incidentally, one morning during that school year it was fifty-two (-52) degrees below zero. The hottest item in town was the jumper cables that were being used to jump-start cars that day. I was glad I didn't own a car and I just walked to class as I usually did except that the snow really squeaked under my feet. That day my "L" (letterman's) jacket made of heavy wool material was not too warm to wear. It was usually good for anything from twenty-five below zero and colder. If I walked very far in that jacket in twenty below weather, I'd get hot and start to sweat.

Upon completing my Junior year, a session with my advisor indicated that I had to go to summer school and acquire at least nine credits in order for me to graduate with my classmates in 1965. With my Senior classes planned and with my student teaching I figured that I had to get nine credits in the summer to have the one hundred twenty-eight credits, the exact minimum to graduate.

Eight credits were considered a full load in summer school, so my nine credits could be considered an overload. I had Introduction to Philosophy, Principles and Practices of Teaching Physical Education, Principles of Insurance and Chorus (my one extra and easy credit) for a total of nine credits. I went to pre-enrollment before leaving campus in May and was all signed up. Phil and I both had our jobs with ASCS and that would start with the feed-grain program measuring about the middle of June. Phil also decided to go to summer school at La Crosse that year. He was not short of class credits like me, he was planning to graduate in three and a half years, which he did. I HAD TO HAVE A CAR. No way out of it, I needed it for my job; I needed to have it to drive to La Crosse every other week taking turns with Phil. I didn't have money for a car! But, I got one! My grandfather Kahler had a 1950 Chevy with eighty five thousand miles on the odometer that had been disconnected for a few years. He didn't drive anymore—occasionally my dad drove grandpa's car on a fishing trip when grandpa insisted that we use his car. Anyway, he sold the car to me for fifty dollars. The car ran quite well and whenever I filled it up with gas I put in a quart of oil or more as needed. I joked with Ernie Knadle at his Mobil station by saying, "Fill 'er up with oil and check the gas!" I used bulk oil so it was only about thirty cents a quart and at that time gas was about thirty cents a gallon.

In Philosophy class I met Beth, a real nice gal from La Farge, Wisconsin, and we got to know each other through dating some during the summer. When Phil and I started our jobs the day-to-day schedule was really hectic. It is amazing what one can do when they have to do it. The following is what my life was like during those eight weeks while I was working and going to school. Get up and leave for La Crosse at 7:00 a.m. sharp regardless of whether Phil or I was driving. Arrive at La Crosse State and be in the Student Union Building having coffee and a sweet roll at 8:30 a.m. getting ready for our 8:40 a.m. class. Attend classes off and on until we both are done at 2:30 p.m. and meet back at the Union before heading for home. We arrived at home about 4:00 p.m. where we took our school books, etc. into our respective houses and picked up our paperwork and canisters of photographs for our jobs. I then went out to measure land, sometimes having to travel thirty miles or more to get to the first job. I measured land as much as possible until dark. I then went toward home, but La Farge was a town I usually had to go through to get back home and Beth was working at the A&W Root Beer Stand. She was usually done working about the time I got there so we talked for a while before I went on home. Once at home I had to finish any paperwork connected with the measuring that I had not completed on the particular farm. Then, if I had anything pressing for school that next day, I had to do whatever was needed before going to bed around midnight. Each day, Monday through Friday, was the same. On Saturday I left the house at 7:00 a.m. heading for my first farm measuring job. I went from farm to farm doing as many as possible that day working until dark again. Then I went to spend some time with Beth before going home. Sunday was also different as I got up about 7:00 a.m., went to early church at 8:30 a.m. and then went to Spring Valley Golf Course in Union Center, Wisconsin to play three or four rounds on the nine-hole course. After twenty-seven or thirty-six holes of generally bogey golf, I usually went to the clubhouse and had a sandwich and a soda pop for my supper. Then, about 7:00 p.m., I went home to study until midnight and go to bed to get my usual seven hours sleep as preparation for another hectic week. THIS WAS THE MOST PRODUCTIVE SUMMER OF MY LIFE. I earned one "A" (Chorus) as I was the only male voice with ten ladies in class. We sang three-part harmony with six sopranos, four altos and me. I held my own (volume-wise) with those ten women—anyone who has heard me sing in church will believe that: I also earned two "B's" and one "C" for a grade point of 2.9—almost a "B" average.

After paying all my car expenses for school and work, I still had over eight hundred dollars left to start my Senior year of college. I had some good times with Beth, we planned to see each other periodically that fall, if possible, and I had some good recreation at the golf course without neglecting my church involvement. Yes, it was a good summer in all areas.

Chapter Eighteen

It wasn't fun when I went to La Crosse to find a place to live before the classes were to begin for my senior year. Every other year I had a place lined up in advance, so this was different, but the results were fine. After checking the paper for apartments for rent I found one down on South Fourth Street. I don't know if I got there first or the two guys from Ontario, Wisconsin (attending La Crosse area Technical School) got there first, but we ended both our hunts by sharing a one bedroom, one bathroom, large kitchen/dining area and large living room area. I had a cot in the living room and it became my bedroom—we didn't need a living room as generally none of us were there except to sleep. Occasionally the two guys got some groceries and cooked some and I had some bread and cold meat there some of the time, but we all ate meals somewhere else most of the time. Our rent was seventy dollars each or two hundred ten dollars total for the apartment. It doesn't take a rocket scientist to figure out that my eight hundred dollars earned in the summer will not cover expenses—my rent alone will be six hundred thirty dollars. Then there is tuition and fees plus that bad habit we all have—eating food!

I better get a job (or two) once I get settled into my classes. My roommates were Jay and "the Kid" as they called each other. "The Kid" seemed to have a little more money, but Jay and I needed to work and found a job on Saturdays at a car wash only five or six blocks south of us. We both worked vacuuming out the dirt before the car went into the wash area. The work was from 8:00 a.m. until 6:00 p.m. so on a nice day we ran more than eighty cars through that place. That job was all right in the fall, but I did not want to be doing that in cold weather (what car wash is open in below zero weather?), so I needed another job.

While I had worked cleaning bowling lanes for Jim Mac Dougal in high school I was taught some of the skills for trouble shooting problems with the automatic pinsetter machines. With that in mind I went out to the Holiday Lanes, a forty lane bowling establishment, to see if I could get a job. I was hired and worked two or three nights per week from 7:00 p.m. to 11:00 p.m. down in the "pit". Fortunately, the machines were the same kind as those in Hillsboro—Brunswick—and I was quite good at solving minor problems such as a deck jam, pin out of range, ball not returning. When I wasn't trouble shooting I was cleaning on a machine not in use. Sometimes I was cleaning the machine on lane forty or thirty-nine when the PA system from the front desk back to me would say, "Out of range on number five." If I was working behind the machine then I ran on the floor to get to number five. If I was working on top of a machine then I ran across the top of the machines until I got to number five. Along the back and across the top over the pinwheel there was a two-inch by ten-inch plank on which I traveled. Each plank was about five feet long with a three-inch gap between machines. So, if I have to travel from number forty to number five, that's approximately one hundred seventy-five feet. The bowlers are waiting for me to fix the problem, so I better run to get there as fast as I can. Anyhow, I enjoyed it, helping others have fun and got paid for it. I think I got a dollar and fifty cents per hour.

In classes that fall the seniors in the physical education curriculum were all in folk dance class. A highlight for the fall was when our class was invited to dress up in our folkdance outfits and go perform at the 1964 La Crosse version of Octoberfest. It was in this class that I became better acquainted with Kaye and we developed a good relationship that lasted until February 1965 when I ruined it with my own stupidity.

Speaking of February 1965, it was around that time that the La Crosse State Men's Basketball team was doing great and fans were hoping that they would get to go to the National Finals in Kansas City, which they did. At some bars, they nearly wore out the record, "Goin' to Kansas City, Kansas City here I come, they got some crazy little women there and I'm goin' to get me one," as it got played and danced to over and over. They didn't win the national title, but did all right.

There were a few more exciting or interesting events during that senior year. The bowling team went with some other competitors to the NAIA National Tournament held at Purdue University. The bowling scores were unremarkable, but the trip of over a thousand miles (round trip) with other students was made more enjoyable by some of us playing cards on top of a suitcase. It was also interesting to see the best of the small colleges competing in various events.

Speaking of bowling, there were two events that were connected with the lanes back in Hillsboro. A few years earlier, Jim Mac Dougal had participated with some others from Hillsboro in the Peterson Classic, a huge bowling tournament in Chicago that ran from January through June each year. It was a tourney that had conditions to "level the playing field" and even keep most of the professional bowlers out of it. The lanes were oiled in an extremely uneven fashion with some lanes very wet and other ones very dry, really testing the adjustment skills of all bowlers. Also, to make it tougher and keep scores down, I was told that the pins in each rack were of mixed weight. Therefore, when you did hit the "pocket" you could not be sure the pins would react and cause you to get a strike. A bowler could never get adjusted to any pair of lanes because the tournament consisted of bowling eight games over sixteen lanes, which means you change to a new pair of lanes after each game. So, having only five shots at a strike on each lane does not give much opportunity for a lot of experimenting. Bowlers who normally threw strikes with a wide curve ball found that the ball was in the right gutter halfway down the lane. Then, on the other lane they would compensate by throwing more in the center of the lane and find the ball going into the left gutter about three-fourths of the way down the lane, because that lane was "dry" and the previous one was "wet". Anyway, back to Jim Mac Dougal, the town was a "buzz" for a while as he had bowled a 290 game, that's right, a spare followed by eleven strikes in a row, a few years earlier. I was excited to get to go to the Peterson Classic and the four of us from Hillsboro hooked up with a group from Pottsville, Pennsylvania to form the thirty-two bowlers needed for a "squad". I was still using the conventional grip at a time when many good bowlers had gone to finger tip grip for more action and curve. I threw a fairly straight line with a small hook as the ball hooked to the left about a foot during the last ten feet before hitting the pins. This was good under these bowling conditions and I was able to average 184 for the eight games and end in fourth place on our squad.

At the Peterson Classic

Another group from Hillsboro that included Jim Mac Dougal and me was the team that went to Milwaukee that spring of 1965 to compete in the Wisconsin State Bowling Association State Tournament. There you bowl three games on a pair of lanes for team score, three games on a pair of lanes for a doubles score (if you have a partner and choose this event) and three games on a pair of lanes for a singles score. I did so-so in the team and doubles competition, but the singles event was my highlight. I started with a score of 233 for the first game and followed with a cool 247!! That's 480 pins, *all* I need that last game is 220 for a 700 series. Man! What an opportunity. I continued to throw the ball right into the pocket, but I must have been unconsciously "forcing it" a bit due to the stress of the situation. I left a solid ten pin, a four-nine split, a solid nine pin that didn't even wiggle and topped it off with a four-six split in the ninth frame. Fortunately, I made most if the spares and did have a couple strikes mixed in with the disappointments for a score of 176 and a series of 656, the highest series I ever bowled in my life.

The last semester of my senior year was the time for me to "put the frosting on the cake" in the form of practicing the skills I had learned in four years with real people—it was called, Student Teaching. My first nine weeks was at an elementary school in North La Crosse and the last nine weeks was a few blocks away at La Crosse Logan High School. When I started the whole semester of practice teaching I thought I wanted a career of teaching high school P.E. and coaching some, but after completing the full semester and having worked in both situations, I was leaning toward wanting a job working with the younger ones. When it came to the time to hunt for a job, I was interested in teaching in a small town in northern Illinois or in Mayville, Wisconsin. I applied first to Mayville and received a response and invitation to go for an interview. I went to Mayville and met with Superintendent Sizer and Elementary and Junior High Principal Ken Sauter. They took me out to the country Club Golf Course for lunch and to discuss the details of the job after showing me the school, the facilities and the equipment. I had a chance to ask a few questions and discover that this was the job for me.

My last tasks to complete before leaving La Crosse was to trade in my 1950 Chevy for a "new" car and get my degree. I found this dark green colored Volkswagen Bug, a 1957 model, and fell in love with it. The dealer gave me fifty dollars trade-in for the Chevy (not bad when I paid fifty for it and drove it eighteen thousand miles) and I had to pay an extra five hundred for the VW. I was scheduled to have the same summer job so with all the extra miles to travel the economic VW would be good.

The day of graduation came and I really don't recall much about getting the degree. What I do remember is that my brother was there with his suit on and out on the lawn in front of Main Hall he did a mock presentation of the diploma to me as he was acting as though he was the President of the College!! Pictures were taken of that event and none were taken of the real presentation so you see who is important in my family—it's family!!

Chapter Nineteen

With my fall scheduled and the teaching job secured, it was now time to unwind after college life and get back to my former summer job so I could make enough to pay for the "new" car before I began my real career. My ASCS job kept me busy from early morning until late at night six days a week and my Sundays were usually spent going to church in the morning and golfing or fishing in the afternoons. The second year of the use of the aerial photographs for measuring the farmers' acres was easier than the first year due to the farmers being much less resistant to the system and I being much more familiar with it. All in all the summer was enjoyable and flew by too fast. Sometime during the summer I went to Mayville to find a place to live for the 1965-66 school year. The Principal had recommended some places that I might want to live. I checked on a couple of them and quickly made my choice. Get this: A two-story brick home with the landlady living downstairs and rooms for rent upstairs. I had the southwest bedroom and another man had the southeast bedroom—there was a bathroom with a tub that had to be shared. My rent was a whopping ONE DOLLAR PER DAY!!

The day before our first Teachers In-service Training Day (my first work day) I moved into my room in the brick house. Incidentally, another factor besides the cost enticing me to live there was the location. To get to my office at school I walked west past one house, walked across the street, went about fifty feet to the school door and went up the stairs to my office. Some mornings I got up early and went to Wibby's Griddle for breakfast before going on to my office to get ready for classes; other days I just made the short trip and skipped breakfast. Breakfast with ham and eggs, toast and coffee was about a dollar or less. Lunches were about a dollar and a quarter.

My contract was to teach Elementary Physical Education, Jr. High boys Physical Education and health classes as well as coach Jr. High football and basketball. I was paid one hundred dollars for coaching each sport and fifty-one hundred dollars for teaching the classes I was assigned, and any other duties.

My morning teaching schedule was easy. Teach Physical Education and health on alternate days to three classes of junior high boys: a seventh grade class, a combined seventh and eighth grade class and an eighth grade class. My afternoons were not so simple. On Monday afternoon I had a first grade, second grade, third grade and fourth grade class for a half hour, half hour, three-fourths hour and three-fourths hour period respectively. Tuesday was the same as Monday, but the classes had different students. On Wednesday I went to Kekoskee to teach a combination first, second and third grades followed by a combination fourth, fifth and sixth grades. Then I went on north to Leroy, another rural school, where I did the same classes as I had at Kekoskee. Thursday afternoon I was back at the city elementary with a fifth grade, combination fifth and sixth grade and a sixth grade class. Friday I went down south near Iron Ridge to a rural school and had a first and second grade class, third and fourth grade class followed by a fifth and sixth grade class which allowed my day to end a half hour earlier than usual. Of course, with the coaching of football and basketball my day at school did not end until about 5:30 p.m. from September through February. My one other required job at school was noon hour playground supervision. That meant that I had all my lunches at the school cafeteria for the high cost of forty cents!! Then I went out to the playground to watch over the activities, break up any fights, listen to first graders tell me about seeing a "Wobin Wed Bwest" in early spring, having a third grade girl tell me that on Sunday they "went by grandmas" and having a fifth grade girl look up at me sheepishly and say, "Mr. Potter, are you married?" and then giggle when she heard me say, "No". I asked the third grade girl who "went by grandmas", "Why didn't you stop?" She responded, "We did, you dummy." In their colloquial speech they often spoke of "going by" someplace when they meant that they went to the place. Some of them "had Christmas by grandmas!!" They were all good kids who were primarily of German and Serbian background I think. The Serbian names were generally identified by their ending in "vich". My dad laughed when I told him there were lots of "viches" living in that town.

Besides my fellow teachers in the Elementary and Junior High School, I met the late Jack Omer, Mayville High School Head Football Coach, as soon as possible before classes started. The plan was for me and my assistant junior high football coach, Francis Stiglbauer, to teach the boys in seventh and eighth grade the same style of football that they will be running in high school for the next few years. My main interest was to get the boys in good physical condition so we would have no injuries if possible. However, I also wanted them to learn Mr. Omer's football plays so they would be prepared to work under his tutorage.

We played six games that year with one of the teams on a *home and home* basis. That team was Horicon Junior High from the little town a few miles to our south. We played them the third and sixth game of the season. We had won our first two games and I was so proud of our line play and the running of George Silcock, a 5 foot 8 inch and 130 pound halfback who ran fast and hit hard when they tried to tackle him. It was the Wednesday practice when George ran the ball and was tackled and hit the ground with the ball under him in a weird position causing an injury. The doctor's diagnosis was a spleen injury and that's nothing to mess with, plus the doctor said he should not play in Friday's game against Horicon. He sat out and the others played their hearts out to no avail as they lost by a touchdown, 13-7. He was given the "green light" to play the remainder of the season and we won all three games including the rematch with Horicon. I had a little family concern when it came to Mayville vs. Horicon as my mother's aunt and uncle lived in Mayville and her cousin lived in Horicon. Anyway, we finished the schedule with a 5-1 record and must have done some good in teaching the Omer system as these same boys had some real good success when they were in eleventh and twelfth grade, winning at least one conference championship. I was not teaching at Mayville then, but I read about it in the newspapers. Then, a few years later, I was saddened to learn of Jack's death at such a young age leaving behind his wife, Donna, and two small children.

My social life during that year was somewhat hectic in one sense and not too active in another sense, the latter being the dating game; more on that later. Early in the fall most activity was around football. Sometimes after the high school game some of the coaches would gather at Butch's Bar in Kekoskee for a beer and the BEST HAMBURGER WITH FRIED ONIONS IN THE WORLD. It was there that we would rehash the game and talk of the "if only" . . . ! On one Saturday afternoon in December Jack Omer and the Industrial Arts teacher, Butch Schultz, and I went for a ride out in the Horicon Marsh, which was frozen fairly well. We drove a ways in one direction and saw a deer. Butch said, "Follow that deer," so I did. We never got stuck with the VW and I wasn't worried as I think my two passengers could have gotten me out if I did get stuck.

In September when leagues started at Sid Silcock lanes and the downtown lanes I joined a team in the Tuesday night league at Silcock's. Fran Stiglbauer, Butch Schultz, the late Jerry Kudla (History teacher) and I got into a league at the downtown lanes on Wednesday nights. It is interesting how easily some people can be amused. This team met every Wednesday night at Kudla's apartment to watch Batman on TV before we went "off to the bat lanes!" It was our way of relaxing before we started bowling. We didn't drink our beer frames like some teams do; we put our money into a kitty and saved it for a big porterhouse steak dinner with all the trimmings and plenty of beer at our end of bowling season team poker party. After a few weeks of bowling at Silcock lanes I was averaging over 180 and someone with the authority asked me to join the City bowling team that bowled in Mayville and traveled to other places to bowl in a city team league. So, I joined them, nothing else to do! When basketball season started I was busy with my junior high coaching job until 5:30 p.m. daily and I had lined up a couple officiating jobs in the area; I had been active as a basketball official during college as much as possible. Then some of the local men headed by Jim Bartelt asked me to be active on the city basketball team. I figured that since they were going to use the grade school gym for the sight of the games, I might as well be a part of that too.

The city basketball team was a lot of fun and I was a regular player. The only bad thing was that the other teams often outmatched us. We did not have much size compared to teams from larger cities. We did have two guys who were 6 foot 4 inches tall and about 250 pounds each and along with me made up our "big men" in the lineup. Menomonee Falls had a team with a front court lineup of 6 foot 8 inches, 6 foot 6 inches and 6 foot 5 inches tall. One time the biggest one of them got a rebound over me, and his elbow came down on my head leaving me with a severe headache. Even though we felt out manned during that game we were shooting the ball well and playing good defense. When the final horn sounded we were on the top end of the score 108-105. That was time for a big celebration, so we all went to Bartelt's tavern about a block south of the school where we played the game. Everyone was drinking and having a good time when I decided that the boys (bartenders) needed a little help. Thus, I got behind the bar and sold drinks just like I was an experienced bartender. One guy was feeling quite good and asked me to sell him a bottle of whiskey. I asked one of the other ones behind the bar how much to charge and collected the right amount. I gave the bottle to its new owner and he promptly began to give everyone else a good shot of whiskey whether they wanted it or not. If they had a glass in front of them, the person got at least a shot of whiskey in it. A few persons got their beer spiked. Regarding the game, it was the greatest upset victory of the year for our team.

Along around midnight Berth Ann and I left the bar and headed over to Ken and Elaine Brockhaus' place for a late night snack. Elaine was a teacher in grade school and Ken, also known as 'Spooker', was one of the other big men on the team. After that Berth Ann and I went to her apartment in Fondulac, Wisconsin, a larger city about thirty miles away. Who is Berth Ann? Where did she come from? I didn't do much dating with my hectic level of activities and teaching/coaching, but sometime in the fall I did date the prettiest "unattached" female that I knew at the time. She was Joan, the girls' Physical Education teacher at Mayville High School. She was nice, but she didn't seem very friendly and not at all loving toward me. Sometime after the new year, Joan and I went to a ski meeting where I met her friend Berth Ann Bockhaus, a speech pathologist, from Fondulac and formerly of Iowa.

It almost seemed like Joan enjoyed introducing me to Berth Ann as though she was happy to get rid of me. I felt that way and believed it so much that I did not even hesitate for a moment when I asked Berth Ann for a first date with her; she accepted and we began dating in a monogamous fashion. We dated usually once a week, maybe twice. Often it was on Saturday night when I was playing basketball like the night against Menomonee Falls. Anyway, that night we went to her apartment and I was very tired and did have a few drinks after the game, so we decided that I would spend the night with her. Based on the standards of the 90's and the new century, we really had some old fashioned values and morals. Get this! We slept in the same bed but she slept under the covers and I slept on top of the covers—she stayed on her side and I stayed on my side. It was not that we did not have strong feelings for each other, but it is that our strong moral and religious upbringing dictated our behavior, and we were mature enough to control ourselves.

The spring of the year after basketball season seemed like a vacation for me. I was involved a little with helping a high school boy trying to throw the discus, did a little fishing and played a few rounds of golf after school during the spring. I was enjoying teaching and a less hectic schedule while spending time with Berth Ann on Saturdays and going to church with her on Sunday some weeks. Her religious background was Lutheran also, though not the same Lutheran Synod as me. One weekend we took a trip to Waverly, Iowa to meet her parents and family. Another weekend we took a trip to Hillsboro for her to meet my parents and family. Sounds like we were getting quite serious. Maybe we were, I know I thought about the possibility of marrying her and possibly asking her at the end of the school year. She was about four years older than me, so emotionally she was probably eight years ahead of me. We planned to spend a whole day together on May 22, 1966 ending with us going to the Spring Mayville School District Teacher's Party at the Country Club. I got up early that morning and drove to Fondulac to get her and then we went to Milwaukee to the Horticulture Museum and the zoo where we met Ken and Elaine Brockhaus. After touring those two facilities we headed out to visit some friends of the Brockhaus'. Then it was on to Mayville where we would freshen up before going to the teachers' party.

My year of hard work was rewarding and I was involved in many social things outside of my teaching. I guess the only negative thing about the social events was that most of them were connected in some way with drinking. Bowling Tuesday night and have two or three drinks, bowling Wednesday nights and have two or three drinks, go out with the coaches on Friday nights and have two or three drinks, bowl with the city team on Saturday afternoon and after the bowling have a couple drinks, then after basketball on Saturday night have a few drinks. Sounds like a lot of activities involving drinking!

Back at the teachers' party we had a couple drinks before dinner and a few after dinner as we were entertained by a man who did a neat enactment of Casey At The Bat among other things. I guess I appeared to be involved with others and my drinking; thus, I was ignoring Berth Ann and leaving her to entertain herself at my teachers' party. About midnight we left the party and I drove to her apartment in Fondulac. We went inside and we got into an argument over me not paying enough attention to her during the party. Somehow this discussion/argument lasted until 4:00 a.m. when, unlike the one previous occasion when I stayed overnight, I walked down the stairs, out to my car and drove for home. I got down to the stop sign at the intersection near Leroy and felt very sleepy. I stopped the car and got out and walked around the car getting cool fresh air on my face, I got back in the car and drove on south through the Village of Kekoskee, around a fairly sweeping curve and onto straight road . . .

Chapter Twenty

What a mess

"Was Jim Mac Dougal and his wife here to see me yesterday?" I asked the nurse that I thought had worked the day before. "Describe them," she said. I did and she replied, "Yes, they were here!" "I REMEMBERED!" I said loudly knowing that was the first thing I remembered since driving south of Kekoskee toward Mayville the morning of May 23,

1966. The following is a chronology of what was apparent or what I've been *told* happened during those *lost* four weeks from early Sunday morning, May 23, 1966 to Sunday afternoon, June 20, 1966:

If you ever drove a Volkswagen Bug from the 1950's you know that the steering is very tight and a quarter inch move of the wheel would put you in the ditch immediately. Likewise, if the wheel was not touched or left in a straight position the car would not wander off the road very fast. Thus, as I fell asleep the car stayed straight quite a distance before it gradually went off the left side of the road and eased along a fairly level right-of-way until it hit a side driveway, catapulted into the air like a jumper off a ski jump flying some seventy to eighty feet before it landed and hit another side driveway. I continued my sleep as the car bounced around, started to roll over and in the process threw me (somehow??) from the car. As the car sat back down on its wheels, they found me lying face down a few feet ahead of the car. Apparently, the driver side door popped open allowing my limp body to fly out as the car tried to flip—had it rolled over it would have rolled on me and you would not be reading this. Adversity strikes again!!

Fortunately, I crashed right in front of a country tavern where the owner's home was under the same roof as the tavern. Someone in that household heard the crash and I was blessed with them being still up, or light sleepers. They called the ambulance and the emergency personnel told someone at the sight that they did not know whether to take me to the morgue or the hospital— apparently there was enough slight pulse to point them toward Waupun and the Catholic Hospital there, St. Mary's I believe. In that facility the main focus was keeping me alive which they did very well. Finally, a specialist from Fondulac was at the Hospital and he told my parents that my breathing was so shallow that I needed a tracheotomy and without one I would soon be dead. This and other medical factors prompted my transfer to University Hospital in Madison, Wisconsin after ten days at the Waupun Hospital.

As you might assume, I did have multiple medical problems. Apparently I hit the ground head first and the force pushed the sixth cervical (C-6) vertebrae out of place toward the left side of my neck causing spinal cord damage above and below that vertebrae. The blow to my head put me in a coma for five days and 23 days amnesia from a concussion. In addition, I suffered a collapsed left lung, a kidney injury of some sort and a broken radius bone in my left arm about two inches above the wrist. From least long term effect to greatest long term effect, the injuries are defined as follows: kidney injury—I heard I had one but any treatment was over before I came out of the amnesia; collapsed lung—I realized that one day in Rehab. when I noticed scars on the medial and lateral sides of my left breast area and asked how those got there. I was told I initially had a collapsed lung and the scars are from the big pin that was stuck through the meat and attached to traction to lift the rib cage aiding the lung back to normal function. They said the pin "was like a huge diaper pin". Broken left arm—was in a cast down to the knuckles of the left hand which inhibited movement of the hand and wrist which may have limited the return of function of the partially paralyzed arm and hand; Concussion—It put me in a coma, left me with some acute amnesia and some long term memory effects that gave me much difficulty in returning to school and I believe affects my day to day memory and recall; Spinal cord injury— the general result is that the cord was smashed, possibly severed in places, above and below the sixth vertebrae leaving me paralyzed from the chest down and partial paralysis of my left arm and hand. The left arm is about half as strong as my right arm. The reason is the fact that the lesion on the spinal cord was diagonal and higher on the left side than the right. I can tap my right thigh with my right hand and feel the taps in my leg down to the top of my knee. On the left side I can't feel that below the waist. I have no muscle control below the waist and only have about five percent of the use of trunk muscles for balance. Therefore, any movement side-to-side or front to back can result in me being flat within seconds unless I have something to lean on, brace myself with or hang onto with one of my hands. I am confined to wheelchair mobility and at times spasms of the leg and / or trunk muscles are so strong I have to hang onto the armrests to prevent being "thrown out" of my own wheelchair.

To facilitate a little understanding about the spinal cord a little extra anatomy is in order. The spinal cord runs from the brain down through the center of the vertebrae and is protected from harm by those bones (as long as they stay in their intended position). While teaching seventh grade health just about a month prior to the accident, I had a student by the name of Lange and his dad owned the local butcher shop. As we discussed the spinal cord the boy offered to bring in a piece of spinal cord from a cow and we gladly accepted his offer. From it we learned that the consistency of the spinal cord is very similar to jello. Amazing that something that soft can have ascending and descending tracts that carry electrical impulses that convey messages back and forth from brain to the body parts and back. To be simplistic and when I need to try to get a young person to understand "why", I compare the brain and spinal cord to the telephone system where the brain is a main hub of the phone system (say in Chicago) and the spinal cord is a large line going across the country with smaller lines going off it toward smaller cities—these are ganglion roots off the spinal cord. Nerves and nerve endings are out beyond the ganglion roots just like smaller phone lines. A phone message may go to Madison, Wisconsin. by way of a large line (ganglion root) and on to a smaller town (Hillsboro) by a smaller line (nerve) and then to an individual house by an individual line (nerve endings). Here's how it works: Your brain gets a call from your calf muscle right leg that says, "I itch". The brain automatically sends out two messages to fix the problem; 1) it sends a message through the spinal cord to the ganglion root leading to the right thigh, the nerve to the quadriceps muscle and to the nerve ending to stimulate the muscle to lift the leg; and simultaneously, 2) it sends a message through the spinal cord to the ganglion root going to the right arm and on to the proper nerves and nerve endings to cause the arm to reach out to the calf and scratch the itch.

Ganglion roots come off the spinal cord below the level of the vertebrae, at least that is how it is in the cervical area. If not, any injury in the neck would have to result in total paralysis from the neck down. Generally, injury at C-6 or C-7 will not result in neck down paralysis; however, a C-5 injury usually will result in paralysis from the neck down, but that is not total paralysis as I have known two men with C-5 spinal cord injury and they both have fair-to-moderate use of their arms with finger dexterity problems and usually can't straighten out the fingers.

Spinal cord injury affects both the motor and sensory systems of the body. Most people we come in contact with only look at the motor part and it is OBVIOUS in the United States where so much emphasis is put on the PHYSICAL. BEAUTY and FITNESS are given great value so the first thought of others is, "Too bad you can't walk." Why do I need to walk when I have a wheelchair to ride in? Walking may be a little overrated, but it would be real nice if I could just stand up. If I could *just stand up*, that would minimize the sensory problems connected with spinal cord injury. The biggest problem with lack of sensation is not knowing how much pressure is being put on the skin of the buttocks when sitting for long periods of time—like sixteen hours a day leading a "normal" life with eight hours sleep and spending the remainder of the day "up" in my wheelchair. Unlike prior to the injury, I do not have the glutial muscles of the buttocks as they are atrophied (wasted away) to nothing. Thus, there is basically skin covering bone where the ischial bones (those are the two bones you sit on that fade blue jeans in two spots after you've worn them a couple years) are trying to poke through the skin. The danger here is the chance of the development of decubitus ulcers (pressure sores in layman's terms). If I develop an ulcer on my buttocks, I would not be able to sit up in the 'chair', thus I wouldn't be able to leave the house to go to work and use my brain. Therefore, it is plain to see that my buttocks is more valuable than my brain; for my brain is worthless when my buttocks is damaged.

Pressure / pain is one sensory area lost and sensation of hot / cold are also lost. Therefore, I have to be careful with shower water temperatures and with winter weather. I need to keep my bath water hot, but not too hot and I need to stay out of situations where the cold air is on my legs for an extended period of time that might cause frostbite without me knowing it.

One of the common problems I have with lack of sensation is I have to be careful in situations that you would think would be totally harmless. Example: I am working on a project with an eight inch by one inch by three foot long board of wood. You hand the board to me, it slips out of my hand and one end starts falling toward my feet. The fall of the board is interrupted when a corner of it scrapes my lower leg before the motion stops as the board rests against my shoe. I feel nothing out of the ordinary so I continue on with my work. At night when I take off my pants and socks, I notice a six inch scrape in the skin of the anterior (front) part of my ankle. An able bodied person with normal circulation and healing potential would not worry about this minor injury, but a spinal cord injured person may "nurse" the wound for weeks with antibiotic salves and bandages while the wound slowly gets worse.

I skinned my ankle one time a few years ago and tried to heal it like I described above. Finally, this stubborn old German gave up and went to see the late Dr. Steven Dorow at Gundersen Clinic in Hillsboro. He suggested and then used the Una-boot as a treatment. The "boot" similar to a soft-cast was put on my foot, ankle and lower leg for a week at a time. After about six weeks I was all healed. With the salve and bandage I used previously the sore got bigger. We can thank "war" for the Una-boot. Dr. Dorow explained that the Una-boot concept started when soldiers came home from overseas with broken legs and other ulcers on their legs. When the casts were removed later in America they discovered that the ulcers were healed in addition to the bone. Consequently, the "boot" was developed and for me and my poor circulation it is a blessing that aids healing of my feet.

While discussing sensation I need to share one experience. My left arm has partial paralysis and the sensation of the forearm is strange. It is hypersensitive to light touch and when rubbed lightly it tingles with a prickly feeling. However, I learned in 1972 about my real lack of sensation in that arm. I was showing a movie on an old reel-to-reel projector when I had some difficulties. I shut off the machine to try to fix it and for assistance with my body balance I leaned my left forearm on the machine. The spot that I leaned on was the steel cover over the projection lamp. I leaned on it for a few seconds, maybe eight or ten, and then went on with the movie thinking nothing of it. The next day there was a mark on my left arm that looked somewhat like the gash I had gotten from Mike Schroeder's tooth in high school on my right arm. Doctors told me it was either a second degree or third degree burn and it took over a week to heal it. It is hard to imagine something that hot and not feeling it! Minor adversity.

Another situation happened twenty-nine years after that projector encounter. I was preparing to go out to my hunting shack deer hunting with my cross-bow. I had just recently dropped my thermos bottle and broke it, so I got a new one from K-Mart and it was the same kind that I had before. I trusted it since it was new so I rinsed it out with water and put the coffee in it. I closed the pour spout top, tightened the cap and put the cup on top. Then I tipped it horizontal and lay it on my right thigh wedged between my right hip and my wheelchair armrest. Within a few minutes my brother arrived and I went out to get into his truck. When I picked up the coffee thermos I noticed that my leg was wet with coffee from the leaking thermos. I lifted the pants up away from the leg to give it some air and went on with the hunting trip. Don fixed the thermos as he discovered that the flip top had been put in backwards causing the leakage. After the hunt, I took off my pants to discover severe burns to my leg. I went to the doctor the next day and it took extensive treatment each day for eight weeks or more before the wound healed. Another minor adversity.

Back to my arrival at University Hospital in Madison, the doctor that did the tracheotomy told my parents that I had a fifty per cent chance with it and no chance without it. Fortunately, I

came out on the right side of that 50-50 deal. The next major
thing that happened to me (fortunately it was still during amnesia)
was the start of traction on my neck to get the bones back in their
proper alignment. First, they must have shaved the two areas
about four inches above my ears where they drilled quarter inch
(or slightly smaller) holes through the skull. Then they put in
metal rods that were part of an apparatus called Crutchfield Tongs.
The rods were put in at an angle and as the fifteen pound weight
pulled on the other end of the apparatus it squeezed the rods
toward the median keeping them tight in my skull. The cable
from the tongs to the weight went through a pulley at the head of
the bed. The procedure pulled my head away from the weight of
my body thus, in time, allowing the sixth cervical vertebrae to
fall in line with C-5 and C-7. Normal time frame was six weeks of
traction, but I got by with forty-one days; that's right, you guess
it, the tongs were to come out on day forty-two so on day forty-
one right after breakfast I heard a clank and a thud. The clank
was the tongs hitting the pulley and the thud was the weight
hitting the floor. The TONGS PULLED OUT EARLY! So I put on
the light for the nurse to come in and see the latest development.
She said, "Well, that's one thing we won't have to do tomorrow!"
X-rays showed that the vertebrae had gotten back in line within
about one sixteenth of an inch!

When you have traction like this they put you on a bed called
a Stryker Frame. It is not really a bed; it consists of a canvass in
a frame the size of the bed frame and another canvass to be used
when it is time to turn over (every two hours). The canvass has a
thick sheet (like a blanket-sheet) on it for a little cushion. When
lying on my back they came in with the canvass and put it over
me, attached the frame at each end of the bed, wrapped two
straps around me to keep me from falling out the side and then
turned me over on my stomach. Last they took the "old" bed off
my back. Ninety-nine per cent of the time this works fine, but
one Saturday night (thank God it was after I was alert and past
the amnesia) I happened to be awake at two a.m. when the young
men came in and put the "new bed" on my stomach, fastened

the ends of the frame and I heard one say, "Ready to flip him, Joe?" "Ya, one, two . . ." "Hold it," I yelled. "What," they asked. "Don't you think you better put the straps on so I don't land on the floor?" "Oh, God, we forgot," they said. I could just see myself lying on the floor with my head still attached to the cable and the weights over the end of the bed. The first accident didn't kill me but that one probably would have done it!! Thank God I was awake!!

Chapter Twenty-One

Since the accident I was in a coma for five days and flat in bed for five more days before moved to Madison. Then I was flat in bed for a while until put in traction on the Stryker Frame where I lay flat on my back for twelve hours a day and flat on my belly for twelve hours a day for the forty-one days of traction (I was changed from back to belly every two hours to avoid sores). Therefore, for at least six weeks I was in a constant horizontal position. I did not realize how much that affected the equilibrium of the body. One day after the end of traction the orderly lifted my head some to fluff my pillow and I DANG NEAR BLACKED OUT. My head and shoulders were raised only about four inches and the effect was tremendous. The next series of treatments involved the tilt table.

The tilt table was a well padded three foot by seven foot board on a pivot with a stopper mounted at the foot end. I was taken in the bed to another room where I was slid over onto the tilt table and secured with straps. They were VERY careful at first and raised the head end of the board five degrees, asked me how I felt and I replied that I was a little dizzy but not too bad. They kept it at that level for a few minutes and then asked if I was ready to go higher and I said, "OK." Slowly my head raised . . . "Whoa," I said, "things are getting black." They stopped and reversed the machine to go down. "How high was that?" I asked when my head cleared. "Only eight degrees when you shouted," they said. "Man, I thought it must have been a lot higher," I said. After going up and down a few times over a period of a half hour I did make some progress. The highest point I made was ten degrees elevation of the head, but that was a start although I didn't stay at that spot very long. After the second day when I made it to ten degrees again and stayed there a little longer, they decided that I would improve more quickly toward getting vertical again if we did that twice a day. That was fine with me and gradually I got up to fifteen, twenty, twenty-five, thirty, thirty-five, forty, etc. until I finally reached about seventy degrees near the end of two weeks working at this project. When at seventy degrees you feel like you are totally vertical (ninety degrees) and want to hang onto the board—thanks for the straps to keep me secure.

I think it must have been July 23, 1966 when Berth Ann came to visit me—it was on a Friday. I did not know about it, but it was a pre-arranged meeting for the doctor to give me some straight facts about my condition and they apparently knew that Berth Ann would be needed to help me through it. She held my hand as the doctor told me that I was paralyzed from the chest down and would "'probably never walk again!" As the old saying goes, that hit me like a ton of bricks! Apparently, I had been told that fact before but it must have been at a time or times when I was either suffering amnesia or just blocked it out with subconscious denial! How did I feel now that reality of the situation had sunk in? Tears, sadness, depression—thank God Berth Ann was there to be with me—she was so caring and concerned.

Later that day or the next day I was lying on my bed and tears began to well up again. Sometimes nurses can think they are so smart that they can make perfect ASSES of themselves. The nurse in charge came over to my bed and asked in a tough voice, "What's the matter with you?" I told her that they had just told me that I will not walk again. To that she rudely replied, "That's nothing new, they told you that before!" I guess she left her bedside manners home that day. She may have been correct,

I'm quite sure they did tell me about not walking before that day, but that day was the first time that it registered in my brain with the full impact. She may be a smart nurse, but not smart enough to realize that sometimes things that are said are not always fully understood by the listener and that denial does take place either consciously or subconsciously.

The next week I did some very serious looking at myself and came to the realization that 1) I was still alive, and 2) God must have a purpose for me in this world. This revelation came to me after a few days of serious grieving about my condition—believe me, grieving is very necessary. Somehow, the doctor knew that I did want to move forward and he tried to get me into the University of Wisconsin Neurological and Rehabilitation Hospital on East Washington Avenue in Madison. Actually I believe it was standard procedure for spinal cord injured patients to go to that hospital for rehabilitation. Anyway, he checked and they put me on the waiting list, which was quite long (I was number eight or ten, I think). So what do I do in the meantime, I asked. The main thing that needed to be continued was the passive range of motion exercises that kept the joints from getting stiff or becoming fused. (Speaking of fused joints, I saw a case like that two years later in Iowa where a man was brought into rehabilitation after being left in bed without any range of motion exercises—fused at the knees and hips) The upshot was that I did not need to be at University Hospital while waiting to be admitted to Rehab. Ironically, my $20,000 major medical insurance that I had with my health insurance through the Mayville School District was about to run out. Since the daily rate at University Hospital was about fifty dollars a day and it was twenty-three dollars a day at St. Joseph's Memorial Hospital in Hillsboro, it would be economically logical to do the waiting in Hillsboro. Besides, I would be "home" where many people knew me and I knew many people. On August 1, 1966 I was transferred to St. Joseph's, just eight days before the twenty-third anniversary of my birthday. Over a hundred birthday cards were sent/delivered to me that day and they perked me up some. Incidentally, the major medical insurance did run out before I was picked up by welfare and Wisconsin Medical Assistance Program. I had to pay a little over a hundred dollars to St. Joseph's Hospital some months later when all insurance was exhausted.

As I got settled into a routine there they kept my legs and other joints limber as well as getting me up periodically from the bed. They lifted me into one of those old wooden wheelchairs with the large wheels in front and the casters in back. That 'chair' must have weighed over a hundred pounds!! It had a high back on it and would have fit a seven foot tall person! Occasionally during August I was able to convince a nurse or staff member that it was *very* important that I go downtown! They knew the fresh air and seeing old friends would do some good for me. So, on three or four occasions I was pushed downtown (approximately seven blocks, one way) and back to the hospital. The late Joanne Stanek was a year ahead of me in school and I considered us to be friends, though not close friends; she was a nurse and worked at St. Joseph's. One day the nurse aide that was planning to take me to town could not do it for some reason, so Joanne asked if I'd like her to take me. I said, "Sure," with a big smile—she was a pretty woman, though I would not see her face much with her pushing me in that God Forsaken Wheelchair. When we got back to the hospital she said with a laugh, "That's hard work pushing you in that chair, next time I think I'll just hook your catheter tubing around my car bumper and pull you to town and back that way!!"

Speaking of catheters, the time had been nearly three months since the accident and I had been totally incontinent of bladder and bowel. The urine problem had been taken care of by the use of a Foley Indwelling Catheter, a relatively short tube made of latex that has one end inserted (with help of K-Y jelly) through the penis and into the bladder. The tubing has a side track that allows one to push air into a small bulb near the bladder end (with needle and syringe) and the bulb of air holds the tubing in the bladder. (NOTE: If Joanne *literally* tried to pull me with her car by the tubing, that bulb would enlarge the bladder neck and the urethra as it pulled out with minimal tension applied) General rule of thumb was that the catheter was changed as often as necessary and usually never left in for more than two weeks with regular irrigation of it and the bladder.

Regarding the bowel, I must have totally been in denial of that business as I do not recall any of the times that the nurses MUST HAVE used suppositories and/or enemas to evacuate the fecal matter. Maybe, since I was in bed all the time at first and was taking some stool softening pills, they just continuously put Chuks under me and cleaned up the mess after the fact—I honestly have no recall of bowel movements until I was in Rehab learning self-care skills.

I did have one interesting experience related to my bladder in August. I don't recall whether he was my regular doctor, or whether he was taking Dr. Boston's place when Boston was out of town, but Dr. Baker was my doctor on this particular instance. He came into my room probably on "morning rounds" and said to me, "I think we will try to see how well you can drain your bladder without the catheter today." I (in total ignorance and not realizing Dr. Baker's limitations in dealing with spinal cord injury side effects) said to him, "Let's go for it." At that stage of my life all doctors were like God and who was I to question anything. If I knew then what I know now and learned in Rehab I would have definitely questioned!! They took out the catheter around ten or eleven o'clock in the morning and encouraged me to continue drinking liquids as I had previously with the catheter in. Around one in the afternoon I noticed that my abdomen area was a little distended, but I had no feeling that I needed to "void" (fancy nurse's word for "pee") the bladder of its fluid. An hour later the belly was stretched more and getting tighter—I put the handheld urinal under my penis, but nothing came out. Soon I broke out in a sweat like the kind I exhibited dripping from my face during a basketball game in high school. That was my first clue that pain would show itself to me through sweating when I could not feel it. I called the nurse and when she arrived I said, "Get a catheter and put it in me before I explode," as my belly was beginning to look like a watermelon. At that point the nurse went through one of those asinine things they like to do thinking they are impressing someone, I guess. She said in a serious tone, "We'll need to get a doctor's order to do it." You know what I'm thinking, "Screw the doctor's order, get me out of this misery." My next episode without a catheter was during rehab when they trained me how to stimulate the bladder so it would drain and not back up like a watermelon. More on that later . . .

I met a nice gal who was just out of high school working as an aide and planning to go to college and Nursing School. She was friendly, seemed intelligent and had a good personality to help her in a profession where caring is essential. Her name was Mary Zenner from Elroy and she was one of the persons who took me downtown a couple of times. She was easy to talk with and she seemed to genuinely "like" me, which was something I had been struggling with in my mind/emotions since the day I was told my true condition and it sunk into my brain. Since I was popular in my school days and felt that I was attractive to the opposite sex, there was a need to reaffirm that now. Mary, in her friendly way, somehow reaffirmed that I was not totally repulsive to the opposite sex or to a person who did not know me before the accident.

During the time at Hillsboro's St. Joseph's Hospital I had very little of my time consumed in therapy, so I had a lot of time to think about questions like: What kind of job will I be able to do in the future? Will I ever be able to drive a car? Will I ever get married? Will Berth Ann marry me? Will I ever date again? Will I ever be able to have sexual relations and/or father any children? Is there any truth to the encouragement that I keep getting: "You'll be walking pretty soon, you are a strong person?" Then there is that old thought that comes up when you feel close to a lot of people and that is, "I wonder what they will think of me now?" Fortunately, I did get that question answered by a man that I admired, former Superintendent of Hillsboro Schools, the late Gordon Shold. He came to me in the hospital and said, "You are the same Jim that you were last year and years ago, you just will probably be doing things in a different way!"

Sometime before my rehabilitation I was living as best as

possible in the hospital, I woke up one morning after having an eerie dream. Many times I woke up in the morning and I knew that I had been dreaming but could not even remember the last part of it. I assume that it has something to do with the after effects of the head injury I suffered in the accident. But, this one morning the dream was so vivid, short, but very vivid. They, whoever they are, say that you only remember the last part of any dream. I guess the subconscious works in mysterious ways. In the eerie dream I was sitting in a wheelchair in the cockpit of a fighter plane and was flying it on a suicide mission. I tilted the wheel up and the plane dove rapidly downward crashing into a ship (apparently belonging to the enemy) and exploded. I was thrown clear from the wreckage and landed on an island in grass that looked to be three feet tall. Then I woke up. I don't know how a trained psychologist would explain it and I never asked one. My analysis is as follows. First, I was 1A for the draft prior to my accident. Secondly, I was flying the plane to subconsciously fulfill my military obligation. Thirdly, I did not know I was going to be in a wheelchair, but my subconscious did. Fourthly, the crash into the ship was my car wreck. Fifthly, being thrown from the wreckage was me being thrown from my car wreck. And lastly, landing in the tall grass may mean that I was momentarily conscious (awake) when I hit the ground when thrown from the car and my eyes opened with blades of grass an inch or two from my eyes causing them to appear to be very tall. That's the best I can do with it—weird!!

I woke up to a load roar and looked at my watch, 7 a.m. and it would be at least another hour before breakfast. What was that noise? It didn't take me long to figure it out. Earlier that year they had a very big rainstorm and it had flooded so bad that the dam holding the water in the mill pond was washed out. The lake was nearly totally drained. The City Fathers decided it was time to dredge the lake because over the years too much silt had washed into the lake from the two streams that fed it. Most of us kids who had swam, fished or boated around on the lake in our early years (back in the days of junior high) knew that the only deep area of the "pond" was near the dam where it was ten feet deep or so. In most areas some fifty yards or more away from the dam the water was only three or four feet deep and in the area from the hospital to the bridge over State Highway 80 the depth was from a foot to six inches in a lot of the places. Those in charge figured that Hillsboro could have a nice lake if they made it deeper and somewhat smaller by moving a large amount of the extra earth. Therefore, every morning, usually six days a week, I got the wake-up call from the large diesel engines of the earthmovers as they scraped up the dirt and hauled it to its new location. Sometimes I heard a double roar as a big D-nine Caterpillar was pushing the earthmover when it got stuck in the mud, which was quite often.

I was making progress with my situation and beginning to come to grips with the fact that I quite well may be living from a wheelchair for the rest of my life. Then it happened when I went to a Sunday morning church service at my hometown church. The church was located a long block from the hospital so my brother came to get me and pushed me up that hill to the church where other hands were summoned to lift me and the wooden "crate" (wheelchair?) up five steps to get into the church. It was after church that I regressed a couple months as many people came to me pouring out their sympathy with "Too bad this had to happen to you, Jim." With that comment, *all* the progress that I had made (to accept my condition and work hard to try to make myself a productive person) was thrown right out the window!! BIG SET-BACK!

Chapter Twenty-Two

It was nearly eight weeks from the time I left Madison and the day I went back and checked into the Rehabilitation part (second floor) of N & R Hospital, as it was called. The days of lying in bed most of the time were over, thank God. I was given a wheelchair to use (looked nothing like the old wooden one) and in a short time the real severity of the broken left arm and the wrist area jammed up came to the fore. The broken arm and jammed bones in the wrist had made it necessary for the cast to be on the arm for a longer-than-normal amount of time. And, the cast came down to about a quarter inch above the large knuckles on the back of my hand as well as holding the thumb tight against the hand inhibiting the movement of the wrist joint and the thumb. Due to the nature of the spinal cord injury (higher on the left side) there was/is partial paralysis of my left arm/hand.

The wheelchair loaner I was "in" could only go in circles because I could not grip the handrim with my left hand to "run" that side. Upon seeing my dilemma the physical therapist notified the two men who worked in the "brace shop" to get and put on a handrim with quad-knobs so I could push the chair with the heel of my left hand against the knobs. Subsequently, the doctor, Dr. Seibens, physiatrist, wrote an order for the brace shopmen to make a "basic opponence" splint to replace the paralyzed basic opponence muscle and stretch the web between thumb and the hand. Initially I could move my thumb (voluntarily) about one-eighth inch away from my hand.

Through therapy and thirty-six years of using that hand I now can move my thumb about one and a half inches from my hand. Doesn't sound like much, but it has been functional thanks in part to Betty Poschell, physical therapist who insisted that I could get some range of motion out of that stiff wrist that only had about ten degrees of extension when she started. She put it in the whirlpool and bent the wrist back and forth while I screamed "Oh, God, that hurts so bad—why don't you just cut that hand off?" I don't think it could have hurt anymore than her bending on it. It was a bad scene, but it was a little easier to take since Betty was a very attractive woman in my eyes. She was fun working with down on the exercise mat, too. She helped me bend over and touch my toes when in a "long-sit" position by putting her body (chest) against my back and pushing. (Long-sit position is sitting upright with legs out in front of you on a mat or bed) I had foot-drop (a situation where in the long-sit position you can't pull your toes toward your head to make the bottom of the feet vertical) and I still could touch my toes with my wrists! Of course, you must remember, I can't feel how much strain is being put on my hamstrings and the pain an able-bodied person would feel! Betty was a neat helper.

While Betty was working on my wrist, an occupational therapy intern was assigned to help me in OT. She taught me how to type and that was great finger therapy—still is right now as I type this rough draft on an old Smith-Corona that I bought at a garage sale. The typing is/was very good for helping to improve the dexterity of both hands but especially the left one. This OT student intern was about my age, single and fairly attractive. My biggest shock came about the second week that she had been working with me. She said, "Tomorrow WE are going to start you learning how to dress yourself." "Oh," was all I could say. I had been up in my bed just recently when a dozen student doctors (three female) observed me lying buck naked on my bed while they prodded and poked to see what types of jerk reactions were going on in my body; checking my involuntary reactions, I guess. So, whatever modesty I once had, was slipping away fast. And, by the time the student OT got done teaching me how to dress myself, I could have been a good candidate for exhibitionist of the year awards! At that point I didn't care who saw me without clothes!

I was beginning to get some movement in the wrist and was developing some skills for transferring to and from the wheelchair. One of my biggest problems, both now and then, was the lack of balance. The lack of any trunk control was the main determining factor in the physical therapists telling me that they were working to make me as functional as possible in the wheelchair rather than wasting time trying to get me up on braces and crutches. The physical therapists worked together to measure me for the proper wheelchair and it had some special modifications to the standard in that the seat was slightly higher to allow for my leg length from knee to ankle. Because of my poor balance the back was made so it went above the scapula bones to give me good support. A few years later I was able to get it cut down about three and a half inches. "This chair will last you a lifetime," the therapist said as he handed me the "keys" to my 1966 Everest & Jennings Heavy Duty Wheelchair. He was almost right as the chair was good and with lots of repairs it lasted thirty-three years. Since my life expectancy was only twenty years at the time of my Rehab, that chair lasted thirteen years more than expected!

It was in physical therapy that I met an interesting person named Jo-Ann G. Furrh. She was in the neurological part of the institution because of the strange symptoms she was having—diagnosis multiple sclerosis. Her husband was a psychology professor or instructor at Platteville State College and they had a seventeen month old son named Thomas. She and I visited often in PT and she invited me to her room to play cards with her which I did a couple times. When she was discharged before my time to leave I expected to never see her again. More later.

Another new experience for me was frog-breathing. Due to the fact that I had the collapsed lung at the time of the accident it was felt that I should do as much as possible to expand my lung capacity and this was accomplished by the technique called frog-breathing. It is a system of taking a deep breath and then with gulping and sucking in more air it forces the lungs to expand beyond their previous capacity. If you repeat this four or five times twice a day you soon have the total lung capacity enlarged. I did this for about two weeks and then the meter read a capacity that was near normal for me.

As I began using my new wheelchair in November I also learned about things like decubitus ulcers and the 'chair had a cushion in it called a "bye-bye-decubiti". It was because of the propensity for the development of decubitus ulcer on the gluteal (buttocks) area that the staff members in Rehab all encourage "wheelchair push-ups" often and with a duration of at least fifteen seconds, preferably longer. The push-up allows the blood to rush back into the area of skin that it may have been forced out of due to sitting. A good analogy is to put your index finger firmly in the palm of the opposite hand, hold it for a few seconds, take it away and watch the palm area go from white to pink to red as the blood flows back into the skin. Excess pressure over an extended period of time forces the blood out of the skin for a prolonged period of time and the tissues die, become infected, become ulcerated and you have a bad bed sore (decubitus ulcer). As my left gluteal area atrophied (wasted away) more, the "bye-bye" cushion had to go bye-bye and be replaced by a thicker one with more protection.

One thing obvious to me and those helping me was that I could not continue working in a capacity as physically involved as before the injury. It was also imperative that I go back to school and be trained for some other profession. I had plans in my head and needed to start slow due to the head injury, amnesia and residual memory problems. In planning, some sessions with the Social Worker, a blind lady with excellent coping skills, and some phone visits with Kaz were helpful for me. Kaz suggested that I might pursue a degree in a "cousin" to physical education, which is Recreation. He also knew an important man regarding my future, Timothy Nugent, Founder and Director of the

Rehabilitation Education Program at the University of Illinois. Kaz knew Tim from College days at La Crosse where they attended approximately the same years. Tim had developed a program at the University of Illinois, which allowed students with the educational capacity to attain a degree regardless of what disability they may have. Kaz made it possible for me to go to Illinois and interview to become a student there.

Those who knew me and know me now are very aware of my positive attitude about life and man's ability to do many things if they are attempted in the right manner and with some confidence. I credit my positive experiences in sports and in work situations for the development and sustaining of the positive attitude. My social worker was aware of it and possibly didn't believe it. Someone ordered a battery of psychological tests (may have been standard for everyone as I saw fellow rehab patients taking them also) to be taken by me. The only result from the tests was that I *seemed to be very unrealistic*. One test had to do with worry and was a true/false answer choice. Nearly every question/statement was, "When in a _____ (situation) I worry about things such as _____." For every one I said *FALSE*. Excuse me, does worry do any good to solve a problem? Get real, Psych. Dept.! Maybe my plans were a little more progressive than ninety percent of the people with a spinal cord injury in the neck area, but THAT does not make them unrealistic!

Through consultation and some trips where I was taken to the main University Hospital Urology Dept. it was determined that my bladder situation was due for a change. They told me that there are three main types of bladders under these circumstances. They are flaccid bladder, spastic bladder and autonomic bladder. In the case of the flaccid or spastic bladder the person generally had to continue to use an Indwelling Catheter. However, when you have an autonomic bladder such as mine was/is, that bladder can be trained to drain with the help of the crede' (Fr. pronounced Cre as in cremate followed by da as in day) method which is nothing more than poking or tapping on the bladder through the stomach (abdominal) skin and tissues with the use of one's fingers, or heal of the hand or knuckles in the case of a quadriplegic with limited finger extensor muscles (can't straighten out his fingers).

With this revelation in mind, it was time for the staff to teach me how to use the condom drainage method, similar to the Texas Catheter system some use. There are two phases to this system using condoms. Phase one is as follows: 1) obtain latex tubing with 9/32 inch hole diameter and 3/32 inch wall width approximately seventeen inches long. 2) cut off two 1/16 inch rings from the end of the tubing. 3) put one of the rings over the tubing about two inches from the end where condom will be attached. 4) obtain non-lubricated condoms with reservoir end (preferred). 5) put the end of the tubing into the reservoir end backwards and unroll about three inches of the condom. 6) put the second ring over the outside of the condom covered tubing end and roll it down about one and a half inches. 7) roll the first ring over the second ring sealing the connection against leakage. 8) poke a hole in the condom end at the tubing end and roll the loose part back down the tubing toward the rings. 9) double check to make sure that it is not backwards and it will unroll onto the penis when needed. I must always have two sets of these tubings so that while wearing one the other is being washed and made ready for use when needed. The condom is changed daily or sometimes every other day. When I was taught this procedure they used rubber bands instead of the rings off the tubing. Four or five twists of rubber bands takes way too much dexterity to do and the band or ring off the tubing does wonderfully well.

Phase 2 of the condom drainage system deals with the attachment and collection bag. Some more products are required to securely attach the condom with a high probability of no leakage and they are skin adhesive and one inch wide elastic "stretch" tape. The procedure starts with the penis being cleaned and dried well with a towel. Then the adhesive is put on the shaft and distributed evenly (I hope) with my finger until it becomes tacky. Promptly I roll on the condom and squeeze it snug against the penis. Finally I cut off about three and a half inches of the tape and wrap it around the condom to help keep the condom "glued tight" yet the elastic does stretch to allow for penal erection without the tape cutting into the skin resulting in an excoriated penis (doctor's term). I know that because it happened one time when I had partially stretched the tape as I put it on causing a wound later. Once the condom is secure the tubing is turned so there is no twist in the condom and it is connected to the Bard leg bag, aka, disposable urine collection bag. There are other brands, but I have used Bard large size leg bags for thirty-six years so that's the best for me. After connecting the tubing to the leg bag, the bag is secured to the leg (personal preference as to which one) below the knee with stretchy latex straps fastened with plastic "buttons" in the holes of the strap. Having the bag that low gets gravity to work for me when urine flows into the tubing and "down" to the bag. An orderly did the initial training and putting on the condom for me the first two or three times, but soon I was able to do it myself and I've done it twelve to thirteen thousand (12,000-13,000) times since then. Do YOU know anyone else who has used over twelve thousand condoms in his lifetime??

The nurses did the training of the crede method of bladder stimulation. One evening nurse liked me and "used" me as an example to teach her daughter about the effects of car wrecks. As the daughter and her date came to see Mom (the nurse) before going to the Homecoming Dance at her high school, the nurse kicked me in the shin as the daughter watched and saw that I didn't even flinch because I didn't feel anything. We hope the daughter got the message; she was not in an accident that night so that was good. Anyway, this nurse was helping me learn to crede every two hours·so she came over to my bed one night shortly after she told me to crede the bladder. Since we had more of a friendly relationship than a professional one, she said to me, "Tinkle, Jimmy, tinkle!" (she was one of the few I let call me Jimmy) I was doing the crede but something subconscious was overriding it—I had a partial erection. So, after she bugged me enough I said to her, "Did you ever try to pee when you had an erection?" She had no response and left chuckling to herself!

Speaking of sexuality, Berth Ann and I met with Dr. Siebens, my physiatrist, (doctor of physical medicine and rehabilitation) to discuss what the possibilities were for sexual relations and having children. We were told that I may not be able to get and keep an erection hard enough and for long enough time to have intercourse. "You'll just have to try and see," the doctor told us. Then, if we can have intercourse, there is the question of the possibility of no climax or ejaculation. This act of releasing fluids and semen out through the penis seems to be very easy for the able bodied person and it happens often with masturbation (self-stimulation). Personally, I never had any problems before injury. Since my spinal cord and total nervous system was "messed up", I had not had any ejaculations due to it taking coordination of some very complicated nervous systems within the total nervous system. Something that was so "easy" as a teenager and young adult is now basically impossible! That's tough to take no matter who you are!

Was being able to father children important to me? Not really, there are many children who need to be adopted and loved by a couple of parents who really care. However, did Berth Ann want to have children? Yes, I feel she did and that would be part of the criteria in our future decision regarding us and marriage. Was the idea of having or not having sexual intercourse (penis—vagina) important to me? Yes, but since I never *really* had penis—vagina intercourse prior to the accident, how do I know what I'm missing. I almost did it once, but . . .

Regarding sexual intercourse and having children, I have noticed a very interesting paradox. In general, the higher the level of spinal cord injury the lower the amount of sensation and physical (motor) function of the body. Secondly, the higher the spinal cord injury the *better* the ability to obtain and maintain an erection as well as father children. Three people's experiences prove this to be accurate. I worked with a patient in Chicago who was a nineteen year old "stud" until he was shot in the lower back while attempting to enter a house and commit robbery. His lumbar vertebrae injury (below ribs) made it impossible to get even a partial erection no matter what the stimulation. The other two were guys with cervical five (C-5) spinal cord injuries who both fathered children. I wonder if God had this in mind when He put together our magnificent bodies with all the intricate nerves and cells and muscles and impulses passed around through tracts: "I am going to fix it so that when this man injures himself, as I know he will, I will take away his ability to walk and use his hands, but I'll compensate for that by letting him have the use of his penis; those who don't lose so much motor control will lose some of their sexual ability." God has spoken. Sounds real to me!

Earlier I spoke about bowel incontinence. As with the case of the bladder, the spinal cord injured person cannot feel when he has to "go" nor can he stop it if and when he has to "go". However, we are thankful that the bowel movements do not happen five or six times a day like the bladder eliminates. Therefore bowel movements can be scheduled on a daily or every-other day basis. As with most things consistency is very important and this deals with the many things that affect the operation of the gastro-intestinal tract—that system where food enters your body through the mouth, gets digested in the mouth, stomach and small intestines, has valuable products reabsorbed through the walls of the large intestines and the remainder comes out as waste called a bowel movement.

While talking about bowel movements, I have a request to all parents. Please, teach your kids about the term "bowel movement" before they are in high school and find themselves in the hospital where the nurse comes to your room at 8 p.m. and asks, "Did your bowels move today?" Or "Did you have a BM today?" and you really don't know what she is asking you so you simply reply, "Yes". In jest you say to yourself, "Sure my bowels moved today every time I rolled over in the bed or got out of it—they are part of me, aren't they?" They moved like my whole body moved!! Poop, do-do and other slang terms for that act should be removed from everyone's vocabulary.

Anyway, bowel movements were something the able-bodied person did without any ordeal and usually took less than five minutes. When I became disabled it became an ordeal that often took nearly a half hour depending on my situation and living arrangement. The last couple weeks in Rehabilitation were spent training me how to manage my own bowel movements since my plans were to be as independent as the architectural barriers of my living situation would allow. Since my plan was to go to the University of Illinois to school and later to be active in the work world, I was working toward having my BMs at night before going to bed rather than in the morning. And, I was told that once on a regular schedule I could do this every other night rather than in the morning.

Why am I going into detail about these basic life activities? Because, when you become disabled, they have a way of controlling part of your life activities; let me explain. The biggest concern for this person with a spinal cord injury was avoiding diarrhea or loose stool that may result in "messing my britches!" Therefore, the major task for me is to maintain solid stool that will remain intact in the bowel until I am ready for it to come out. To do this adequately I need to use knowledge about what affects consistency of stool and by trial and error discover other things that pertain to it. First, we must realize that everything we eat and drink has an effect on stool consistency; second, we must realize that certain medicines affect (kills the good bacteria in the bowel that is needed for good digestion) stool consistency; and third, our level of activity affects stool consistency. To illustrate the latter my own experience is good proof. While in the hospital, in bed most of the time with no physical activity I was given Pericolace (a fairly strong stool softener to keep me from being too constipated). When I went to Rehab and was up in my wheelchair daily and more active, my medicine was changed to Colace, a stool softener that was half as strong as Pericolace. When I was out of the hospital and actively moving about at school, I no longer needed any pills to prevent constipation (the greater the activity level, the less possibility of constipation). On the contrary, off and on over the past thirty-six years of living with this disability all medications related to the bowels have been in the category of anti-diarrheal agents—I drank a few gallons of Keopectate over the years! Regarding the second item that I stated has effect on stool consistency, I have to be careful in the case of anti-biotic medicines and remember which ones caused me to be "loose" after taking them and advise the doctor next time that, "I don't take anymore penicillin or amphicillin or any other cillins!!" Then, they always ask, "Why?" So, to get them to remember, I crudely say, "Because they give me the shits!" And, "I definitely don't need that problem!" Regarding the first item (diet) I learned over time that good healthy fresh fruits tend to give me loose stool especially if I eat more than a little bit—I believe it is the citrus as I have had the same trouble with vitamin C tablets. Also, I am asking for trouble if I drink more than two twelve ounce cans or bottles of beer, sometimes one can could be a problem.

In addition to the situations mentioned above, there is a hidden cause of a chance for loose stool or bowel problems. That is "nerves" or "stress" situations in which the "pressure is on" prior to a big event such as a test in school or certain job deadlines or other requirements. Able-bodied people have often been observed frequenting the "facilities" such as a coach prior to the "big game" where his nervousness leads to bowel difficulties that need immediate attention. The disabled person has this problem magnified due to their inability to "run to the bathroom" and if one worries about having "messed pants" it enhances the probability of doing it!

The last week or two in rehab I worked on getting into a regular bowel movement routine of every other night so it would carryover to my next life projects. I received training in safe transfer from wheelchair to commode, how to use dulcolax suppositories to assist and how to do digital stimulation of the anal sphincter with a plastic/rubber glove on my hand. In addition, during these last days I solidified some plans such as getting accepted at La Crosse State to take a few credits and got an appointment to go to the University of Illinois to see about going there for graduate school if I did OK at La Crosse.

To summarize my condition at the day of discharge from rehabilitation, January 7, 1967, it involved basically total paralysis from my breastline down (no muscle use in that part of the body and no feeling in that part of the body), no sensation in the buttocks area so much precaution needed to avoid decubitus ulcers (pressure sores), no feeling or control of the urinary system so need for the continuous use of the external catheter, no feeling or control of the bowels so must have routine for regular times to do it or will have many problems, no feeling of hot or cold or pain in the area of paralysis so care is needed to avoid injury, very poor healing in the lower areas of paralysis due to poor circulation, paralysis of the left arm/hand has left it with half strength and poor dexterity of the fingers as well as the obvious which is confinement to either a sitting or lying position in my wheelchair or in bed or in a car seat.

Now that you know what is in the previous paragraph you can easily understand why I say what I say when someone says to me, "It's too bad you can't walk," and I respond with, "That's the least of my problems!!" The wheelchair is my means of "walking," but it does not solve many of those other problems that are part of spinal cord injury.

The Rehabilitation Hospital discharged me with a month's supply of any bowel/bladder pills I was taking at the time and set a check-up for six weeks hence. They also sent with me the tubing and gallon jug I had been using for urine collection at night, something necessary since my accident and for as long as I live.

If I said, "Everything I needed to know in life, living with a spinal cord injury, I learned in Rehabilitation," I'd be lying. True, many very important things are learned there and set a good basis for all the things that one must learn to live day to day in the real world. Frankly, you learn a little bit about planning, but you don't realize how important it is and what an ongoing activity it has to be to function with a limited amount of frustration. I did learn that real quickly the first time I went to a store and discovered that I should have called first because I could not get into the building, due to architectural barriers. Or the time shortly after discharge when I went to an event and after a few hours there I needed to empty my legbag before it burst. I went to the restroom and (1) I couldn't get into the facility without a lot of assistance and (2) once inside the room I could not get close to the toilet to empty my bag, so the assistant helped me make a rapid trip outdoors to drain the bag where all the local dogs do "it". Not on a tire, but behind the tire where I can lean over and brace my head against the back of the car by the trunk to get the tubing out of my sock so I can unclamp it and drain the bag.

One of the great attributes that probably cannot be taught is "patience". I had an upper hand on it as during my growing up years I watched my father in many situations where he demonstrated great patience. Thus, I think I may have inherited it or at least the propensity to develop it. Either way you look at it, during rehabilitation you have no way of knowing how much patience you will need in future situations. Sometimes I think that the Nurses or other Staff members purposely take their time in answering our "call" light just to help us learn some patience!! At the time you get frustrated, but if you learn patience from it then it can turn into a positive experience, not a negative one. Like when the physical therapist was bending my left wrist it was a very negative experience, but the fairly good functional use of that hand I've had for the past thirty-six years definitely has made those experiences positive.

Mark these words: *NINETY NINE PERCENT OF LIFE IS ATTITUDE.* People who know me well, know I have a very positive attitude. I can say in all honesty, "If I didn't have a positive attitude, I would not be living today!!"

When I was in Rehab. they installed a trapeze so that the bar hung out over the middle of the bed. It was there so I could grab it and pull myself up to a sitting position since I had no trunk muscles with which to do this task. They also sent one home with me on my first home visit so dad could hook it on the bed I used at home. Was there a trapeze over the bunk type bed I would be using at the dormitory at La Crosse State in three weeks? No, of course not. Would I take mine with me? No, of course not. So, I

better learn how to get myself up in a sitting position in bed
BEFORE I get there. Would there be a trapeze on the bed in my
dormitory room at the University of Illinois? No, so I better learn
how to get up without one!! Gee, those beds don't even have side
rails like the ones in Rehab., so I better learn something new. It
is physically impossible to simply turn over from my back to my
side so I could use my hands and push up the top part of my
body and sit up that way, so I had to learn a new way to turn over.
I had three weeks to learn something.

Sometimes "trial and error" is the best teacher and after many
errors I discovered that I could get rolled over by reaching my
left arm across my body to my right and by reaching my right arm
out to the right of my body; then with rapid movement I "threw"
both arms to the left simultaneously as a means of starting the
body to turn. If I got a "good one" I would roll far enough to grab
the edge of the mattress on the double bed and pull myself over
on my side. Occasionally I could grab the bed edge on the first
try, but usually it takes (I said takes, not took, as I still use this
method) three or four attempts before I can muster enough turn
of the body to make it—and now it is even harder to do because
of the weight I've gained in my belly. Once I get that belly going
in the right direction it helps, but getting it going is harder than
before!!

I was taught early on that I needed to sleep as much as
possible on my stomach due to the fact that once I get going in a
regular routine I would be up in my 'chair' *sitting on my buttocks*
about sixteen hours a day and I had better give the skin a good
rest overnight or I'd soon have breakdown of the skin. In reality I
spend about, on the average, seven hours on my belly and an hour
on my right side; and, I can't lay on my left side due to the tubing
going from my penis to the collection jug down beside the bed.

I must sleep on the side of the bed so that as I lay on my
back the wheelchair is to my right. This is so that I can transfer
into the 'chair with my right arm reaching over to the right armrest
of the 'chair and having the necessary strength to lift and pull my
body over to the 'chair missing the wheelchair tire. To hit the tire

would be a bruise and could lead to breakdown. Care MUST be taken with each transfer to avoid any chance of injury. Since my right arm is twice as strong as my left I feel it is much safer transferring in that direction. I lift my upper body over into the 'chair and then I use my arms and hands to carefully guide and lift my legs off the bed so the feet land softly on the footrests.

Earlier I spoke of learning how to dress myself but I never detailed the procedure of something that for twenty years (twenty-two minus the first two years of my life) had been a simple one or two minute job. Not anymore. Although I wake up lying on my stomach or side, my first acts of the day leave me on my back. These initial acts are (1) since I don't have any feeling below the waist primarily I first turn on my right side and with my hand check my "plumbing" to make sure I've had no accidental leaks during the night and again with my hand I reach and feel my buttocks area to make sure I have not had any accidental bowel "action" overnight, (2) push myself up to a sitting position so I can reach down and uncross my legs with my hands, (3) lay down on my back and crede (stimulate) my bladder causing it to drain until it is empty or as near empty as I can get it, (4) change the condom as previously described, and (5) attach the condom tubing to the leg that has been washed out and made ready for the day's use. Now I can start to get dressed. The first part is to get into a sitting position as described previously. The pants, socks and shoes to be worn that day have been placed in my wheelchair before going to sleep so they are handy in the morning. After sitting up I reach into the chair seat and get the clothes, putting them on the bed to my left.

Dressing begins with putting on my socks and leaving the top of the right one pushed down off my ankle. Next I strap on the legbag starting with the top latex strap just below the knee on the front of the leg and the bottom strap just above the ankle and tuck the short tubing at the bottom of the bag into my sock pulling the sock up over it. Then I put an extra strap around my leg and tubing just above the knee to hold that section in place to avoid kinking. It's time for the pants. I take the waist area in both hands, lean forward as far as my belly will allow and pull them onto my feet, ankles and legs—both legs at the same time. THAT negates the old saying: "He puts his pants on the same way I do, one leg at a time." Meaning that "he" is no better than I am! Does that mean I am better than them 'cause I put my pants on two legs at a time? Duh . . . not really! Now I put on the shoes one at a time! Once the pants are up by my lower thighs I lie (fall) back on my back pulling up the pants as I go. Here's where the rolling comes in handy again. I roll to my right a little and with the left hand pull up the left side as far as possible. Then with three or four attempts I finally roll far enough to the left to use my right hand to pull up the right side clear to the waist. Now a short roll to the right lets me finish getting the left side to the waist. Snap the pants, zip them up and buckle the belt (don't use a belt anymore since the time the buckle cut into my belly) completes the task. Finally, I grab my wheelchair handrim with my right hand, put my right elbow firmly into the mattress and flex that biceps muscle to sit up—if that won't work, then it goes back to the rolling to the left to get into position to push myself up to sitting and transfer into the wheelchair.

I spoke of being careful recently and it is especially necessary when my feet are bare as in use of the commode or shower. In those cases I take off both footrests before transferring to avoid scraping the skin anywhere. If I just flip the footrests to a vertical position the danger is worse as the bottom of the footrests are very rough from them scraping periodically on concrete as in going off a curb backwards where they come down on the concrete and scrape as I back away from the curb (a situation I've been in many times due to no curb cuts). A scrape on my feet takes a looooonnng time to heal!!

Chapter Twenty-Three

Fourteen weeks of rehabilitation and a total of seven and a half months of being confined to a hospital and getting treatment and training was over. The security blanket was lifted and I was supposed to be ready to live as independently as possible in a world full of architectural barriers (something I was totally unaware of prior to my injury). To begin with, I got home to my folks' house that had only three steps up to get in the front porch (higher at back porch) so dad had gotten a four foot by eight foot sheet of half or three-fourths inch plywood to ramp the front. It did not make it so I could go up it independently, but at least it made it possible for someone to push me up and into the house. At that point in time I did not need to be able to come and go independently because wherever I went I had to have someone take me. AND, I was getting ready to leave February 1, 1967 to go to school so there was really no need to fuss about it then.

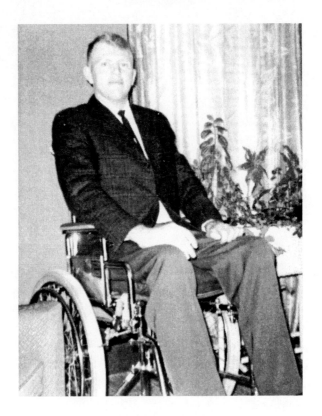

I have "new" wheels

During those three weeks at home I had my appointment with the Rehabilitation Education Center Director/Asst. Director at the Univ. of Illinois, in Champaign, Illinois. On the day of the trip my brother was "off" from work and he took me to the meeting. It was on that trip that I was reminded of another problem/blessing, which was some excessive sweating from my head, neck and shoulder areas. It was a problem due to the fact that it made me VERY uncomfortable when the temperature was ten or twenty degrees below zero and even with the best car heater, I still was chilled all the time I was sweating on this trip. It is a blessing as it is my body's way of telling me something is hurting or something is WRONG in my body that I can't feel. Incidentally, the doctors told me that my "sweating mechanism" was messed up by the spinal cord damage and that is why I DON'T sweat at all if the surrounding temperature is eighty, ninety or over a hundred degrees! Ironically when I was able bodied I did sweat profusely whenever the temperature got much over seventy-five. Thus, there is another precaution I needed to be aware of and take—stay away from spending a lot of time in hot places where I could get heat stroke or heat exhaustion due to no sweating.

We went to the meeting and I was impressed with the program there. They said that I could attend and could start in summer school, if my grades were good at La Crosse.

Soon school started at La Crosse and I was there living in White Hall, the same dormitory I was living in during my sophomore year previously. The Wisconsin Medical Assistance Program and Vocational Rehabilitation worked together to finance my needed education and arranged for an assistant to help me overcome the architectural barriers. From rehab. I took home a portapottie type piece of equipment that I could use with help to get to the inaccessible commode and shower. My assistant moved me as needed in the pottie on wheels to the set destinations. Then, my assistant helped me to get to and from classes and in and out (up and down one step) of the dormitory.

With physical problems minimized, I should be able to devote all my attention to study. Due to the nature of my head injury and the amnesia that followed the coma, I was still not able to remember things very well which made the class work challenging. So I only took ten credits, two three-credit Recreation classes and one four-credit statistics class. At the nine weeks period I was in the D-F range in all three classes as I could not remember what I had just read in the book—read a chapter and remember only the last paragraph! Somehow during the second nine weeks I improved very much, began to enjoy the classes some, and ended the semester with three C's for grades which was good enough to allow me to get into the University of Illinois for graduate school and be part of the group in the Rehabilitation Education Program as previously mentioned.

While attending LaCrosse State I was scheduled for a check-up at Rehab in Madison. It was for a day in February and it turned out to be a cold day—about ten degrees below zero for a "high." Since I had no help available at home to take me for this trip, it was determined that Medical Assistance would arrange for it and pay for it. They contacted an ambulance transport company to take me and the men arrived about 7a.m. to pick me up.

Early indicators told me this was not going to be a very enjoyable trip, no matter how positive my attitude was! As I rolled down the sidewalk to the parked ambulance, the men got a bed on wheels out of the back of the ambulance, rolled it over by me and asked me how I wanted to make the transfer. To that I responded, "I'm not riding two hundred fifty miles on that damn thing!" Then I added, "I'd like to ride in the front seat and see where I am going." "OK," they said, and I transferred from my 'chair into the front seat of the vehicle. The vehicle was about a fifteen year old hearse converted into an ambulance, I believe.

Once on our way the ride was basically uneventful. We got to Rehab on time and I met with the Doctor, various therapists, the Social Worker and some nursing personnel. I was able to grab a little lunch while there and somewhere round 2 p.m. all the things were completed so we could head for La Crosse. We headed up I-90-94. Somewhere between Wisconsin Dells and Mauston I heard a bang! The driver stopped the car as we had a blow-out on the left rear tire.

The heater did not work real well in the vehicle, but the driver left the engine running while the two of them worked to get the jack out of the back and lift the car to change the tire. I did have to have the window down a little to avoid carbon monoxide poisoning—the exhaust system on that old "beater" was not too great either. The driver came and sat behind the wheel after about twenty minutes. He had a bewildered look on his face. "Did you get it changed?" I asked with enthusiasm and optimism in my voice. "No, the jack won't lift the car high enough to get the wheel and oversized tire off the car." While he sat beside me in the car warming himself, the other man went to the nearest farm home by walking through the snow and across fences only to find no one home. When he got back the driver stood outside the car trying to "flag" someone down to get some help. Finally, a State Patrol Officer stopped and he radioed ahead to Mauston to have a wrecker service come out so the hoist on the back of the wrecker could lift the rear of the vehicle. We waited. And waited. And waited. After about forty-five minutes since the officer made the call, the driver got out again to flag down somebody, anybody, to see about getting help again. Another State Patrol Officer finally stopped and again a call was made to some wrecker service to get the help we needed. After about a half hour the wrecker showed up, lifted the back of the car enough to do the job. That was fine, but then they discovered another problem with the lug nuts or the spare being different from the wheel/tire that was flat. SOMEHOW after another forty-five minutes they got the spare on the vehicle and we were ready to go to the destination—HOME.

While all this business with the changing of the tire was going on I sat chilly in the front seat of the vehicle. About halfway through the changing ordeal, the driver told me I did not have to have the window down so far—I had it down two to three inches. Upon his suggestion to raise it some I turned the crank and "clunk," the window dropped down two inches. He said, "Try it again." So, I cranked it as he said and after a half turn it "clunked" again dropping the window another two inches. He finally went outside the car and pulled the window up as I cranked the handle to get it within about three inches of the top and we left it there because it stayed that time!

Sitting in one spot for so long and with limited liquid intake, my bladder began to become irritated causing me to sweat. Thus, we were ready to head for La Crosse with the sun gone down, the temperature headed for minus twenty, a three inch gap allowing cold air in the window on my sweaty face, neck and shoulders and we were almost out of gas!! We stopped in Mauston and got gas; then it was a freezing seventy miles of Interstate road home. NEXT TIME I found my own way to go someplace!!

With that semester over I had learned some about living

outside of the hospital setting and knew that I would have to be more independent once at the campus in Illinois. However, I also knew that the facilities would make it possible to be more independent there. Now, I had to spend three weeks at home with my parents in Hillsboro before summer school started. Dad made it possible for me to use our tiny bathroom with the help of the pottie chair on wheels and my parents made the old dining room into a partial bedroom for me as all the bedrooms were upstairs when I was in high school. It wasn't as good as we would have liked it, but it would work for short periods of time, if we could keep our cool.

Chapter Twenty-Four

Arrangements were made for me to fly down to Champaign-Urbana, Illinois by starting at La Crosse Airport on Northwest Airline. It was my first time flying in an older plane with about forty passengers and once in the air it seemed like I could see the side windows vibrating from the engine propellers nearby; and that gave me a little fear. It was a "puddle-jumper" flight as we landed in Madison, flew on to Milwaukee and landed there, then flew on into Chicago's O'hare Field where I connected with Ozark Airlines to take me the last leg of the trip. The Ozark leg was on a newer jet plane with about thirty other passengers. That part seemed safer to me! The Rehabilitation Education Program had a shuttle bus there to take students to their living quarters on campus (bus had wheelchair lift for easy access). Since I was a graduate student I was assigned to the graduate student dormitory so that is where I went.

The rooms were very nice and were more like private little apartments in the graduate student dormitory. However, there was a real problem with accessibility and mine was not like the undergraduate dormitory rooms with central bathrooms. My bathroom was not functional for my use, so I soon transferred out to one of the undergraduate dormitories and had a really neat roommate, Vincent Falardeau, who was a graduate student and future French teacher. He had been at the University for a few years and was a great role model for me as he was a person with a cervical-five (C-5) spinal cord injury that left him with slightly more functional disability than I had. He had developed his triceps and biceps muscles as much as possible, but due to paralysis he could not straighten out his fingers. "One of the first things you need to do is go over to Rehab. and buy yourself a raised, padded toilet seat," Vince advised me the morning of the second day I was there sharing a room with him. He showed me what he used and I thought that was really neat, so I went and bought one for fifteen dollars. I've had it recovered a few times with new padding and am still using it now, thirty-five years later!! Vincent helped me learn a lot of the things about living with a disability that could not be learned in a Rehab. Hospital. Trying to live independently is also a great teacher of things as you learn the skills you need (I learned the skills I needed).

Prior to classes beginning we had a new student orientation at the Rehabilitation Education Center where we learned the rules and regulations about using the bus system and other services of the Program. The Director, Tim Nugent, spoke to us and he made one comment that I will never forget and it helped me understand how he started that Program to help persons with various disabilities get a college education. That comment was, "Remember, A PROBLEM IS THE ABSENCE OF AN IDEA." It now seems so simple—no matter what the *problem*, it is definitely going to seem smaller once you have an *idea* how you might solve it!! I have *tried* to live by that concept.

When it was registration time for classes my advisor suggested that I take two classes that summer. Each class was one unit of credit and equal to four undergraduate credits. So those two classes made a full load for summertime. The total requirement for the Masters Degree was eight units so if all went as planned and I did well in them I'd have a good start toward that degree. But, in the middle of the summer I had a small somewhat superficial sore starting on my buttocks. I decided to spend more time "off my butt" so I dropped one of the courses and decreased the strain in my body. I guess the pace was a little too fast for me at that stage of my development as a person living with a specific disability. The summer term ended with one unit successfully completed and my buttocks sore healed up fine.

One really neat thing happened on or around the Fourth of July. There was a big program held at the football stadium where about fifty thousand or so got together to celebrate the University of Illinois Centennial. Toward the end of the event after it was quite dark, all or most of the crowd held a lighted match at the same time making a nice glow in the stadium for a few seconds. When the activity was over a friend of mine showed me a shortcut way to roll home in our wheelchairs—through the cemetery!! We were about a mile or more from our dormitory so any shortcut sounded good to me; and, by that time I had developed fairly good arm strength for wheeling the chair without getting tired as easily as previously.

Another event occurred during the summer session that was very necessary. After corresponding by mail off and on with Berth Ann for the past year, I received a letter stating she was going to visit me in Illinois and the date was set. Our visit was cordial and we shared enjoyable time together hugging and reminiscing. As we discussed our future I knew that mine was going to be questionable at best for a few years. She, however, needed to get on with her life and I knew that. I felt sad, but realistically relieved, when she told me, "Jim, after knowing you the way you were before the accident, I just can't bring myself to accept you like you are now." I wished her well and told her to have a good life. I've heard people talk about having "closure" and I guess we finally had closure of a chapter of my life that was hard to let go of! We are still good friends today.

After a brief three weeks off it was time to go back to the U. of I. for the fall semester. Have you ever felt that you are destined to fail at something, or that someone is trying to tell you NOT to do something? Read on to see how stubborn we are at times like these. I packed my bags, dad put them in the car and he, mom and I headed for the La Crosse Airport where I was scheduled to take a flight out at about 11:00 a.m. that Sunday morning. When time came to get on the plane, there were about fifteen steps up to the door so the airline people brought out a narrow, highback, slightly padded seat chair with two wheels in the back. On this chair they could pull me up the steps and roll it between the seats once on the plane. I transferred from my wheelchair to this narrow chair and fortunately looked back at my cushion on my wheelchair where I noticed a wet soiled spot. The reason they had not suddenly taken the 'chair away to luggage is that I needed to take the cushion with me and sit on it in the plane. And, when I said, "Hold it!" and "I can't go." they knew something was wrong. "I pooped my pants," I said to the man nearest me, "I'll have to take a later flight." So I got back in my wheelchair and headed back to the waiting room where mom and dad (thank God) were still waiting to see my departure. I told them of my dilemma (remember me saying something about "nerves" causing loose stool, on previous pages of this story) and we began discussing relatives that lived in the La Crosse area. After a couple phone calls, we found that Dick (cousin) and Faye Goldsmith were at home and we could go there to resolve my problem. When we got to their place they covered a bed with something that would protect it and I, with some help from mom, got cleaned up and lay there while she washed and dried my pants. I probably could have just changed clothes, but my luggage with extra clothes in it was already on the plane going to Champaign, Illinois. So, now I was scheduled for the next flight out which was somewhere around 4:00 p.m.

This time I was on board the plane without problems and was headed for Madison, Milwaukee, Chicago before I needed to change planes to Ozark. I had time to get from the Northwest terminal to Ozark because the personnel there were going to take care of me and get me there on time for the 5:30 p.m. flight; however, my personal wheelchair was checked through to Champaign and they put my cushion in an "airline" wheelchair and me with it. You know the typical "airline" wheelchair: solid arms on both sides so a paraplegic needs to be almost totally lifted into it PLUS it has only three inch diameter wheels on the thing so it has to be "pushed" by someone other than the person seated in it! Talk about a way to "cripple" a disabled person!!

My flight was announced, people began to get up and go to get on the plane. Why didn't they put me on first like before, I asked myself with a momentary feeling that I might be left behind. Finally I was able to talk to a worker who told me, "The pilot will not let you on the plane because you can't walk." "What?" I responded, "Ozark has been flying persons with disabilities in wheelchairs for years, what's the deal?" "This particular pilot does not let anyone who can't walk on his plane, and he has that right," replied the worker. I was sick, damn mad, pissed off, frustrated and above all HELPLESS as I sat there in a TOTALLY WORTHLESS DAMN WHEELCHAIR THE LIKES OF WHICH SHOULD NOT BE BUILT!! I couldn't even go to get a cup of coffee or anything. It was like being tied to a pole along the highway some place where no one gives a damn, AND, that is what I'd have liked to do with that pilot! Guess how long I got to wait like that for the next Ozark flight hoping that one has a pilot who is not an asshole. Close, if you guessed 10:00 p.m., but it was 11:00 p.m. when I finally got on the plane and landed in Champaign about 11:30-11:45. I called to see about getting into the dormitory at that late hour and was told the doors were being locked at midnight, but they would alert one counselor to watch for me and let me in. Finally, it was the end of one sad long day. That bed felt GREAT!

I had problems with the plane flight, but I discovered later that they were not over. Prior to classes starting and the dormitory being nearly full, residents had to get meals at restaurants in the area. Fortunately many were wheelchair accessible due to the impact of the Rehab-Education Program at the school and about one hundred to two hundred persons in wheelchairs being "in town" most of the year. I went into one such restaurant off-campus and it was ramped up to the door in an umbrella fashion as the door faced the corner of an intersection. The lunch was good and I paid for it, rolled out the door, turned to the right and discovered the umbrella effect of the concrete under me. As my weight shifted to the left side of my chair and downhill to the front left caster, my right rear tire was off the ground so I could not turn to the right. There was a curb cut there, but I missed it and the left side of my 'chair went down the ramp as the right side stayed up on the curb causing me to tip over and be thrown out of my chair. The result was bruising of the meat around my left ischial tuberosity (sitting bone on left buttocks). When I got back to the dormitory I used my hand mirror and checked my butt for damages, but I did not find any. Each day before dressing I checked to see any damage and found none. Then, after I was all registered and starting to go to classes (ten days since the bruise date) I discovered a dark area under the skin in the general area of the wound. The handwriting was on the wall (way back before I left Hillsboro) if I could have only read it!! I called Dr. Seibens at the Rehab. Hospital in Madison and told him of my problem. He said I had better come to Madison and have him look at it, and he added that I better not plan to stay in school this semester. So I called my parents, they came and got me, took me to see Dr. Siebens and then home. The doctor said that he felt I could heal the sore up with a certain medication and by staying off my butt for a period of time. Adversity strikes again!

It was during this time living with my parents and being confined to bed—again—that I felt my biggest bout of depression and frustration. When you live independently for a few years, lose all your independence, gain back a degree of independence and then lose it all again, you have a tendency to think, What's the use. I loved my parents, but I HATED being dependent on them by having meals brought to me in bed and by having my mom bring things and take things away so I can have my bowel movements in bed. That's in bed in the dining room/bedroom/bathroom where I existed for over four months. You can do anything if you put your mind to it and have the right attitude. Due to my sore on the gluteal area of the buttocks, I could not sit on the porta-pottie chair as I did before when living there so I had to learn how to have BM's in bed. Without getting descriptive, it takes many items normally not associated with that act. On the bed I needed a Chux (pad to cover area of bed), toilet paper roll, a paper or plastic sack, bar of soap, a half-gallon of water in a gallon ice cream pail, a washcloth, a latex glove and a can of air freshener. These items plus a hand mirror leaning against a shoe and decent light so I can see what I'm doing made the task possible. Now, please, a little privacy and NO VISITORS!!

It was prior to one of the just previously mentioned events that I hit "rock bottom" one day and due to someone not coming to my aid as rapidly as I desired, I simply said through my depressed state, "I should have died in that wreck!" Never before and never since have I been that low, but I pulled out of it soon and when I began to be able to be up in my wheelchair for an hour and down for three hours, then up for an hour and down again, I began to see real progress toward my goals. Then I went to up two hours, down two hours, up two hours, down two hours then up two more hours before in bed for the night. Later it went to up four hours and down one hour then up for four hours again until I got to where I could be up in the wheelchair all day long without any down time. The buttocks area was healed . . . for now. Soon it was Christmas and then mid-January and time to go back to the University of Illinois to attempt my first full semester.

Chapter Twenty-Five

Vince Falardeau was still in the same room that I left last fall so it was back to familiar territory when I got back to school after something special—an uneventful air flight!! I took a load of course work that I thought I could handle and I did it. I continued to learn from my fantastic roommate as he was a person with a higher spinal cord injury teaching me what I should be doing. He was student teaching that semester and he was like a clock— he had everything figured in minutes and could tell me all that he had to do and the exact amount of time it would take him to do it. So, I knew not to ask him any questions if he was leaving for school and it was after 8:10 a.m.

Vince was the one who told me all about the University of Illinois Gizz Kids Wheelchair Athletic team. Tim Nugent founded the Rehabilitation-Education Center and program but he also was the founder of the National Wheelchair Athletic Association and the National Wheelchair Basketball Association. The Gizz Kids Basketball Team was very good at that time and had won some National Championships; I think it was the spring of 1968 when I watched them defeat the Detroit Sparks to win that National Championship right there in the UI Fieldhouse.

Wheelchair basketball is not made for everyone who needs to use a wheelchair. Old friends from high school days often asked me if I played wheelchair basketball adding that they figured I would be good (based on my able-bodied skills) since I sat tall in my wheelchair. Here are the facts: A person with no trunk balance has no business trying to compete with others with more ability. The only way I could shoot the ball is to put it in my right hand and "throw it" not "shoot it" at the basket while I hang onto the 'chair with my left hand to keep from falling out of the 'chair!! Most spinal cord injury persons whose injury is at or above the mid thorasic level (middle rib cage) will have limited trunk balance; however, there are always exceptions. Besides, I don't feel that the Gizz Kids team was developed to help me (or those like me). It was/is very important for those who did not have the kind of high school experiences that I had; i.e., persons who contacted polio in their grade school or early high school years or possibly someone with a childhood amputation.

In addition to basketball, there are other activities involved in the competition that culminates with the National Wheelchair Games. These are swimming, track & field, table tennis, archery, bowling and possibly more. Vince was a National Champion swimmer in his class group—Class I-A. He suggested that I might try some events . . . more later.

One Saturday morning Vince was going someplace and I was interested in his car and hand controls, so I went out with him to his car to watch. I saw he had a two door (I knew that was necessary) and his had bucket seats with a console in the middle. He went to the passenger side to get into the car so I watched closely as I figured I would have to get into one that way due to weakness in my left arm for pulling the wheelchair into the car. He sat on the bucket seat, folded his 'chair and pulled it into the backseat area where he had previously removed the seat. Then, he transferred his butt somehow over the opening between the seats to the driver's side, started the car and drove away leaving me with my mouth open and my brain going "a mile a minute." My immediate thought was "if he can do it, so can I". When he returned, I got information about his controls and in May, 1968 I ordered controls for the car I planned to buy that next summer.

That spring term I was able to ride home for Easter break with a student from Mauston, Wisconsin. He also took me back to school. Memorable part of the trip was on the way to Wisconsin it was the day the news came over the radio about the assignation of Martin Luther King. Kennedy in 1963 just before Thanksgiving break and now King in 1968 just before Easter—both times I was riding home from school in someone else's car.

Soon the semester was over, final exams passed and I had all my plans set for an internship in Therapeutic Recreation (yes, I learned about the therapeutic option that I could take for my degree and I had to take the undergraduate level internship to better prepare me for this new field). I went home to Hillsboro and told mom that I had ordered hand controls for the car I planned to buy that summer after internship was over. Her first response was, "You'll never get your wheelchair in the car!" I said, "We'll see!" I thought she taught me to NEVER say never! Anyway, my internship was scheduled from about mid-June to mid-August.

Still being dependent on others for travel, my parents took me to Des Moines, Iowa for my summer session at Younker Rehabilitation Hospital under the supervision of Angie Anderson, Supervisor of Recreation Therapy. A friend described Des Moines as a "big little town" with small stores and the small town atmosphere. Where I went for training was connected to Iowa Methodist Hospital and it had the Nursing School and Nurse's Dormitory connected to it. Certain elevators took a person down to the tunnel that led to other buildings.

The housing arrangements for my summer stay in Des Moines were somewhat "out of the ordinary" due to my disability. When I left the University I was told I would have an apartment there. When we got to the address I was given to report for the summer, we were sitting in front of the Nurse's Dormitory!! Mom went in to the front desk and inquired about my apartment. We WERE in the right place! I was assigned a one bedroom guest apartment on the ground floor adjacent to the apartment housing the House Mother, the supervisor of a dormitory full of lovely young ladies who all had the ambition of becoming Nurses! THANK YOU, JESUS, I said softly to myself after I realized that the scenery was very nice there. NOW, please don't get the wrong idea. There were no ladies' rooms on that floor—they all were upstairs in their rooms. However, I did see them occasionally in the lobby or in the snack/hairdryer room right across the hall from my apartment. Occasionally I went over for a candy bar and one night a lady who was just leaving spoke to me. I responded and we visited for a while in the hall. During the visit we discussed my problem of keeping my pants and shirts looking neat—"I can't do it very well," I said and I offered to pay her a quarter for each shirt and pair of slacks that she washed and ironed for me. She agreed that it was a fair price and we were both satisfied. I don't recall her name, so let's call her Linda.

Linda was a very attractive woman about twenty years old and had a wonderful personality. She also had a boyfriend who was in the military stationed in North Carolina. One day after about three weeks of knowing her she brought my clean laundry to me. I thanked her and paid her the paltry sum; then she told me about her boyfriend who was coming home to see her the next weekend. She didn't do it to make we envious but she did it to preface inviting me to go out with them on Saturday night. I said, "Wow," other than to go outside the front of the building, I did not go anywhere for about four weeks. I immediately said I'd love to go and I finally had something different to "look forward to." Unknown to me in advance I was in for a real education. Saturday night arrived and her boyfriend arrived driving an MG convertible.

Linda and I went out to the car and she introduced me to her boyfriend. I took a look at the car and my first response was "what a challenge this is" as I noticed that the top of the car was about level with my shoulder as I sat in my 'chair and when I looked down to the seat it was about fifteen inches lower that the seat of my 'chair. "That's a long way down," I said, "and it will be a long way back up when we get where we are going, but we will cross that bridge when we get there." I safely got down into the seat, folded up the 'chair and they put it standing up on the backseat—thank God the top was down as the 'chair stood up a foot or more above the top of the car.

We found that Linda had a choice of sitting on the shifting lever or on my lap and she chose my lap, which was nice. We went a few miles to a nice downtown bar and had a couple of mixed drinks. They helped with a little lifting to get me up from the car seat to my 'chair seat. After the drinks they said we should go to a more relaxed environment for more fun. So, back down into the car and off to some place else. Again with help I got into the 'chair and went into the bar with them. It was a large building with picnic tables, a bandstand with a group of banjo players on it and a lot of people shucking peanuts and throwing the shucks on the floor. It had a country atmosphere and the beer was flowing swiftly all around. And, as the banjos played the crowd was singing, "Iowa, Iowa, that's where the tall corn grows." After an hour or two there, we headed back to the dormitory on the hill. They helped me back out of the car and I thanked them for a wonderful night. Then I went to bed.

The Chief Physiatrist, Dr. De Gravelles, at Younkers Rehab. was a real inspiration to me. He was probably thirty to thirty-five years old, about six foot three inches tall and walked with braces and crutches. You see, he got polio when he was in medical school, but what an attitude about life. One day I saw him leave the hospital as he threw his crutches in the backseat of his corvette convertible and sat at the wheel to drive away with hand controls and the top down. His staff meetings were also very educational for me. He arranged to get braces for me to try to walk with them on the parallel bars. I couldn't as I jackknifed every two steps but at least I knew it was not possible for me!!

Dr. De is what everyone called the chief and he had an interesting background—he spoke with a unique accent, they called it New Orleans Cajun Canadian French, I think. Anyway, he had trouble saying R's. I had developed a superficial ulcer on my butt and he told me to get a different cushion to sit on for relief. "I want you to dress it with fuwa by fuwas (4"x4" gauze pads) and get yourself a wubber wing (rubber ring) to sit on," he told me. So I did as told and was able to complete my internship. The reason I was in Iowa was to get the experience of learning to work with Physical and Occupational Therapists as well as Social Workers, Doctors and Nurses. It was also enjoyable to work the odd hours of 1:00 p.m. to 9:30 or 10:00 p.m. sometimes and weekends at times. The credits I got for the summer were eight undergraduate credits that did not apply to my degree, but the experience was invaluable or (as the advertisers say these days) PRICELESS!

When the session was over the co-workers and my supervisor had a little party for my "going away" and they presented me with a scrap book full of pictures and humorous items from the total experience. I was thrilled with it and still have it today! On Saturday after my last day of duty, I said my goodbye to Linda and thanked her for her help. My parents arrived to get me about noon or 1 p.m. as it is about three hundred fifty miles from Hillsboro to Des Moines. I was not thrilled about going back to live in a house with a semi-accessible bathroom, but I was looking forward to gaining some independence by getting a reasonable priced yet dependable car to drive to the U. of I. in the fall.

While I was away, dad replaced the old sidewalk to the front door with a concrete walk that ended flush with the porch floor. Thus, I could come and go as I pleased once I got that "new" car.

Dad and Don had been looking around for a car and had found one at a car lot in Mauston. It was a 1966 Chevrolet Impala, six cylinder, no power steering, with about fifty thousand miles on it. It was nearly three years old and the price was good so I/we bought it. Dad and Don put on the hand controls for me and I was ready to start driving again with my learner's permit. Dad was the lucky one who got to go with me as I practiced. One thing you must know—almost all of dad's traveling in a car was done with him behind the wheel and he rarely if ever rode in the passenger front seat. I started driving and headed out of town on the old highway 33 going west (this is back when the road was narrow with barely two lanes and then the ditch on both sides). Whenever the car got about a foot away from the centerline and was probably a foot from the edge of the road, it appeared unsafe to my dad and he said, "Get out of the ditch, Get out of the ditch,

God damn it, Jim, Get out of the ditch!!" The next time I asked
him to go with me he said, "You go by yourself." So I did and I
began to get much better with the hand controls. One day I was
heading up a hill and I approached a cattle crossing sign; as I
crested the hill I saw a black object and immediately my reflex
caused me to hit the hand brake lever and push the brake down.
The object was the black top of a truck, but it could have been
the black top of the back of a Holstein cow. At that point I knew
I was ready to take the test and get my license to drive (again).

My "new" Impala

I had to prove to my mom that I could get my 'chair into the
car. The first couple times that I put my 'chair in the "new" car I

had a little help. But, it wasn't long before I had developed a system of just the correct order for each of the moves that I have to make to do this task, which is quite simple for an able-bodied person. Just a few simple steps do it:

1. Roll to passenger side of the car to the rear of the door, put on brakes and open door.
2. Roll into the open space between door and seat. Set brakes.
3. Remove pin and take off left armrest of w/c and place it on floorboard of car.
4. Grab front left corner of w/c seat with left hand and right armrest with right hand to scoot buttocks up toward the front of the seat.
5. Place left hand on the car seat and reach around my back with my right hand and grab the left w/c tire with it.
6. Push up on the tire to clear it with my buttocks and lift body over to the car seat.
7. Brace self with left hand up against the ceiling of the car above the door opening and work with right hand to unlock brakes, remove w/c cushion and put it on floorboard, lift up in middle of w/c seat to fold it up, put on "special" C-shaped piece of steel (my dad made it for me and still use it today) over the handgrips at the top back of the w/c so it will not unfold while I'm putting it in the car, pick up the w/c by the footrests and spin it around so the foot plate hinges rest on the door sill.
8. Lay over on the bench seat and reach the seat adjustment lever at the side of the seat on driver's side. Push lever and guide seat ahead by holding onto the steering wheel.
9. Sit up again and fold the back of the right seat forward and tuck it under my right armpit.
10. Rebrace self with left hand on ceiling and with right hand, while holding seat forward pick up front of the w/c with two fingers and pull it forward so front casters rest

on the doorsill. Regrasp w/c higher by top of footrest braces and pull the rear wheels up over the ledge and into the backseat. Tip the top of the w/c back against the back of the backseat.

11. Slide seat back in driving position.
12. Reposition brace hand and adjust buttocks so the right hand can pull in the left leg and then the right leg.
13. Grab steering wheel with left hand and close door with right hand. Slide over to drive.

Chapter Twenty-Six

Back at the University with my car to get around as needed I was ready to do my thesis project and finish whatever class work was left. I did those things and later discovered that due to the limited number of respondents to my research project, it did not qualify as a thesis and was changed to a "special project" worth the same amount of credit as a thesis except I would have to take the comprehensive exam to get my degree. The '68-'69 school year was a busy one and still had a few highlights.

With a car on campus it was easier to have a date now and then during the year. One weekend I went to St. Louis to see a former girlfriend for the weekend. We had a good time renewing our friendship and both felt the weekend visit was too short. Later in the spring I had developed a friendship (we had lunch together in the coed dormitory cafeteria a couple times) with a beautiful gal who looked like the famous Cleopatra of the movies. She was a Catholic and at that time in my life I didn't know what I was except that I did believe in God. I had come to the conclusion that religious denominations were NOTHING MORE THAN an economical means to spread the word of God. So, "Cleopatra" and I went to the Catholic Mass one Sunday, then went to dinner at the cafeteria followed by a nice pleasant afternoon out by a lake in a park about twenty miles west of the School. It was a fun day.

Since Vince had completed his training in the spring semester of 1968, he was gone from school and I had a new roommate named Mike Hibbs—or as he used to say when he called his parents collect, "David Michael Hibbs, H-I-B-B-S!" He and I played chess once in a while but he always beat me, I did come close once! He was a quadriplegic like Vince with a little more difficulty using his hands.

Using the facts that Vince had told me I tried out for the Regional Wheelchair Games and made the team in track and field. If I did well in the regional meet I would be able to go with the team to New York City for the National Wheelchair games. In this type of competition there were five basic classes of disability in order to attempt to make the competition more fair. Vince was a class I-A, the class of greatest disability, and they go up the ladder with I-B, I, II and III (class that included guys like Tom Brown, bilateral amputee at both knees and Ed, who was a post-polio paraplegic who can walk with a slight limp). For the Regional Wheelchair Games Meet I was classified as a I-B and competed with the others in that class doing field events of discus, shot put and javelin plus one race (60 yards) that I should have stayed out of—my leg flew off the footrest and dragged in the cinders beside my 'chair until I stopped and got it picked up and back in place; then I was thirty yards behind! Never raced again. However, I did take three blue ribbons in the field events winning each one. I think my discus throw was thirty-six feet—a little over a hundred feet shorter than my best in high school. So, I was really excited about going to New York City where I planned to participate in bowling and other events. I was given a new bowling ball that was only thirteen pounds and drilled to fit me—A gift from Jim Mac Dougal and Jack Dempsey, my former employers. I had practiced some and managed one game of 147 that I thought was great for me as many games did not get up to one hundred.

The National Wheelchair Games were held between Spring Semester and Summer Session. About May 30, 1969 we boarded the Gizz Kids Bus, left Champaign about 2 p.m. and stayed in Washington, PA right after crossing the West Virginia strip separating Ohio and Pennsylvania. The next day we went across PA to New

Jersey before dropping into the Big Apple. We went to a hotel and after some difficulties using the commode in the bathroom part of our room, we settled in for a good night's sleep. Suddenly I woke up and knew why. Roar . . . roar . . . roar . . . roar . . . every ten to fifteen seconds a jet plane started down the take-off strip and up into the air. After I got up I looked out the window to the north across the four lane highway where I watched planes taxi down to the end of the airfield, turn around and begin take-off.

We were in Queens and the airport was La Guardia with a zillion flights a day. Around 8:00 that morning I left the Hotel and went to one of the facilities where the games were held. There I met with the classification officials and discovered that for the National Games I was classified, a Class I, so I had to compete with some persons with more ability than I faced in the Regional. A quick review of some of the distances in Class I for the events that I had succeeded in winning at regional and I soon found myself outclassed. But, never fail, I could still compete in bowling and ping-pong (table tennis). That morning I managed to win two table tennis games before being defeated, and in that case I beat myself as I thought he was a higher class person who was misrated like me! He was an amputee and that was all I saw. However, he had some paralysis also and somehow I let him psych me out and beat me. I still got fourth place in a class that I thought was too high for me. Then in the afternoon I went bowling with thirty-one others in Class I and managed to roll a 330 series—that's a solid 110 average—and I think I finished sixth in the group. I was pleased. Later in the day we went to the outdoor races and I watched a U. of I. man run the mile in his wheelchair in a time of about four minutes and fifty seconds—I was impressed to say the least!!

A couple hours passed and we were at the ending ceremony with awards and a banquet preceded by a cocktail hour during which I had my first taste of Scotch. The meal was good, the program was short and soon we were getting on the bus to head back toward Illinois. The bus driver must have slept all day. We started out that night I suppose ten or eleven o'clock and he

drove straight through to the U. of I. We only had one stop for a
meal where we all got out of the bus for a little exercise, some
food in our bellies and we were back on the road arriving at
Champaign about 5:00 p.m. the next day (Sunday).

After a very brief visit at home I returned to school for the
summer during which my task was to analyze my data, gather
more support materials from the available resources and write
my special project paper. I did that and managed to pass my
Comprehensive Exam plus find a little time to play some bridge
during the course of the summer there. But, somehow it couldn't
be problem free.

Around the first of August I was transferring from my bed to
my wheelchair when my hand slipped sideways on the sheet
causing my rear-end to not quite make it over into the wheelchair.
Actually, my buttocks landed so that the tip of my tailbone
(coccyx) came down right on top of the tire of the 'chair. As with
my injury earlier that cost me a semester of school, I immediately
got back into bed and checked the area for damage. Finding no
problems apparent, I went on with my work of getting papers
turned in and taking that test. Then, about eight days later a
dark area developed on the point where the body met the tire. I
had a doctor send me to the Carl Clinic and Hospital in Urbana,
Illinois, the twin city of Champaign. The doctor said that I should
have surgery on the problem area and I was glad I was done with
school. Adversity strikes again!

I packed my few clothes and other belongings into the trunk
of my car and drove over to check into the Hospital. I had two
real nice experiences in that Hospital. The first had to do with
my roommate who was Dr. Tom Curraton, a Prof. at the University
who specialized in physiology of exercise and good fitness. He
was eighty-three years old (if I remember right) and was in the
hospital for some treatment that is common for all men if they
live long enough. He and I talked about fitness and he said that
he still started each morning by swimming a mile!! NINETY-NINE
percent of Americans don't start their day WALKING a mile never
mind talking about SWIMMING a mile!! Tom was quite a man.

The second experience had to do with the surgery. I was taken into the operating room and put on the table lying on my side in a position where I could see myself in the glass doors of the supply cabinet nearby. I was only given a local anesthetic and I could stay awake throughout the entire surgery. I could watch, and I did, in the glass when I saw the doctor make an "S" cut down and around the coccyx. Then with tongs I saw the assistant move the skin and other flesh away so the doctor could smooth the rough bony prominence by actual chiseling off the bump on the bone using a chisel and a hammer. The only thing I felt was the jarring as the hammer struck the chisel and it rippled up the spine going from vertebrae to vertebrae. Just a light thud repeatedly was felt. About a month later I was healed enough to be discharged as long as I didn't try to drive myself to Hillsboro. I said, "Great," and I called my parents to come and get me— again!!

Chapter Twenty-Seven

From September 1969 to that same time the next year I was active checking out possible jobs through the National Therapeutic Recreation Society (NTRS), the professional organization I joined after my graduation with the degree. I applied and was given the title of a Master Therapeutic Recreation Specialist when I registered with NTRS. I soon found out that the new field I was educated to work in seemed to have very few jobs available. I thought, "Gee, I spent two years getting trained to do a job that doesn't seem to exist very often. Now I'll have to live on my two hundred dollar a month social security disability income check," I said to myself, "Thank God my parents are still loving me!" Some days they may not have loved me, but they did tolerate me and help me through that year.

I had ambition so I applied to work as a substitute teacher (still had my State Teacher's Certificate) at Hillsboro, Wonewoc and Elroy Public Schools. The going rate of pay was just twenty dollars a day, but I was quite pleased with that. Any amount was a lot of money to me. I worked only few days (maybe six total) in Wonewoc and did not get called to Elroy, but I worked quite a few at Hillsboro. I taught Jr. High Mathematics and Science and English as well as classes of High School Biology, Chemistry, English and Industrial Arts. Then I got my big chance. My former eighth grade teacher, Mr. Bernard Braithwaite, was teaching his last year before retiring after forty-some years of teaching. He taught classes of remedial mathematics and asked me to substitute for him while he had some minor surgery completed. He always liked my command of basic math when I was in eighth grade so he knew that I would do a good job for him. On top of his confidence in me, he said that I would probably work for five weeks in a row and that made me eligible for the same "per day" pay as a regular teacher in their first year. Consequently, I got a seventy-five percent raise up to thirty-five dollars a day for that work. With that five week block included I worked about one-quarter to one-third of the year as a substitute teacher.

I woke up at an early hour one morning to the ringing of the phone. It was the school calling for me to go in to substitute teach. I went through my usual ritual and got out of bed and into my wheelchair. After a bite of breakfast and a little time preparing in the bathroom, I looked at the indoor-outdoor thermometer in the kitchen. Outside temperature was a cool minus forty-two! The small amount of snow that had blown over the sidewalk squeaked loudly as I rolled to my car which was parked in Al Jefferies' driveway (retired neighbor who spent the winter with his wife in Florida). I got in and the seat was colder than the ice (thank God my butt could not feel how cold it was) due to the plastic seat covers. I wonder if anyone ever got frostbite on their butt!! I could have and not even known it. Anyway, I turned the key and to my surprise it started—nothing like an old six cylinder Chevy in cold weather. After a short warm-up time I almost broke off the shifting lever to get it in gear to start backing up. I had no power steering so I had to stop every few feet to use both hands on the steering wheel—one arm was not strong enough with the other hand on the hand control accelerating. When I got to the top of the street at the stop sign before Highway 33/82, I watched closely while moving and, with no cars coming, I cranked the steering wheel while the momentum provided the speed necessary to make it around the corner. Once at school I had a good day.

The highlight of the year at HHS as a sub came in February when the basketball team was scheduled to play on Friday night and Mrs. Elaine (Hunter) Hanna worked as librarian in the high school. She asked if I would like to speak at the pep rally and I agreed to it. She went out to the center of the court and looked at totally full bleachers—six rows of fans (students) over eighty-five feet long on the side of the court. The students cheered her and then when it was quiet she said, "I would now like to introduce to you probably the greatest athlete ever to attend Hillsboro High School, Jim Potter." I rolled my chair out to the center jump circle to the sound of continuous clapping and cheering; when I looked up at the group, I discovered the largest STANDING OVATION I had ever seen in my life and it was for me. Tears welled up in my eyes, big time, but I held them back long enough to say "Thank you." I then said a few words that hopefully would inspire the team to play their hardest at the game that night. Unfortunately, I think I recall that they lost to Westby in a close game.

In addition to the teaching experience that year, I had a big surprise before Christmas. I received a Christmas card from Jo-Ann, the person that I had met over three years earlier while she and I were in the same hospital in Madison (my Rehab.). She included a note stating that she and her husband were divorced and that she and her son, now four years old, were living near Bayard, New Mexico with her parents. She said that her multiple sclerosis had given her so many "ups" and "downs" that she could not live and work and raise her son independently, so her parents rescued her like mine rescued me that year. Off and on from Christmas until June she and I wrote letters back and forth as well as talked on the phone. We shared a mutual caring and love for each other that may have been partially based on the comfortable nature due to both of us having similar but very different disabilities. One thing led to another and she invited me to go down and visit her. My first thought was that this would be a great test of my ability to be independent and see some country too. So I called AAA and got a trip-tic that planned the trip for me once I told them the daily number of miles I expected to travel. (Three and a half days, Hillsboro to Albuquerque, NM.)

At that time I had been disabled for three years and I still had a little fear of the unknowns of the world. I missed that feeling

I once enjoyed, the one I had knowing that if I was threatened I could simply stand up with my height and size that usually intimidated most individual men—the unarmed kind. One way to overcome fear is to go someplace strange, if I return unscathed my fears go away. If not I'm probably dead. Either way is good because living in fear is pure hell and you might as well be dead because you are not *really living*.

June 20, 1970 arrived with sunshine and I left Hillsboro on my first long solo drive. I drove to a town about seventy or eighty miles west of Des Moines, Iowa and spent the night in the motel suggested by AAA. The trip went smoothly and I found gas stations when needed as well as drive-in restaurants for food. My second day took me across the state of Nebraska—flat as a pancake was my impression—and I ended the day in Ogallala, Nebraska at a small motel. There was about eight inches up to get over the threshold and into the room. I needed some help and the woman working at the office was small and told me she was sixty-four years old. She boosted me up that ledge like she was a "spring chicken." The next day I gradually watched the mountains approaching from the west and saw my first ice cap in June. All except thirty miles that day were traveled in Colorado as I left I-80, went to Denver on I-76 and then took I-25 down to Raton, NM where I spent the third night. The next day (Friday, I think) I went on down through Santa Fe and to the airport in Albuquerque where I was scheduled to meet Jo-Ann who was flying in on a small plane from Silver City. Seeing that I was ahead of schedule I drove to the Motel where I had reservations for the night—I wanted to locate it ahead of time so it would be easy to find later. Then I drove back to the airport to wait for Jo-Ann to arrive. Once there on land, the skycap helped her with her luggage and she managed with her walker quite well. I got to the car, pulled my wheelchair in behind the seat and then when she was ready to get in, she stood outside the door and handed her folded walker to me so I could lay it across the top of my wheelchair in the back. She then got into the car and we went to the motel to rest before going out to supper.

Jo-Ann gave me a lesson about MS and her condition that night after I had gotten into bed she came out of the bathroom in her nightie without her walker. She stopped by the doorway and got my attention asking me to look at her, which I did. She appeared to be so proud of herself and suddenly she fell like a tree under the sharp grip of a buzz saw. Her pride went to tears in about three seconds and I felt so sad for her, but there was nothing I could do or say to help. She picked herself up with the help of the mattress at the foot of the bed and using the bed to steady herself she walked around to the side and got in. We got a good night sleep and were ready for more travel on Sunday.

We headed west on I-40 and made two stops along the way to Williams, Arizona. We enjoyed looking at the Painted Desert and then took a short tour of the Petrified Forest park area before heading on down the road. We stayed at a motel in Williams that night and then spent most of the next day going up to the Grand Canyon, viewing what we could of it from the car and then going back to Williams for the night. We drove to different areas there in the Canyon Park to see as much as possible below and did find one place where we could see way down to the river below. While we were in the park I had an embarrassing and difficult to correct problem—my condom urine drainage system was leaking around where the condom attached to the penis and I needed to somehow replace it without getting too much wetter. It would take way too long to drive back down to Williams and the motel. It seemed that everywhere we drove in the park there were a lot of people there. We finally found a slightly secluded spot and Jo-Ann got out of the car so she could stand by the door to block the view of the onlookers and that would allow me to put my feet out the door so I could get my pants down off my paralyzed butt enough to get at the task area and change the condom. It worked and within about ten minutes the flow was going into the legbag as it was supposed to go in the first place. Also, I forgot, but Jo-Ann first had to use her walker to go to the trunk to get my "condom box" (a stationery box with my supplies) so I'd have the necessary materials I needed to do the job.

Tuesday morning we got up and went to a restaurant for breakfast. We then talked about our plan to go south and Jo-Ann said that it was a real pretty drive down Oak Creek Canyon south of Flagstaff and it was generally quite cool there. I thought it was a good suggestion and we would be off the Interstate that we had been traveling mostly since Albuquerque. At Flagstaff we turned south on State Hwy 89 toward Sedona, AZ. It was a highway carved out of the side of the bluff that followed the side of the canyon. It seemed cool at first, but soon got warm and we really did notice it due to no air conditioning in my '66 Chevy. We had the windows open and as I was driving faster and faster around the sharp curves I tried to get cool. Because I don't sweat when it's hot, I was beginning to get overheated. My driving became a little wreckless as I was just TOO DARN HOT. It may have been only ten or fifteen miles from Flagstaff to Sedona, but it seemed like a hundred to me. We finally got to a motel, but they only had the "swamp cooler" and no refrigerated air so we went on. When we did get to one with A/C we stopped and Jo-Ann was weak too. So, I just blew the horn until someone came out to see what the problem was. I was so weak with heat exhaustion that the man had to lift me out of the car into my 'chair with little help from me. He then pushed me to the room and helped me to bed. I was able to muster enough energy to get my pants and shirt off while the man went to get a bucket of ice cubes. When he got back I bathed my legs and whole body with the ice and did finally get my temperature down somewhere near the normal range. Saved from adversity. Before we got to the motel a bank sign said it was 107 degrees at 2:35 p.m. I guess the breakfast we had was close to noon when we ate it! I'm not sure, but I bet that was a record "high" temperature for the date in late June. Finally with my body temperature lowered, Jo-Ann and I both fell asleep.

We slept until after 9 p.m. and got up to leave for Bayard before 10 p.m. I then decided that I would never do any daytime driving in Arizona again. We looked at the map we had and somehow the road we took turned from blacktop to gravel about three miles out in the country. I turned around and we went back for instructions to get us to the Interstate (my safe zone). We had to stop at a rowdy tavern where I finally got someone's attention to get advice. Once we got on I-17 and then I-10 we went fine to Tucson where we stopped for the day at 5:30 a.m. We spent the whole day in the air-conditioned motel and didn't check out until 7 p.m. that night. The TV station news said it was 119 degrees in Phoenix and 121 degrees in Tucson that day. Thank God we were not out in that heat—we would have both been dead from it. After eating some, about 8 p.m. we got on the road and went down I-10 east until we got to Lordsburg, N.M. where we turned northeast on State Hwy. 90 and went on to Silver City, Bayard and to Jo-Ann's parents' house. We got there safe a little after midnight and they were expecting us as we had called to let them know our plans.

It was nice there where the Godec's house sat in the shade of trees, but it did get hot there some. I stayed there about two weeks and learned to get quite good at a game called Perquacky— a word spelling game. I also learned how to play Mexican Dominoes and had the worst food experience in my life. We all went to a 4th of July event where there was a big picnic. Jo-Ann decided she would be a smart-ass at my expense. While we were getting our plates filled with good food, she said to me, "Here honey, have a pickle." I said thanks and took it. I chomped down on that "pickle" taking a big bite and having about an inch of it in my mouth I started chewing it. In seconds my mouth was on fire, the kind that won't get put out with a simple glass of water—I drank a half dozen after that. It was a fresh Jalapeno!

The biggest thing in the Bayard/Hurley, N.M. area is the Kennicott Copper mine where Jo-Ann's dad worked for forty years as a tin smith, called a "tinker", or commonly called a sheet metal worker these days. I had one of those interesting "small world" experiences in Hurley, N.M. the day I took my car in to Sears Automotive for an oil change. While the work was being done I browsed in the store and bumped into a man from Holman, Wisconsin that I played basketball against in high school and went to school with at La Crosse State. He was teaching out at some Indian Reservation. He recognized me even though I don' t think he knew I was in a wheelchair all the time. He looked familiar, but I couldn't call his name.

A few days after the Fourth I left their home and Jo-Ann went with me as she wanted to visit her cousin in Denver. Since I was going right past Denver it saved her plane fare to Denver and I would have company part of the way home to Wisconsin. We got into Denver on a Friday night and visited a bit after supper at her cousin's home. I did not want to spend the night there due to some accessibility problems so I left at 11 p.m. and headed for Lawrence, Kansas where Dennis Degner was now living and attending school (graduate school in engineering) there. I got to Dennis' place at about 2 p.m. and stayed a while. He put some blankets on the floor and helped me get down to take a short nap there. About 6 p.m. he helped me up in my chair, we visited a bit and then I left for Hillsboro on my final leg of the trip.

This last part of the trip turned out to be a bit scary as I went over a railroad track just outside a town and it sounded like I had a flat tire on the car. I stopped, but couldn't get out of the car in the ditch. Finally I got a passerby to stop. He checked all my tires for me and they were all OK. I drove on and headed into Iowa on some State road (I don't think I-35 north and south was completed yet). I traveled at the fifty-five mile per hour speed between towns and after a while a car (or pick-up truck) got right up close behind me. I slowed down to about thirty mph and he slowed down too. I sped up to sixty-five mph and he was soon right on my bumper, so to speak. I was a little frightened and felt helpless if there was danger behind me. We soon came to a small town and I turned off on the second street as though I was going home. Fortunately, he did not follow me and just went right on by staying on the highway. I went around the block and followed him—at a distance behind him. He was traveling faster than I and soon he was gone out of sight. Once I got on I-80 in west Iowa I felt safer and traveled faster. When I got into a small town near Dubuque, Iowa I had some weird mechanical sound in the car. Fortunately, the gas stations were not like they are now—all self-serve. At 8 a.m. on a Sunday morning I found a Service Station open that not only pumped gas but changed oil and did some repairs like many of them did back then. They diagnosed my problem correctly and said it would go another hundred miles or so and get me home before I would have to fix it. I was pleased and arrived in Hillsboro at 11 a.m.—late for church, but HOME.

Chapter Twenty-Eight

In my search for a job in therapeutic recreation I was mainly interested in a job working with physically disabled in line with my internship experience and because of more rapport with patients due to my own injury—some empathy or at least understanding. I also was not interested in working in a large city. Des Moines was big enough and it was less than a half million people in 1968. But, one out of two isn't all that bad!!

In September 1970 I applied for a job at Schwab Rehabilitation Hospital in Chicago and was hired the day I interviewed there. While in the city and about two hundred forty miles from home I looked and found a place to live. I secured an apartment that they rented monthly at the beautiful old Shoreland Hotel located at 55th and South Shore Drive. It had a lot more space than I needed due to a large living room/dining room with a kitchenette, a bedroom and a bathroom with a twenty-four inch wide door and a six inch step up into it. By this time I had plenty of experience in having BM's on the bed and "sponge baths" the same way so I felt it would work for me since the commode was right inside the bathroom door allowing me to dump my urine bag and fecal materials in it and flush it away. It had a nice double wide sink in the kitchenette which was good for shaving and other personal hygiene. Then I could fill my pail three-quarters full and take it into the bedroom and do the sponge bath there on the bed to properly clean the butt and crotch as well as any other areas hard to reach while sitting in the 'chair with no trunk balance. I had all my meals at the hospital cafeteria or in the Hotel Restaurant just off the lobby on the ground floor.

On September 30th I moved into the Hotel Apartment on the fourth floor and I started my job on October 1, 1970. The Hospital was located in the fourteen hundred block of South California Street just north of Ogden Avenue. It was a fairly poor neighborhood and the Hospital had a security guard on duty around the clock. The day guard usually came to the locked (key card) parking lot, surrounded by an eight foot high chain-link fence with barbwire on the top, to meet me when I got to work at 1 p.m. and the night guard escorted me to my car when I left at 10 p.m.

The longer I worked on that job, the more I realized that I needed to be cloned! I felt that it would be important to be on the job in the mornings to go to patient staffings and learn more about them. I felt that I should be there each night to conduct leisure activities for those interested after their day of other therapies. I felt that I should be there afternoons and evenings on the weekends to fill any void with some meaningful use of free time and a Chicago organization had volunteer entertainment that I could/should schedule for the patients. So, if there were two of me, maybe I could do the job the way I felt it should be done. I didn't have any means of taking patients into the city for any public entertainment even after I had a summer evening assistant we still didn't have a vehicle for him to drive and haul patients in wheelchairs. Coincidentally, at that time Art Ruben was Recreation Director at the Rehab. Institute of Chicago and in addition to regular trips into the community with patients, he was planning to take a group of patients to Europe!! Oh well, money does those things!!

Jo-Ann came to Chicago and spent Christmas 1970 with me and my family in Wisconsin. After a few days she flew back to New Mexico with ideas of planning our marriage for the next summer. With a little more correspondence we set the date for late June 1971.

I lay in my bed sleeping on the morning of June 6, 1971, a Saturday, when the phone rang and it was my brother. His message was sad as he said that dad had died of a heart attack the Friday night before. I knew he had previously had heart trouble, been to Marshfield, Wisconsin Clinic for treatment, and carried nitro pills with him all the time. This time they didn't help as he had a massive coronary attack while traveling home from La Crosse with mom. So I went to Hillsboro for the funeral and to be with family.

It was tough to get ready for a wedding mentally just after being in the same church for dad's funeral. But, three weeks later we gathered there and Jo-Ann and I were married in a double ring, double wheelchair ceremony! After the wedding we all went to the gymnasium of the old high school for a nice reception. The old gym was serving as a type of community center for teen dances and receptions, etc. We must have had a dance after the reception as we did not leave there until after dark, probably 10 or 11 p.m. to go on our big honeymoon. Saturday night, Sunday and Sunday night we stayed at the big Holiday Inn in La Crosse. On Monday we drove back to Hillsboro and Tuesday we went back to Chicago where we lived at the Shoreland Hotel for half a month before we found an apartment with two bedrooms in Forest Park, a western suburb of Chicago.

Jo-Ann's son, Tommy, was with his father in California but was going to join us before school started and live with his mother and me; thus a need for two bedrooms. So, in mid-August I called on my brother Don and his wife, Mary, to help us move to the new pad. I had purchased some used furniture at a couple locations, so when Don and Mary arrived we first had to go rent a trailer and then pick up the items I had purchased before we moved the things from the Hotel apartment. All in all, it was a long day for our helpers and they finally got the last things into the apartment late that night. Jo-Ann and I stayed at the Hotel yet one more night and Don and Mary just got the bed mattress on the floor before they both collapsed with exhaustion on the mattress and fell fast asleep until morning. Both bedrooms of the apartment were just inside the east wall of the building and the building wall was only about eight feet from the street called Harlem Avenue, which is Illinois Highway 43. It was just north of the stoplight on 16th Street and traffic noise was quite hard for us to get used to. Don and Mary were so tired they did not hear a thing!

Tommy was six and he flew into O'hare Field soon enough to be with us a short time before he started first grade. He was very bright and somewhat bored in school. He had flown on a few airplanes already at his young age and was able to build things with his lego toys. One day he said, "How do you like my 747?" as he "flew" it with his hand in the living room! Tommy flew to spend the next few summers with his father and was with us during most school years up through fifth grade—more on that later.

Often during our marriage Jo-Ann and I talked about personal bodily functions in such a relaxed manner that we referred to it as peanut butter and jelly or P B & J topics. We had found some comfort in going to a Northern Baptist Church in Oak Park as Jo-Ann was Southern Baptist from her past and she didn't care for the Lutheran church. We also attended a lot of Hour of Power on TV on Sundays at home. Anyway, at the church we became friends with Mr. and Mrs. Brown. One day they were guests at our apartment and she had to use the bathroom (had the raised toilet seat on the commode) and she was a short person. Jo-Ann forgot to warn her and after they left Jo-Ann noticed the puddle in front of the commode. We laughed, Mrs. Brown must have gotten a shoe full due to her stream of urine going under the raised toilet seat and over the top of the porcelain commode!! Just like P B & J!

After two and a half years on that job, the hospital was suffering financial problems due to retroactive denials of payments for Medicare patients (by Medicare) who may have been treated for six months or more. The Jewish Federation of Metropolitan Chicago had been subsidizing the Hospital so management decided it was time for some cutbacks. My position was one that was to be cut. Some time later, a part-time worker doing a few activities was replacing me, but I couldn't look back. Potential adversity looms!

I got word about the job being deleted about the end of March, 1973 and I was devastated by it even though I felt like my role there was a lot of "spinning my wheels," so to speak. When I told Jo-Ann she almost had an exacerbation of her disease and she was totally upset. With my positive attitude, my most valuable asset, I told her that they were giving me some time to find a job but I didn't have forever to do it. I checked with the NTRS where I had found the Schwab Rehab. job listed originally but to no satisfaction. Nothing was available, at least not in a place that sounded feasible for my/our situation. When in doubt, check the want ads, someone said one time. So, I did. I looked in the Chicago Sun Times and I couldn't believe it: "Wanted: Activity Director for Nursing Home. Contact Lester Oken, Administrator, Normandy Terrace Convalescent Center, Chicago, Illinois.

It was about mid-May and I called Mr. Oken, gave him a brief description of my qualifications and arranged for a personal interview. At the interview I learned that it was a three hundred sixty bed facility that had all levels of residents from the profoundly retarded to elderly who were primarily self-care and lived as independently as possible but getting their medications properly and assistance in personal care areas as needed.

Chapter Twenty-Nine

I left the interview at the Nursing Home with a good understanding of the tremendous challenge that lay before me in the new job that I had just accepted for a salary about the same as I had been making at Schwab. My boss at Schwab was happy I had found employment and after discussion I only worked a few more days with my vacation time covering the remainder of the month thus receiving a full month's paycheck at the end. So, I had a few days off to relax before reporting to the new job on June, 1 1973. My title was Activity Director and I inherited a staff of two full-time and one half-time worker. I'm a firm believer of the old saying, "If it ain't broke, don't fix it," so for the first couple weeks on the job I was getting oriented to the situation, to the workers, to the residents and to the ongoing program. I also went back to "school" in discussions with the administrator and the Director of Nursing, Mrs. Biordi, to learn about the various government regulations related to the Nursing Homes and the requirements of the Activity Programs. I learned that the previous "supervisor" was an Occupational Therapist who came in to the facility about twice a month as a consultant.

At the outset, Mr. Oken had promised me that if I was doing a good job after three months he would give me a raise. After early analysis of the program I felt that the previous program was a good one for a small Nursing Home, but was NOT NEAR what needed to be happening in this facility. During this early period one "summer" worker was hired as she had worked there the previous summer before going to college for nine months. She was Donna Biordi, daughter of the Nursing Director and she was young, bright and had a good personality for working with people though she was only about twenty years old. Shortly after meeting her I knew she was going to be a great asset to me in the development of the "new" program I had vaguely constructed in my mind. She had good typing skills, was easy to work with and eager to help. I knew that she would only be working during the summer so it was imperative that I set a time frame for the completion of the revised program. I told her we needed to have the program constructed and implemented before Labor Day.

By the summer of 1973 Jo-Ann had been having some problems off and on especially with tension headaches, either directly or indirectly related to her MS, and thus she was very glad I secured that job. Our biggest worry was for us to be without the insurance we so badly needed to get the medical care she needed periodically. At times her energy level was even lower than normal, but most of the time I knew that she would do as much as she could at home which usually consisted of doing some housekeeping chores and cooking an evening meal for us. And, to still keep her hands "working" she did some needlepoint work which kept them more functional. In her prime before the MS hit she was a very skilled pianist and musician and an "A" student at Baylor University. My main jobs at home that were time consuming were laundry and getting all the groceries. I stressed that Jo be very explicit about her grocery lists so I wouldn't have to go to the store twice each week. There was a laundromat about three blocks from the apartment so my Saturday (or Friday night) job was loading the baskets of clothes in the car trunk, hauling them to the laundromat, taking them into the place, washing and drying the clothes and repeating the procedure to get them back home safe and CLEAN. It wasn't easy and when the snow was one to two feet deep I sure was glad Tommy was there with us to help me.

One Saturday I went shopping for groceries and while I was

in the store this stranger, a woman, came up to me and began "preaching" to me with "You know, God meant for you to be a whole person; if you believed strongly enough you would be healed of your affliction." And, I sorta fell for it for a while and lowered myself to her level by stating, "I don't believe what you said is Biblical." What a mistake. She then opened up with quotes from the Old Testament. She went on and on, then I (though furious on the inside) simply said, "Keep it to yourself, Lady, I got groceries to buy!!"

Another time I went to the grocery store and filled the cart nearly to the top. To push the cart in the store I grasp the cart handle with my left (weak) hand and it becomes my steering wheel while my right arm pushes the 'chair making the power to move it. The clerk bagged the groceries in five or six bags, I paid her and pushed the loaded cart out the door and down the gradual slope of the parking lot to my trunk, then opened the trunk and loaded the groceries in the trunk. Next I pushed the cart over to an area by a light pole where there were other carts to make it easier for the guy assigned to collect them from the lot. I went to my car and got in, was about to slide the front seat ahead and pull in the wheelchair when I was approached by a real "do-gooder." He said politely, "May I help you?" "No, that's OK, I can get it fine," I replied. "Oh, let me help you," he went on grasping the handgrips on the back of my folded 'chair. "No, that's OK," I said slightly irritated with his persistence. "Oh, I can do it," he said lifting the back of the wheelchair. I said with a smile, "OK, go ahead," and I lay down in the seat. Now, anyone with a half a brain knows that you cannot put a twelve inch wide folded wheelchair through a gap of five or six inches (or less) between the seat and the door jam. He tried and he tried and he tried; I just smiled. Then he said, "I can't get it in." Finally, I thought, I'll get to go home with my groceries. I said, "Stand back please and watch" then I slid the seat forward and sat up, grasped the chair and pulled it in with one simple swift motion. "Now, see how easy that is *when you know what you are doing!!*" Those were my last words to him and he never bothered me again.

My job took me daily, and some Saturdays, to Lawrence Avenue just off Lake Shore Drive at 4800 North and we lived on Harlem Avenue (7200 West) and Sixteenth Street (1600 South). It was about a fifteen mile trip one way and each morning I left home at 7:15 a.m. for a forty five minute ride down Eisenhower Expressway and up Lake Shore Drive. At night, especially in the summer with cars overheating, I could leave work at 5 p.m. as scheduled and usually get home at 6:30 p.m.—exactly twice as long to go home as it was to go to work. After staying until 6 p.m. one night working in peace and quiet on the new program, I was shocked to discover that I could be home by 6:45 p.m. and save forty-five minutes of burning up gas for nothing. I also discovered that if Donna and I worked on the program in one hour of quiet each night, I would not have to go to work on Saturdays. That way I could get my shopping and laundry done on Saturdays leaving Saturday night and Sunday for much needed relaxation as well as time to spend with my family.

Tommy flew in from spending the summer in California with his dad about a week before school started and we were again a "family". By then I had the new program implemented and, of course, there was always the need for ongoing adjustments. It was somewhere around this time in September when I was allowed to hire another worker and I really got lucky. Her name was Alexanne Osinski, a Catholic nun who had more skills than I had seen in one person. Music, art, writing, dealing with people who were hurting; you name it, she could do it—and do it well. What a blessing!

The end of September came and I looked at my check— same as before! Oops, guess I'm not doing so well or Mr. Oken forgot about the raise he promised. The program was running quite smoothly and I felt good about myself and about my staff. So, I called his secretary and made an appointment to talk with him. Incidentally, just prior to the meeting I had learned about the Medicare requirement for having a "certified" person as Activity Director and how much money the business would lose if I were not there. I guess that is called getting a little leverage in case I needed to use it. I asked him why I didn't get that raise in September. He stammered and fumbled a bit as though I had just stuck a gun in his belly, then said, "Well, Jim." I thought, get ready for this, Jim! Then I smartly put him out of his misery by taking control of the conversation. I said, "OK, am I doing a lousy job, a fair job, a good job or an excellent job?" He responded without looking me in the eye, "You know I'd be cutting my own throat if I answered that question!!" I got a decent raise!!

Christmas was just around the corner and there was some talk among some of the Department Heads about a Christmas Bonus. Having been there a mere seven months (almost) I had the idea that I would not be getting any Christmas bonus—Gee, I nearly had to beg for a raise! The central kitchen was located across the hall from our "activity room" that included twenty square feet that I called my "open" office. I always did believe in the "open door" policy and it was very easy for me to have it as there was no wall or door around my desk and me! We were in the basement on the west end of the building. One day the Director of Food Service came to the "office" and beckoned me to the hall outside. He said, "Did you get your Christmas Bonus yet?" A little befuddled I responded, "I didn't think I'd be getting one." "Oh, yes," he said, "There is one up there for you." I asked, "Did you get one?" (Dumb question, of course he did) "It's none of my business, but how much did you get?" "Hundred dollars" was his reply. "Well, I sure won't get that much being here only part of the year." "I don't know, but you probably will," he added, "Go check, I'm curious." So I went up to see the administrator and asked if he had anything for me. He calmly put his hand out to shake mine and said, "Good job." He then handed an envelope to me. I thanked him and he said, "Go ahead and open it if you wish." So I did and it was a check for a hundred dollars!! I looked up at him and the true emotion of the moment took over as tears welled in my eyes and ran down my cheeks like a baby. I think (now) that the tears were the outcome of feeling really appreciated after many forty-five and fifty hour weeks. The Director of Food Service saw me as I rolled into my work area and he came to inquire. "Well," he said inquisitively. "You were right," I said. "And you deserve it, Merry Christmas, Jim." "Thank you," I said sincerely looking him in the eyes. "Merry Christmas to you." I went home for the holiday as it was December 24th and after five o'clock.

Jo-Ann and I hugged and cried when I showed her the check. She was so proud of me and I knew that we sure could use the money, with the Christmas gifts and all the extra money that is needed at that time of the year. Another thing that made it so special is the fact I had never previously gotten any kind of bonus at Christmas or any other time.

Before I knew it, I was nearing my anniversary at that work place and I received a real surprise in the mail. I got a letter from NTRS, my professional organization, stating that I had been recommended for a teaching position that was opening up at the University of Iowa. I was satisfied with the work that I had done at the Nursing Home and since about third grade I had a yen for teaching. Academia may not be my forte as evidenced by my B-C grade averages in high school, college and graduate school but it sounded intriguing to me. Maybe it had something to do with the fact that my best buddy, Phil Eastman, was a Professor at Northern Illinois University after he got two Masters Degrees and a PhD. Maybe I was subconsciously jealous of him! However, I doubt that because I was "full" of education by the time I had persevered enough to get my Masters. In reality I thought I might like teaching at the college level.

Curiosity won and I made a call to John Nesbitt, Chairperson of the Recreation Education Program at the University of Iowa, He set up an interview day and I drove out to Iowa City to check out the opportunity for a new experience. I was offered the job and accepted it. I gave notice at the Nursing Home of my intent to end the employment with them as of the end of July. "How are we going to make this move?" Jo-Ann asked me. Fortunately we did not have a two-story house full of things to move and what we had fit nicely into a U-Haul truck. Who drove the truck since neither Jo-Ann nor I could possibly do it? My good buddy Phil to the rescue! He drove the truck and helped load and unload it along with friends. Man, when you are disabled, it sure is great to have friends!

The apartment we landed in was out on the east side of Iowa City and about two miles from East Hall. There was a short step up into the apartment, but it was not so bad and it could be ramped quite easily. The early August move gave us time to get settled before I had to begin my new job. East Hall was in the part of campus east of the river in the "downtown" area and the Recreation Education Department was on the top (fourth) floor north off the elevator. The city had about twenty thousand residents and the student population was about twenty thousand students in undergraduate and graduate classes.

Chapter Thirty

The last week of August was time for work-meetings and in-service training as well as getting organized for a *really* new experience. I found out that my job was supposed to be sixty percent teaching, twenty percent service to the University and community, and twenty percent research and writing. When I got my teaching schedule of one general Recreation course, one therapeutic Recreation course, one Recreation leadership course and one leadership laboratory class, I realized then that about ninety percent of MY time would be needed for teaching. "Oh well," I said to myself, "We'll see how this goes!" I was a bit overwhelmed to say the least.

Just trying to stay ahead of the students by reading and preparing lectures was a task and when it came to developing tests that really tested student knowledge of the subjects I really had my work cut out for me! They gave me the basic textbooks to be the guide for the classes, but how the material was taught was up to me. I soon found that I was "low man on the totem pole" as the saying goes. There were four or five full or assistant professors and three or four "instructors" (like me) who were teaching and working on their Doctorate Degrees. I was not working on a Doctorate and had no desire to do so. I soon developed good relationships with all the other faculty as I needed them for advice quite often, which they supplied as much as they could afford.

I soon learned that there was a bit of a riff between the

Chairperson and the faculty for some reason unknown to me. I soon found myself "in the middle" as I always believed that a person works for his boss, but, if I was going to survive and keep my sanity through it all, I had to "ride the fence" without getting splinters if I could do that delicate task. I soon realized that I did not have the time or the energy to get "caught up" in the BS that floated around and my dedication had to be to my students in my classes.

Classes began and I managed to do my best. I did not have the intent to do so, but I was about to embark on a task that would literally leave a "mark," a permanent mark no less, on the University of Iowa campus. I decided to give my students in Introduction to Therapeutic Recreation class an introduction to a reality obvious to me.

After developing a set of criteria for the students to work with and use as a guide for their endeavors, I presented an assignment to the class in late September. There were about sixty students in the class and there were about one hundred buildings on the campus. There were a few "large" buildings and they were assigned one to a student. The "smaller" buildings were assigned two to a student. The task was for the students to survey their building(s) and, using the guidelines that I had gotten from the American National Standards Institute (standards for architectural accessibility), report the status of the building in terms of architectural barriers found. It was discovered that ninety-five percent of the buildings had some form of "barrier" to the functional use by a person in a wheelchair and all needed "help" if you expanded the concept to include the blind persons. My students had gathered some very meaningful data and I sure did NOT want it to go the way of too much research—put into a book and stuck on a shelf someplace to gather dust. I wanted it to be the key that would unlock some progress on this campus.

During the second semester I shared some of my ideas with my boss and he arranged for me to meet with the Academic Vice President of Student Affairs (I believe that was his title). I met with him and he was most cordial to me. I told him of the GREAT

NEED for something to be done about this overwhelming problem. We discussed that it was not only the campus, but the whole community that could be improved, though that may be totally out of our control. We planned to have a "wheelchair awareness day" involving members of the Administration, Faculty and some City Officials as well as a few businessmen or women. We planned it for late April or May when the weather was nicer—God forbid they have to go through the hassles of snow and cold that I had to deal with on a regular basis in the winter!!

The "big day" arrived and since we had borrowed twenty-some wheelchairs from the VA Hospital there, we were ready to "issue" them to the volunteer participants. I met with all of them to give them the guidelines for their behavior—I was not going to follow them around all day so they were on the "honor" system in that regard. I did give them a little break, "Don't soil your pants just because you can't get into the bathroom that you've been using for years at work—in those cases, and ONLY those cases you are allowed to get out of your chair to do your "business"— all your other business should be done from sitting in your 'chair. No standing up to reach that object on a high shelf—you have to beg someone to get it for you." I think some of them felt a little uneasy about that last comment of mine as they began to think about their own personal relationships and how well (or poorly) they had developed them. Some may have thought, "Do I have any friends to help me if I have to beg?"

The Awareness Day was a huge success and the cooperation from the Vice President was awesome. He began to get the "financial" ball rolling in the Capitol and funds came forth to take care of many of the problems. Not only did they focus on the buildings, but also the curbs got their attention and soon the concrete was flowing to fill in the curb cuts with ramps that met the ANSI Standards. By the end of my second year there over fifty percent of the buildings had "cleared up" the architectural barriers to make them at least basically accessible and the new curb cuts made street to sidewalk travel for me a breeze. Probably the GREATEST AWARD that I ever received in my life was a simple "Letter of Commendation" sent to me through campus mail from the Vice President. The letter gave me great pride and in my humble manner I filed it in a folder with other University materials. I don't know where it is "exactly" today, but I could probably find it if needed for something—like an ego boost someday if I'm "down."

Have you ever cried since you were a baby? Most of us "grown" men try not to do it very often or in front of other people. Some men don't cry because they are "tough" or think they are tough. Some men don't cry because they keep everything inside until they have a heart attack. Some men cry "at the drop of a hat" as the old saying goes. Sometimes crying can be very cleansing and healthy, at least for me. I had one of those last experiences just before Christmas 1975.

The first mistake that I made was assigning two classes a "term" paper to be due around December 15th. Hindsight tells me that sure can put a cramp in a teacher's time when grades are usually due to be turned in a couple days after Christmas. Final exams were over, students and teachers were home on Christmas "vacation." I had the exams graded and had a pretty good idea what most of the students would be receiving from me in terms of grades. However, I still had eighty of the ninety-five term papers to read and grade. Thank God I restricted the assignment and told the students to leave out the fillers, it's not a novel, and keep them under twenty pages typed, double-spaced. So, I ONLY had fifteen or sixteen hundred pages to read!! And, it was about a week before grades were due. The weight was heavy, figuratively and literally—no way I could lift those term papers all at once!

It was time for me to take a break from reading, reading, and reading so I went into the living room and turned on the TV. I had seen some of the episodes of "Little House on the Prairie," and being somewhat of a sentimentalist, I enjoyed them and at times was "touched" emotionally toward the end of them. That day they had a real "beauty." It was the one Christmas episode where the father worked extra hours to get the mother a new stove and get Laura a saddle for her horse. Laura also knew that mother needed a new stove and bought one for her by trading her horse to the local merchant (for his brat daughter)!

Tears welled in my eyes at the emotional gift opening scene and the hugs and tears that ensued on the show. Then it happened; the weight of the job, my disability and maybe the weight of the world just had to come out. I cried, and I cried and I cried! It must have lasted a half-hour to an hour. Sounds weird but I sure felt better afterward. It didn't get my work done, but I tackled it better afterward.

There is a rule, written or unwritten, that at a major University an instructor can only teach for three years without getting a PhD. Since I had nearly completed my second year, it was time to start looking for a job, as I did not want to wait until the last year and possibly be left out in the cold without a job. Also, I came to the realization that I sure would like to get out of the area where I have to deal with the cold and snow. The worst part about the snow is the amount that I drug into the house (apt.) each night in the winter and had to sit in the kitchen for quite some time before I could ever feel comfortable in the living room. Had to melt off!!

One of the greatest ego boosters in life is a job that you can do and enjoy. Such was the case with Jo-Ann that first year in Iowa City. She wanted to have a way of contributing to the family financially as well as with her love and support at home. Somehow it came to her attention that there was a job opening in the Iowa City School District. The title was Code-a-Phone Operator, which meant that she would have a device in our home, called a Code-a-Phone and it recorded all the messages from teachers who could not make it in to work. Her job was to get up VERY early, get the messages off the machine and when a reasonable hour approached she called people from the substitute list that showed the subjects they could or would teach if called in to substitute. Sometimes she was lucky and got the phone call the day before and could do the arranging for the substitute teacher in the evening prior to the day they were needed to teach. Jo-Ann prided herself in doing everything right as much as possible and did this job very well. She did have some very stressful days when there was illness abounding and five to ten subs to try to get—a job occasionally impossible to complete. The job went well the first year and much of the second year when apparently the stress of the job caused her to have an exacerbation of her illness. Consequently, she had to quit. The bright side was that there was a disability clause in the group insurance plan that provided her a small disability check after her termination.

Jo-Ann didn't have too much social life outside of the home. We did become involved with going to a Baptist church there and they had small prayer groups—we had one that met at our home with two other young couples joining us. They were very interesting and self-fulfilling.

In addition, we socialized often with Don and Ruth who lived in the apartment right above us. They usually came down to visit and one night they asked us if we ever played the card game called Rook. I said that I had played some when I was a kid, but hadn't for years. Jo-Ann said she had never played it, but was willing to learn. We played, I refreshed my memory and Jo-Ann learned. We played men against the women as that put one experienced player with a novice on each side. We had loads of fun, and laughter filled the apartment many nights. The laughter usually started when Don and Ruth arrived and jolly Don would sound out, "Let's fly the bird!" He meant, let's pay Rook.

While in Chicago I went to an NTRS Annual Symposium held in Champaign. On the way home my car stalled and I was able to run it with the "hot" light on until I got to a service station. I didn't dare stop earlier (although I should have) due to being stalled with night coming on and no way to get help. When I got to the station it was determined that I had a cracked block on the car and would have to get a new (different) one. So my '66 Impala was replaced with a '69 Chevy Caprice that served me well (except for the new transmission I had to have put in) until it was near the hundred thousand mile mark. I saw a pretty '74 Malibu in Iowa City and traded for it, in the spring of 1976. It was a clean copper colored two-door hardtop. The mechanics transferred my hand controls and I was in business again.

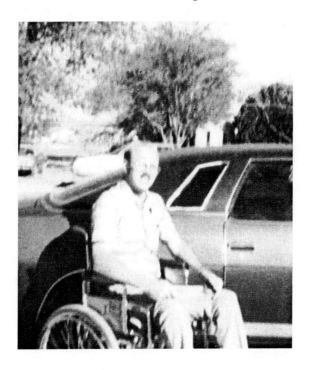

My "new" Malibu

In relation to the snow I talked about "dragging it into the apartment," in early April I thought it was time for me to start looking for a different job in a warmer climate. I was interested in Arizona, New Mexico and Texas. I checked with NTRS and nothing seemed to look "right" for me of the few jobs listed. So I tried another avenue and found that "The Lord DOES work in mysterious ways, His wonders to perform" to slightly change the quote from the Bible. Follow this chain of miracles, if you will. I contacted Gordon Howard, Supervisor of the SPI Program. SPI was the acronym for Special Populations Involvement, a program where Gordon supervised the work of Graduate Students as they conducted research in recreational activities for the group called

Deaf-Blind. Yes, people who are deaf and blind. Anyway, he knew people all over the country in the field of therapeutic recreation so I asked him if he had contacts in those southwestern states. "Sure, I might be able to help you, Jim," he said after I explained my plight. Two minutes later he was talking with Dr. Joe Teaff at Texas Women's University, Denton, Texas. Joe said that something had come across his desk recently about some job out west of Abilene but he couldn't find the paperwork. He said it was a State job. That was a start!!

The very next morning the miracle happened. One of the students to whom I served as advisor came into my office and said she was looking into jobs following her soon to be realized graduation. She was looking into jobs in Texas and had in her hand a list of all the State Hospitals and State Schools in Texas. Without allowing my intent I asked her politely, "Could you get a copy of that for me, I'd like to have one on file," I said half lying in the process. "Just go to the office and ask Ellen (secretary for the Recreation Education Program) to copy it for you or let you copy it," I told the girl after she consented to letting me have a copy. After she left and my work with her was complete, I went down to the basement of the building.

After getting off the elevator I made a right turn in the basement to face a long wall that contained a five foot by seven foot map of the United States. I looked with great interest at the cities west of Abilene, Texas and committed a few of them to my short term memory. I then looked at the State Hospitals list and the second one was the state Hospital in Big Spring, Texas. "That must be it, thank you Jesus," I whispered to myself. I quickly and clearly wrote down the name and phone number for the Director of Personnel, Mr. Chaney. Doug was his first name. I had a short period of time before my next class to teach and I was prepared for it, so "There's no time like the present" I thought as I went up to my office and dialed the phone.

Upon getting into conversation with Mr. Chaney I first asked him if they still had a position open in Recreation Therapy. "Yes," he said, "Are you interested in it?" We soon got to me telling him educational and experiential qualifications. "You are qualified for the job," he said. He promised to send me application forms, then paused, "You don't need these, just send your resume and proof of your education along with a letter signifying your desire to be considered for the position of Recreation Therapy Supervisor." I responded with, "Thank you very much, I will send it right away."

I sent the materials to Mr. Chaney and waited. And waited. And waited. Soon it was three weeks passed and I "took the bull by the horn" calling Mr. Chaney on the phone. "Mr. Gatewood was supposed to get back with you," he said after I told him my dilemma. He transferred my call to the Rehabilitation Department and the secretary told me that Mr. Gatewood was in a meeting, but he did want to talk to me so, "Please hold on." "Gatewood speaking," came the quiet voice over the phone lines. We talked for about a half hour and set up an interview day where I would drive down there to look over the situation and see if I was interested in another big move.

Dr. Nesbitt had someone cover my classes while I took time to make the trip to Texas and back. After two long days of driving I got to the Holiday Inn ready for a good night's sleep before the interview. Locals gave me directions to the Hospital and I filed them in my mind for the next morning. It came before I was totally rested, but I got up and after breakfast went to the facility, arriving at the Allred Building as instructed, after getting directions from someone—maybe patient, maybe staff member, I really didn't know! As they say, "Not all the monkeys are in the zoo!!"

Mr. Gatewood was a truly professional looking man in his suit and tie without a wrinkle in either one. He took me to meet the staff in Recreation Therapy including their temporary leader, Ann Trawick. After a series of conversations with many individuals the interview ended with Mr. Gatewood offering me the job, discussing salary and job promotion opportunities as well as me signing on the dotted line indicating my intent to show-up for work on June 15, 1976.

That night back at the motel I ran into a man from Coahoma, Texas, a small town just east of Big Spring. He was very friendly and went with me to look around town before it got too dark to see things such as a apartment complexes for our possible living in the future. We went down west third street and the man calmly said something about that being the "red light" district and quickly followed with, "Don't go there, the news will beat you home!!" The next morning I went to an apartment complex with an opening and while talking with the manager of the complex agreed to rent one on the first floor as of June 1, 1976. I wrote him a check as security deposit and headed home.

Chapter Thirty-One

The semester ended, the grades were in and I cleaned out my office. While doing that I had to do some reflecting on the past two years and my "career" as a college instructor. I never did have any time to do any research, I believe my teaching was adequate, nothing spectacular for sure, but I was proud of my service to the college and community in terms of the changes in buildings and sidewalks for better access by those of us with disabilities. In addition, I was active on a community committee regarding the use of Block Grant Funds to better the community.

Reminiscence led my mind to the relationship I had developed with Reed Edmondsen, a student in the Recreation Program who was on the University Golf Team and a big help for me to experience the unbelievable in a leisure pursuit of golfing. Somehow Jo-Ann had contacted Reed and had him get her Christmas gift for me—a two way chipper, a special unusual weighted golf club. Reed was from a small community southwest of Iowa City, Wellman, Iowa, where he grew up golfing at a course with an unusual characteristic. It had sand greens, the only type of green where a wheelchair with its occupant could go without ruining the green. In the summer of 1975 and spring of 1976 he took me out (I drove) to the course. The first time we started on number one and progressed VERY slowly through the entire course of holes. My arms were "milk toast" by the time we finished and it wasn't from swinging the club. On a couple hills he pushed me so I could keep up with him. We both decided our favorite hole in terms of distance was the par three number six so we parked the car outside the course a short stone's throw from the number six tee. We played number six down a grade and then turned around and played back up to the number five green (brown!). How did I play golf with no trunk balance? I parked the chair slightly at an angle toward the ball on the tee off to the right of my 'chair. Using his driver in my right hand and with my left hand holding onto the 'chair I could get a good swing and hit the ball somewhere between eighty and a hundred yards consistently. Then I would use my weighted chipper for my approach shots to the green. Once on the green with the ball, Reed helped push my chair on top of (or in) the sand to position for a putt or two as needed. When we completed the hole we raked the green (sand) smooth for the next time we got there. I got to where I was averaging bogey four on each of our outings. It was great fun.

There was another student that I took a liking to from my experience of him being in my first Introduction to Therapeutic Recreation class. We somehow, without any conference in private, had developed a mutual respect for each other. One day he stopped me in the hall outside my office and asked if I had some time to talk. I said, "Sure Larry," and we talked in my office. He had been in undergraduate school for somewhere around eight years—you know, changed his major almost as often as he changed his pants! The guy was gifted, very bright and could have been successful at almost any career including being a doctor or a lawyer, in my opinion. After ten or fifteen minutes of talking with him I asked if he wanted my advice. "What the heck do you think I came here for?" he queried. I laughed and then said, "Larry Young, you need to learn how to 'edit'." And I didn't mean change majors to Journalism so he could edit newspapers! I meant that he should look at all his interests and the progress he had made toward making a career in that interest become a reality. Then start scratching off the ones that cannot be realized within a year. I said that getting your degree in something did not lock you in to spend the remainder of your life working in that career. He then said, "That's easy, the way you put it; I know that I need to finish up my degree in therapeutic recreation, get out of school and get to work."

Due to the fact that Tommy was spending that school year in California with his dad, we had an empty bedroom in our apartment. Larry decided that all he needed to do to complete his degree was take two or three classes in the spring of 1976 and do his internship that next summer. Since he lived in Clinton, Iowa, a little over a hundred miles to the east, he approached me with the idea of him commuting to school in the spring as he would only have classes two or three days a week and asked if there was any possibility of him staying with Jo Ann and I the few nights per week as was needed. Since it was the end of the day when he asked, I suggested that we both go to my home and talk with Jo-Ann about the idea. Larry had a neat personality so I pretty well knew that he would have Jo-Ann like putty in his hand before long. And, he did, so we made the arrangements for him to fulfill his plans and stay with us, as needed.

Chapter Thirty-Two

Since my dad had died, my mother was living at home by herself and I believe still working in the school cafeteria preparing meals for the kids at HHS. I talked with her on the phone often and I shared with her the upcoming move to Texas indicating I did not know if I could afford to hire professional movers and asked if she had any ideas on the subject—like some help from my relatives and/or friends in Hillsboro. She got right on it and in a few days called me back with a plan that sounded feasible to her. What did I think of it? Sounded good to me, and it was going to "kill two or three birds with one stone"!

Don Hubbard is the older brother of my high school classmate, Ron Hubbard. Don had a small Moving Business in Hillsboro so was experienced in moving furniture and driving a loaded truck. Ron lived and worked in Houston, Texas. Their parents were both living and in there sixties I think. The plan was this. I would secure the rental of a Ryder truck large enough to haul our belongings and Don would drive it to Texas with his parents going along. Then they would take a bus to Houston to see Ron. After their visit was over they would fly back to Iowa City where their car would be left during their extended trip. In addition, they agreed to bring my mom along on the trip, during which she would ride with me to Texas. Jo-Ann was not in this picture because she packed up things for the move and then flew to New Mexico to visit her parents while all this mess was going on—less trauma for her disease.

The day arrived for packing of the truck and once complete the Hubbards took their car to a place for safe keeping until their return. We all stayed in a motel that night and got an early start on the road the next day with them in the truck and mom and I following behind in my car. We had reservations in Wichita, KS the first night and that was about halfway. We went on the next day and had some truck trouble near Oklahoma City, OK. However, Don called the magic number and the Ryder personnel instructed him to continue to drive (one of the duel tires was flat) on into Oklahoma City with information on how to get to the Ryder business address for repairs. He did as instructed and fortunately (the Lord was with us, again) the other tire did not blow before we got there. We had a two-hour delay and then were back on our way for an uneventful seven hours to Big Spring. I told Don to take the first exit off Interstate twenty when they got to Big Spring and then stop so he could follow me the last couple miles to the apartment complex.

It was somewhere in the neighborhood of 10:30 or 11:00 p.m. when we pulled into the complex. Mom got out of the car and instructed Don as to where he needed to drive to get to the back of the apartments for unloading with the least distance to carry the furniture. Unfortunately he couldn't back up to the door as he did in Iowa City to load as the apartments were in a square shape with a swimming pool in the center of the square—the doors all faced the pool. To back up to the front door he would have had to have his truck in the pool! They unloaded all the furniture completing the task a couple hours after midnight and most of it was just placed one thing against the other in the living room. Upon completion, we all headed for the Holiday Inn to get a well-deserved night of sleep with plans to NOT get up very early. The next morning we met for breakfast at the motel around 10:00 a.m. and Don called the bus terminal for information about the next bus toward Houston. He also called the Ryder dealership there to get directions for taking back the one-way rented truck.

After breakfast and Don's phone calls we sat and visited a bit before they had to go take the truck back and get a cab to the bus station in time for their trip. Don and I had really not discussed his fee for the things he was doing for me so we got our heads together then. It was sort of a "you scratch my back and I'll scratch yours" situation. They got a "free ride" to Texas, even if they were still five hundred miles from Houston and I got my furniture moved. Don said the bus fare to Houston for them was going to be one hundred fifty dollars and if I would pay that amount, he would call it even. "That's more than fair to me," I said as I gave him the cash and a big thank you!

Chapter Thirty-Three

My job at the State Hospital didn't start for two weeks so we had some time for a "vacation." Mom and I at 33 years of age had never seen the Carlsbad Caverns so we decided to take a day and drive over to see what it was all about, besides a big cave. It looked like a good one day trip as it was about one hundred eighty miles away, if we took the route with more "major" highways north to LaMesa, TX, west to Hobbs, NM and southwest to Carlsbad, NM. We left my new abode and got to the caverns between 11:00 a.m. and noon. We went on the tour with the group and it was shortened by quite a bit by us coming to the area where there was "no wheelchair passage." I was actually sorta glad it was shortened as I was still a little tired from spending the previous afternoon trying to at least get the new apartment set up so we had a place to sleep. We didn't want to do much else as Jo-Ann was scheduled to fly into the Midland-Odess Air Terminal the day after our Carlsbad trip, which she did. Mom and I went to get Jo and brought her home.

.

After the move—boxes, boxes, boxes

The landlord had Bert Sheppard change the bathroom door to a large size and for the first time since leaving the University of Illinois in 1969 I had the luxury of using my padded toilet seat and have BM's like the "normal folks". I still couldn't use the shower, but lets not get all the privileges at once! More later . . .

Jo-Ann's visit with her parents was short but she was glad to get away from any anxiety associated with the move. As she looked at the piles of boxes in the living room she had the same bewildered look on her face as I had the first day. I assured her that we did not have to do all the work in one day or even one week, but we wanted to get a lot of things done while mom was there with us to give a bunch of help. We got some help with the heavy things—dressers, etc. and Don Hubbard and his dad had put the beds in the bedrooms right away when unloading the truck. Soon things were in fairly good order and Jo and I took mom to the Airport to fly home to Hillsboro.

My work began and I soon learned that Mr. Gatewood was also the pastor of a small church called Salem Baptist, a few miles east of town. Upon discussing Jo-Ann's background, Mr. Gatewood invited us to come out and attend services at "his" little church. We did that when we could and developed some good relationships.

Tommy joined us in the fall and went to school at Big Spring that year. He enjoyed using the swimming pool on warm days and seemed to do well in school. One day he came home with a cat that he had found. It was just a little stray kitten and was so cute that it didn't take much begging for us to let him keep it. He called it "Samantha" and that was so cute until we did a little physical examination of the cat and told him we needed to change HIS name to "Sam." Then Sam became Sam-cat! I guess a one syllable name was not good enough for a cute little cat.

Tommy joined Boy Scouts to the satisfaction of his mother and was fairly active in his troup. The Saturday after Thanksgiving he was supposed to take brownies to a Scout Bake Sale at the mall located a mile to the west. I got up and was ready to take him to the event when I looked outside to see a layer of white stuff on the ground. We headed for the car and Tommy had to push me due to about four solid inches of the wettest snow possible on the ground. Without him I could have never gotten to the car. To get to the mall we had to go down a fairly long, steep hill and up a short steep hill to FM 700 where there was a stoplight, then left on FM 700 over to the mall. We went down the long hill and came up toward the stoplight only to see two or three cars spinning their tires and sliding backwards in their attempt to get through the green light. Doesn't look too good I thought.

Drawing from my experience of driving on snow and ice in Wisconsin, Illinois and Iowa I thought of a way to conquer the situation. Momentum is the key! I drove up within about fifty feet of the sliding backward cars and spun my car around on the slippery road headed back where I just came from. "We going home, Jim?" questioned Tommy. "No," I said, "You watch!" I headed back toward home until my tires nearly were slipping and then spun the car around in the road once again. I gained speed going down that hill and when I got up behind the other cars I maintained my momentum, turned into the left lane, cut left into a service station, went past the pumps and up the steep short hill to FM 700. Turning left I went on to the mall and left Tommy there with the instructions to call home when he was done unless one of the other fathers offered to take him home. I didn't expect that much snow all winter down there in Texas and I sure hoped this was not an indicator of the type of winter coming up.

Chapter Thirty-Four

Chuck McCall worked in the Industrial Therapy part of the Rehabilitation Dept. at the Hospital. He was a recovering alcoholic who had apparently been in the Alcohol Treatment Program at the Hospital until his discharge when he was sort of taken under the wing (so to speak) of Mr. Gatewood and given a chance to make good of his life. He was a conscientious worker and part of the time he taught a class called "Personal and Social Adjustment" (PSA). He also worked in the "work therapy" program there.

Within days after we moved. into the apartment I discovered that Chuck and his wife, Janine, lived straight across the full length of the pool on the east end of the complex. Chuck was extremely friendly and a really nice guy, Janine was nice too. Many evenings we would sit together at his apartment and drink coffee while talking philosophically about life and various issues. We had a good relationship and one weekend his dad came to visit him. In a short time I had a good relationship with his dad.

One very hot August night Chuck and I were visiting and "out of the clear blue" (as the old saying goes) I said, "Chuck, I want to go swimming sometime, will you help me?" "Sure, Jim, I'd be glad to if I can do it," he responded. I told him my problems that had prevented me from doing any swimming previous to that, such as, the need to do it early in the morning while my bladder was empty before I put on the condom for the day, the fact that the pool deck was very hard so cushions would be needed when I got out of my 'chair before going into the pool and, of course, the help (lifting) needed to get me out of the 'chair and back into it after the swim. "Let's do it this Saturday," Chuck said with enthusiasm feeling really needed in an area outside of his job. "OK," I said, "It's a deal!"

Saturday arrived and a quick call to Chuck at 9:00 a.m. confirmed he was ready to help me. We met at the pool and he was more hesitant than I was as he finally came to the realization he was about to help a paralyzed good friend into a pool of water where he might drown! "Are you sure you can swim?" he asked with reservations in his voice. "No," I said reaffirming his anxiety, but I set him at ease with, "I had a good roommate at Illinois in worse shape than me who I saw swim like a fish!"

Chuck got me into the pool safely and I floated on my back swimming a modified version of the backstroke. Periodically I turned to my belly down and did the crawl stroke for a short while. I had a wonderful time in that gravity free (almost) environment and felt so "free" that I stayed as long as I could which was about a half hour. "We'll have to do this again soon," I told Chuck as he was helping me get back into the 'chair. "Sure, anytime you want," he assured me. Before I knew it the summer was gone and I NEVER SWAM AGAIN!! Chuck was a good friend until . . . read on.

About three months into the job my title was changed from Recreation Supervisor to Referral Coordinator and consultant to Recreation Therapy, with that my duties changed drastically. In this position my responsibility was to make sure that each Unit Treatment Team received information about their patients getting treatment in Rehab. Therapies at the patients' staffing (Team meeting discussing the patients) and bring back referrals for new patients and patient treatment changes. I supervised Lois Meek (aka "Granny," as she affectionately was called), Bertha Turner and our secretary Elsie Neill. Lois, Bertha and I attended staffings covering about nine Treatment Teams on campus. The four of us shared a nice room about twelve feet by fifteen feet in the northwest corner of the building.

The Allred Building was originally an open area for Occupational Therapy on the north end with the gymnasium on the south end. When the Rehab. Administration and other offices replaced the Occupational Therapy area many walls were installed totally messing up the equalization of temperatures during air conditioning and heating periods. As the weather got colder "Granny" felt it most and brought a thermometer to lay on her desk to show the boss how cold it was back there. One day I looked at "Granny" and she appeared tired. I said, "Granny, you look tired." She said, "I'm getting sleepy, you know that's the last thing you do before you freeze to death!!" "What's the temperature there?" I asked with concern. "Right now it says fifty degrees," she said looking at her temperature gauge. "I'm calling the boss, we *have* to do something about this," I assured her with doubt in my mind. Some things are out of our control— sometimes out of human control!

Mr. McCall, Chuck's father had a fairly serious case of phlebitis (a blood clotting problem) and took Coumadin (a blood thinner) to help control the problem. He was in his sixties and retired from an oil company job but maintaining fairly good health. Unfortunately, Chuck had the same problems as his dad and also took Coumadin. One morning, December 29, 1976 to be exact, Chuck was teaching his PSA class held from 9:00 a.m. to 9:50 a.m. It was about 9:25 a.m. when Chuck came into our office and said, "Bertha, you got any Tums?" Seeing he looked a little pale she asked, "What's the matter?" "I got a little indigestion, must be from my breakfast," he answered. He chewed the Tums quickly, swallowed and got a glass of water from our little kitchen area and drank it. He came back into the office with his face flushed and sweat pouring from his forehead. We had him sit down and put his head down a minute while Lois called for a nurse working in Staff Development next door to our department. The nurse looked at him, talked with him a bit and then without hesitation said, "I am calling the ambulance, this man is very sick." Soon the ambulance arrived, put him on the stretcher and took him to the nearest local general hospital where he was . . . DEAD ON ARRIVAL!! Apparently, a blood clot from his leg loosened and went to his heart causing a massive coronary that killed him. He was thirty-four and my best friend. I was sick and in hindsight could only think about the things we could have or should have done to get him to the hospital sooner. As I drove back home from the funeral and burial held in Cisco, Texas east of Abilene, Texas on December 31, 1976 I could only say on NEW YEAR'S EVE, "It's NOT going to be a HAPPY NEW YEAR!"

Chapter Thirty-Five

We had already moved three times since we were married; I hated the thought of doing it again and Jo bawked at it more than I did, but I rationalized with Jo, how are we ever going to get away from throwing our money away on rent with nothing to show for it? How much longer do we want to try to tolerate the nightly noise upstairs in the apartment above us costing us sleep? She agreed that I could begin to look for a house with a yard in March. I looked at a lot of houses that were almost accessible (usually a six inch ledge by the door needing a ramp), but once I got into the house found that the kitchen, dining and living rooms were fine; however, the hallway leading to the bedrooms and bathroom were invariably only about forty inches wide. That made it impossible, or extremely difficult to make the corners from the hall to the rooms in a wheelchair, especially a 'chair as long as mine was—about four feet long from my toes to the back of the rear times. My realtor that I had helping me find possible houses had suggested many in the twenty to forty thousand dollar range and I looked at them, but nothing seemed to be a "fit."

After suggesting that maybe a slightly older home might fit our needs better, the realtor said, "Oh, I have this one that has been on the market for a year, but, due to the three steps up to get into it, I held back suggesting it to you." I replied, "Maybe I better take a look at it." I rounded up some "muscle" to help me get into the house on East Fifteenth Street to check it out. I was impressed in a positive way and with help the next day Jo and I both went to look at it. The only ugly thing about the property was that the weeds were two feet tall in the front and fenced back yard. It had a wide carport adjacent to the house, thirty-two inch doors throughout, big living room, three nice sized bedrooms, sufficient sized bathroom, a storage area by the carport and three doors to the outside—front, back and side to the carport. I studied and knew it could be ramped best up to the carport door with the ramp running lengthwise of the carport along the wall to the door. Yes, that would cost some, but the inside advantages were great, so we decided to seal the deal after finding out that our payments would be less than we were paying monthly in rent at the apartment. We hired Bert Sheppard to build the ramp and moved in on May 1, 1977. He also changed the bathroom door from twenty-four to thirty-six inches for easy access to the commode and tub. He built a padded shower seat and using a shower hose and sprayer I was now finally able to bathe in a nearly normal manner. How refreshing!! If you don't believe me, try "sponge" baths for a few days, a few weeks, a few months, or a few years like I had to do.

Speaking recently of weeds in the yard, Tommy had a yen for adventure and a day or two after we moved into the house he went out the back door to have a look. I was off work so it must have been a Saturday or Sunday and was in the master bedroom in the back of the house when I heard this screaming and crying like the proverbial "stuck pig" in the first part of butchering. I rushed to his aid going out the side door, down the ramp, around the outer side of the carport, through the fence gate and through the thick weeds for about twenty yards to get to him. As I got my education about grasses and weeds in west Texas with grass burrs and goatheads sticking to my wheelchair tire and consequently being jammed into my hands, I saw Tommy holding up one foot (no shoe, no sock) with a great number of those burrs and goatheads sticking in it. I instantly knew why he was crying as I was near tears with the pain in my hands. I finally got to him, picked him up with my right arm and sat him on my lap where he

252

road with me back around to the front of the house. His mother took care of him and soon the tears were gone. That very same day I hired some guys to clean off all weeds and mow the lawn down like it should be.

Once the weeds were gone, I could see there was new grass growing under it all. Unlike the north where I grew up, I later learned that new grasses began to spring up (maybe that's why the season is called spring) in March, not May, in west Texas! Anyway, the property sure looked better.

Indeed, 1977 was not a happy year. Jo-Ann enjoyed Tommy being with us so much that in the spring she decided to go to court and get custody of Tommy so he would be with us each school year and live with his father in the summers. She wanted it in writing from the legal sources. Tommy's father, Dean Furrh, came to the hearing and the custody was won by Jo-Ann. That spring Tommy joined a Little League team and, though he was not a great player of baseball, he seemed to enjoy the comradery of the team. He had previously been somewhat of a loner, possibly due to his high level of intelligence, and certainly was well versed in entertaining himself.

We hadn't lived in the new house for even a week when, with the daily high temperature around ninety degrees we soon discovered that the swamp cooler on the roof did not do anything for cooling the house. While we are spending money we might as well spend some more and get central heating and air conditioning because I know I can't live without refrigerated air no matter how good a swamp cooler works—they make me hot and humid instead of just hot. So, we contracted to have the new unit put in and was it ever nice. ·

One highlight of the year came in June when Larry Young asked ME to come to Clinton, Iowa to be his Best Man at his wedding to his college sweetheart, Jane, who had completed her studies to be a nurse. When I told Jo about that and the fact that I wanted to go do it in July, she said, "Good," and we had been talking about getting her daddy to come over from New Mexico to "check out" our house (he could fix anything) for us. Her dad showed up as planned a day or two before I left for Wisconsin where I spent a few days before I drove two hundred miles or less down to Clinton for the wedding and then went back to Hillsboro for a few days before going back to Texas. When I got back home I bought a cheap lawnmower—push type power rotary mower—so I could mow my lawn or have it for someone else to mow for me. I tried pushing it with my toes against the back of it and the handle bar area up by my chest while my hands were on my wheelchair tires pushing. Every little while my footrests or toes would get up on the rear tires of the mower causing instant "brakes." I told Jo's dad that I needed fenders built on my mower to prevent that from happening. Tony, her dad, aka A.J. "Tony" Godec, said in his drawl, "Weeell," paused for a while as he was thinking and added, "Let me see what I can do." He asked where a sheet metal shop was located and left only to return soon and begin "tinkering" (no pun intended as his profession was that of a tinker) out in the storage shed that I had converted into a makeshift workshop (at least I had a bench and a vise). "Come and try this out," he hollered from the carport, indicating that he had them made and mounted on the mower already. I tried it and it worked great, never again did my feet or footrests hit the tires.

Now any ambitious young high school boy could mow our lawn in forty-five minutes to an hour depending on whether they hurried or just took their time. After having the fenders on the mower I was so excited to mow it that I got right at it on the next Saturday after the fenders were installed. It was a hell-o-va-lot of work but I took great pride in doing it myself. It took me four and a half hours!! One Saturday it was so hot that it did not get down to ninety degrees until nearly ten o'clock so I started mowing then—bet the neighbors loved me!! I mowed until about midnight and only had the front yard done (about one-third of the total). A full moon and the street light nearby provided light.

On another Saturday it was not so hot and I was out mowing about 11:00 a.m. when a car came by the house, stopped a little ways past when he realized what he had seen out of the corner of his eye, backed the car up to the front of my lawn and stopped.

He walked over to me with his camera, talked with me for a little while and took some pictures of me doing my mowing. He was from the Big Spring Herald, local daily newspaper, and he put a nice article with pictures in the Sunday paper the next morning. I was pleased and proud of my accomplishments.

Speaking of newspapers, it is amazing to me how the delivery of them to homes has changed since I had my paper delivery responsibilities in high school. When I delivered I put the paper where the customer wanted it; either in the screen door and close it or on the porch in a box for it. I collected for it every week *after* delivery and if they did not get one paper that week, the money left for me was less than a week's total. When I was a subscriber I instructed the paperboy to put the thing inside my screen door at the top of the ramp—very simple. Then he'd forget or a substitute would deliver it and, God only knew where I might find it—one time it was in the middle of the neighbor's front yard. One kid had his mother drive him around on the route and he threw the papers from sitting in the front seat of the car!! Since I had to pay in advance, I had no recourse except to quit the paper if unhappy or call the boss of the delivery persons. I called him and it helped—for a while! When asked what his job was, one paperboy said, "My job is throwing papers!!" That says it all.

Chapter Thirty-Six

That summer Tommy went to spend it with his father. When the summer was over Tommy decided that he wanted to continue living with his father and did not return to us. Jo-Ann wished that we could do something about that but neither she nor I had the energy or financial resources to put up any kind of a fight. Needless to say, she was not a "happy camper" during that fall. One day in November, November 22, 1977 (anniversary of John F. Kennedy's assassination, a man Jo thought highly of) to be exact, Jo-Ann had a physical therapy session as she had been having some treatment sessions for a few weeks. I came home from work to find her in bed sleeping—nothing unusual as she was often in bed all tired out from her attempts to enhance her physical condition in spite of her MS. I fixed my supper, watched TV some and went to bed at my usual time—she was still sleeping so I did not wake her. I got up quietly and saw she was still sleeping the next morning—often she had sleeplessness during the night and once sleeping well, I did not bother her. About 9:00 a.m. I called to talk with Jo-Ann and no answer. At 9:15 a.m. I called again and no answer. At 9:30 a.m. I called again thinking she could not possibly still be in the bathroom or too far from the phone, but after twelve rings there was no answer. Bertha Turner lived in the next block by the apartment we lived in first in Big Spring and she and Jo-Ann had become friends. So, I said to Bertha that morning, "I don't think things are good at home with Jo." "What is it, Jim?" she asked with concern. "Jo doesn't answer the phone and I've tried three times in the last half hour," I said. "Will you go with me to the house?" She agreed and I got someone to "cover" my ten and eleven o'clock classes in case we weren't back in time. We drove to my home, went in and found Jo-Ann still in bed. We shouted and then shook her, but could not wake her. I called the ambulance and they came and took her to the nearest local hospital where "her" doctor worked. She was in a coma. We later found out she had taken too many Valium, whether accidentally or on purpose, it didn't matter, however it happened it appeared to be her way of reaching out to get the kind of care she really needed. Since I was busy "doing my thing" at work, I guess I was not really aware of the amount of difficulty she was having. Thank God she came out of the coma after a while, got better, and it was time to get her some help. Mr. Gatewood went "to bat" for us checking with government officials in the State and the Federal levels to see about financial help to pay for a visiting or live-in helper. No luck! Another adversity to handle.

Jo-Ann was in the local general hospital for about four weeks so I had a little time to think and come to some very difficult conclusions. The first was that I never again wanted to come home to the scene that I discover on November 23, 1977. Secondly, it would be impossible to pay for the services of a live-in or visiting helper for Jo out of my meager salary. Third, the nursing home costs to give her the care she needed were nine hundred dollars—more than my take-home salary. Fourth, we would have to get a divorce in order for the nursing home to accept her disability check and the remainder of her costs would be covered by the State of Texas from funds designated to help people in her situation. So, I filed for divorce about December 15, 1977 and she waived the necessity for her to attend the hearing, as she entered the nursing home around December 21, 1977. After the sixty day waiting period the judge notified me to come to court—Big Spring was the County Seat for Howard County—for the hearing and the final decree. Only when I signed the papers and looked at the date did I really feel weird—it was February 14, 1978, Valentines Day! The gossip that went around for the next few months was hideous, but I had to ignore it and I believed the old saying although I changed a couple words, "Unless you've rolled a mile in my wheelchair, don't pass judgment."

I visited Jo often during the first three months that she was there. Then, we had a "falling out" which apparently was all my fault. It was on a Saturday when I did not show up to see her at 1:00 p.m. or so like I had been doing for the last few weeks. I got there about 4:00 p.m. and was met with, "Where you been" not "Hi, how are you?" So, I told her the truth. "Juli, the music therapist at the Hospital, and some other friends and I went bowling this afternoon and that's why I'm late." She blew up and said something very uncharacteristic, "Then you can go to Hell!!" I said, "OK, I'll go," and I left. I don't think she expected that from me. And, it was a long tine before I went back to see her, but I don't hold grudges forever and I later did go visit her—I don't recall how much later it was. I'm not all bad; I paid her phone bills there and have paid them for the last twenty-five years. We are now good friends again.

Chapter Thirty-Seven

It didn't take me long to realize that cooking (fixing) my own meals at night after a long day's work and eating them alone was not much fun. I then started to eat some meals at the local restaurants. Juli and I spent some time together mostly on weekends and on Sunday we often watched football games together while she was cooking a good pot roast in the crock-pot, for our supper. We enjoyed going bowling on Saturdays and it was then that I discovered I needed glasses. I looked at the automatic scorer and said, "Is that score 138, 136, 168, 166 or 188?" Juli then asked in amazement, "Can't you see that, Jim?" An eye exam the next week showed I was near sighted some and had a stigmatism causing the blurred vision. I got glasses for the first time at age thirty-five.

In May that year one of the local service organizations had a tree sale and I bought a pecan tree to plant. On a Saturday soon after, I borrowed a posthole digger, the manual kind, from "Pee Wee" who lived a short distance west of me. I told him what I was going to do and he somewhat sarcastically said, "Good luck!" If I can mow my lawn I can plant a tree while sitting in my wheelchair, I thought optimistically. I picked a spot in the back yard where the tree, when grown, would not get up against the house or into any of the wires to and from the house. I set my 'chair so the spot to dig was just to the right of my right caster (front wheel). I took the digger in my right hand with the handles together and jammed it into the ground a few times while maintaining balance with my left hand hanging onto the 'chair. When I had enough dirt loose to pick it up I pulled the handles apart with each hand on a side, but I couldn't lift it up (or later out of the hole) with both hands due to no trunk balance. So, I slid my right arm down between the two handles causing it to grip the dirt. Once I had it as tight as possible, I gripped the handle low and forced (wedged) my upper arm down against the other handle as much as possible and lifted the whole thing up with my right arm. I shook it and poked the dirt out with a small tree branch and repeated the task over one hundred times before I got down about thirty inches where I couldn't grip the dirt anymore. Then, after all that, Pee Wee showed up and said, "Can I help you finish that job?" Hot, tired and a little frustrated I said, "Sure," and he helped "plant" the tree!

In 1978 I joined St. Paul Lutheran Church (Missouri Synod) and was comfortable since it was quite similar to the one I grew up attending. Juli was also a member or regular attendee there, so we had that in common. While involved in that church I taught Sunday School one year and was Financial Secretary a few years and Treasurer for two years. I was part of that congregation for eighteen years.

Marriage was not in the forecast for Juli and I, so later in the year when she started dating a guy that she eventually married, I was not surprised—we had some good times together and we did "football picks." We each picked who we thought was going to win each game in the NFL every week AND, we have remained friends and have just completed doing our "picks" for twenty-four straight years. Life situations have changed for both of us many times, but the "picks" have continued in spite of our moves and other changes.

Tom and Beverly Greiner moved to Big Spring in 1977 and Tom was Evaluator for Industrial Therapy, a Certified Vocational Counselor, with whom a good relationship was developed. Beverly worked as a secretary at the Hospital also. Many times they invited me to their house for meals and card games.

Sometime during 1979, Jo-Ann had a visit from an old friend. Micki Dwire had made the trip down from Alamosa, Colorado to see her friend from "Girl Scout Days." Micki grew up in Silver City, NM only a few miles from where Jo grew up and they had developed a friendship through their common Girl Scout activities. As a matter of fact, Micki, her husband Ron and their girls, Sharon and Amy, stopped to visit with us briefly when we lived in Forest Park, Illinois. Also, Micki and the girls came to visit us right after we moved to Big Spring on the day of the "big fire" at the local refinery. That was after she and her husband had divorced and they had taken up residence in Alamosa, CO. After Micki had visited Jo that day at the nursing home she came over to the house and visited with me showing much concern about how I was "holding up" after all that had gone on the past year or so.

The fall of 1979 brought some bad news from back home in Hillsboro. Mom had been in to the doctor for a checkup, they found cancer of the uterus and she had a hysterectomy. However, the surgery did not get all the cancer and she was left with the miserable experience of taking chemotherapy that made her very sick.

Also during 1979 I got to know George Colvin and he invited me to join the Big Spring Club of Civitan International, an international organization geared to help communities build good citizenship and was a major supporter for local, State and International Special Olympics. Civitan became one of three major sponsors of Special Olympics through contributions of thousands of dollars and volunteers to help with the events.

While I was active in Civitan in Big Spring, Texas the International Organization had a project that I really enjoyed working on. It was called the "Candy Box Project." My job was to secure a business where I could put a candy box somewhere near their cash register where customers would take an individually wrapped red and white peppermint candy or a few of them and put some change in the slot for that purpose. The sign said, "Your Change can Change Things" or "Your Change Changes Things." You see, a member in Kentucky was concerned about who would care for his mentally retarded son after the boy's parents had passed on from this life. The profits, excess over the cost of the candy, were used by Civitan International to build homes where individuals like this man's son could live after their patents were gone. The project was a success.

Also, while a member of Civitan I volunteered to talk to a group of high school students at a Leadership Seminar held in Georgetown, Texas at the University there. I used some of the material on Personal Adjustment and Social Adjustment that I used regularly in my SLACS (Social, Leisure And Coping Skills) classes at BSSH. Some of the students had friends who were having trouble with alcohol and/or drugs listened intently to me. Many came up to me after the talk and with tears in their eyes thanked me for my message. I felt like a "million bucks!"

Micki was very concerned about mom when I told her of the cancer. She had lost a brother-in-law to cancer at a fairly young age, so she kept up with all the nursing information and latest treatments for cancer. After her visit with me, she and I corresponded by mail on a weekly basis and talked on the phone some. In early spring of 1980 she came down to Big Spring to see me for a couple days and later on I went up to Alamosa, CO to see her for a couple days. On her visit to see me we went to the grocery store together, bought some good food and she cooked a meal for us at my house. Somehow I felt that that was the kind of thing that would hold a marriage together and it was a wonderful day.

Micki and I set the time for the wedding in late May 1980 to be married in her Methodist church in Alamosa with Tom Greiner being my "best man." He and I drove to Alamosa and after the wedding he quickly flew home to his wife as she was expecting their first baby "any day now." After the wedding and a short reception, Micki and I went to the graduation ceremonies at the Alamosa High School where Shari was graduating. Then Micki and I spent that night at the "Baca Grande" about fifty miles north up the San Luis Valley past the Great Sand Dunes National Monument—places we visited during my previous trip to Colorado. The next day we drove to Denver and flew to Wisconsin to see my mom. We spent a few days with her and flew back to Colorado where I drove back to Texas and she began packing for her and the girls to move to Big Spring.

Chapter Thirty-Eight

By the time Micki and the girls, Shari (to be 18 years old in a few months) and Amy (to be 14 years old in a few months) got down to my home, I had sold many of the items that would be duplicated on their arrival. Thus, we had room in the house for their additions. Shari took the back bedroom and Amy the one by the kitchen/dining room. We settled in and arranged for some responsibilities with the main daily household chores making for less tension in the home. I continued my job responsibilities and Micki took the summer "off" from a nursing job to get the house in order and spend some time with the girls prior to the hectic schedule coming up when school started. Shari went to Howard Junior College, Amy started her first year at Big Spring High School and Micki was busy choosing a job as a nurse as September arrived.

Speaking of September, it was September 1, 1980 when my sister, Shirley and family, and my brother, Don and family were called to St. Joseph's Memorial Hospital as mom was asking for them and telling the nurse that the end was in sight. They went to her side and, without a lot of time passing, she passed on to a better place. I got two calls that day, one saying she was not doing well and the second saying that she was gone. Tears welled up in my eyes, but I was sure glad that day that I had taken the time off work and got to spend some time with her in late July and early August. The hardest thing I ever did in my life was saying good-bye to my mom in August knowing full well that I would never see her alive again. And, when I left Hillsboro that day I told my siblings that I would not be flying back up to attend the funeral when that time came. On the day of the funeral tears came to my eyes again a few times, but they really got heavy when Dr. Butler, Hospital Chaplain at BSSH, and wife Mary Butler, Director of Nursing at BSSH, sent over to my office one single rose for me. Needless to say, it was extremely thoughtful and touching thing for them to do.

"You didn't go home for your mother's funeral?" someone said one day in derogatory manner as though it was a mortal sin. "No," I said emphatically, "I remember well my flying experience going to the University of Illinois in 1967, AND, the last time I flew the dumb airline lost my wheelchair." On that occasion I had flown to some NTRS National Symposium for training and when I got back to the Midland International Air Terminal they could not locate my wheelchair. They were very kind and gave me a chair to use, but that didn't suit me at all. It wasn't as bad as the one they "parked" me in at O'hare in 1967, but based on needing a wheelchair that fits you when you are a spinal cord injured person, it was terrible. Fortunately, I did get my own chair four days later and was very thankful to have it, but the posts that telescope into other posts when you unfold the wheelchair were BENT!! Since I needed to fold it and unfold it every time I got in and out of my car, repairs were necessary. I have NOT flown since!

Prior to Micki and I getting married, I had taken a basic Accounting class at Howard College to rekindle my high school interest in accounting and work toward a possible degree. I loved it and did great receiving an "A" in the course. Also at night school, I took a course in Economics—didn't like it, didn't do too well. So, since I couldn't get the intermediate accounting class at Howard college night school, I took it at University of Texas—Permain Basin in Odessa sixty miles away two nights a week for a whole year. The class work was "tough", I got a "C" and learned from it that I NEVER again wanted to be an accountant! Too many rules and standards that we were supposed to memorize—again my brain trauma from the accident reared its ugly head.

The seven-year-old '74 Malibu was up around a hundred thousand miles so I traded it in for a 1979 Oldsmobile two door with a big engine and lots of room for my wheelchair in the backseat area. The front seat was a bench seat which I prefer and it only had thirty-some thousand miles on it. I got it just in time to test it out on a short trip. Phil Eastman was Professor of Mathematics at Boise State University in Idaho and Paul "Doc" Tatter was living in Santa Fe, NM so when Phil called and told me he was planning a trip down to Santa Fe on his new Goldwing motorcycle to see Paul, I told him I could rendezvous with them at the motel I chose. I drove up there on Friday, we visited on Saturday and I went back home on Sunday. The "new" car ran great so Micki and I planned a trip for the summer including visits to her previous home in Birmingham, Michigan, visits with some of her relatives in Minnesota and a few days staying with my brother and family during the time that took in my twenty year high school class reunion. We also visited with friends in Dallas, TX on the first leg of the trip. It was a good two-week "getaway" from my job and the Texas heat. While in Michigan the "X" under my wheelchair seat broke. The repairman we contacted said he could not weld it to stay so put a "sleeve" on it with a larger piece of pipe. That sleeve held it good for the next twenty-plus years.

At BSSH I coached a volleyball team made up of mostly Recreation Therapy staff members. I was just as strict with them as my High School coach in that I told them they could serve any way they wanted to as long as it got over the net and did not go out of bounds. Whenever one of them missed a serve they looked at me to see how mad I was and watched my frowning at them. If looks could kill, they'd be dead on the spot! We won a few championships in the tournaments with teams from the various units.

Early May, preferably in late April in west Texas is usually a time before the weather gets too hot for anything outdoors. Thus,

JIM POTTER

my staff and I developed an annual track and field competition among the patients at BSSH. Since it is also a time when the spring winds blow sand around sufficient to make the sky red at times, I named the event, Sandstorm Relays. There were some running and jumping events as well events using softballs and frisbees. Unit teams competed against each other for the championship and individual winners were given awards.

When you work at the same place for a number of years many days, weeks, months and years blend together when doing the same thing. I was a little different when my referral coordinator job changed to Supervisor of Occupational Therapy on a temporary basis. That experience lasted until a new Registered OT was hired and I developed a class of Independent Living Skills (ILS) that my assistant and I held in a house (former residence of a doctor) on campus. After about a year things changed in the department and I was back in the "office" as supervisor/consultant for Recreation Therapy and started teaching a class that I developed as a spin-off from the ILS class. It was called Social, Leisure and Coping Skills with the acronym SLACS. I loved the teaching of it and it was one of the most popular classes when judged by the patients. More will be said about this class later.

The Occupational Therapist hired was Nat Hart, a Big Spring native who had been away in the military and attending school to get his degree. We became good friends and spent some time fishing together. George Colvin came to our house one day and brought his son, Jay, with him. He met Shari and soon they began dating. They got married in the summer of 1981 and in the fall of 1982 Micki was a grandmother to Travis John, aka TJ as everyone called him. Around this same time David Keyes and his wife moved to Big Spring where he was employed as a physician's assistant at the Veteran's Memorial Hospital—I called him the PA at the VA! They were active in the Lutheran church with me and we became good friends.

I had not been fishing or hunting for a long time and really missed them. I had no idea about hunting in Texas, but there

266

were fishing opportunities (lakes) in the area where I could be doing some fishing—I usually needed some help to get close enough to the water. Therefore, if I could get Nat or Jay or David to go with me, I could get back to one of my favorite leisure pastimes. On any given Saturday morning I ought to get one of them to be available for fishing if I asked them ahead of time. Not always! But David did go with me more than the others. In the summer of 1984, David and I were fishing two or three times and for some unknown reason I did not get overheated because I was sweating profusely most of the time. I didn't have an ulcer on my buttocks so that cause was ruled out. I thought it could be bladder infection, but my urine was flowing fairly well—still the sweats. Then, one night, after having previous nights of some sweating, I soaked the bed with sweat. When Micki came home from work, she always worked nights (11-7 shift), I was still in bed sweating terribly. She said, "That's it, you are going to the doctor and I am having them keep you there until they find out what is wrong with you." "OK," I said, reluctantly, "I guess you are right." Adversity takes another form.

Since my experience with the general practitioner (doctor) in Illinois where he told me to "Stay off it" after the diagnosis of infection in my foot, I had little faith in them, so my "family doctor" was my Urologist. Dr. Cowan was a neat man who had been caring for my urinary problems a couple years and I went to see him after Micki called the office and told them it was an emergency and he needed to see me. After some discussion he decided to put me in the hospital so he could properly get me ready for an IVP, an Intravenous Pylegram, aka, a kidney X-ray. That night I discovered that "properly get me ready" meant about a three bag enema to totally clean out the bowel for a clear picture of the kidneys—God those X-ray tables are hard! I feared more for bruising my butt on the table than I did about the dye I was about to drink!

"Well, Doc," I said as Dr. Cowan came into my room with the results, "What did you fine out?" "We have to do another test, an ultra-sound test." "Why?" I replied with concern. "Your kidney is fine as we found no problems, but off to the right side of the picture there was something we could not identify; the ultra-sound should answer that question, so they will come up and get you when they are ready."

Soon the door opened and a pretty woman in her early twenties arrived at my bedside. "I'm here to take you down and do the ultra-sound test on you," she said. She got an orderly and they helped me get on a cart to go for the procedure. Suddenly I felt like I had died and gone to heaven as this beautiful young lady put (rubbed) some kind of oily substance on my lower chest and belly. This made the test equipment move smoothly over the area so she could get pictures of it. Back in the room a while later I snoozed a little and was awakened by Dr. Cowan, "Jim," he said, "I have the results of the last test." "Ok, lay it on me," I resigned. "You have a gall bladder full of rocks," he went on, "And you will need surgery to remove it." "Gall Bladder?" I exclaimed louder than usual, "So I been having gall bladder attacks all this time and since I don't feel the pain like able-bodied people do, that explains all the sweats for no obvious reason!" "Who would you like to do the operation?" he asked. Reviewing my limited knowledge of the surgeons in the hospital there, I quickly answered, "Dr. Crockett." He was a young, good surgeon with a great bedside manner that made anyone feel comfortable when they were about to "go under the knife". "I will contact him and arrange for him to stop in to see you yet today." Dr. Cowan assured me as he left the room.

Cheerful, like I always saw him, Dr. Crockett dropped in to arrange my surgery. "I hope you can do it soon," I said after we talked a bit about the procedure. "How does tomorrow morning sound?" he said, "Someone cancelled, so I am available and if we can get it scheduled in the operating room, we'll do it first thing in the morning." "Very good," is all I had to say. His last words as he left the room were, "I'll have the anesthesiologist see you yet tonight to get things started."

The worst part about surgery or any other procedures in the hospital that require the patient to have an IV put in his body is

"Putting in the IV." One time it hurt so badly I had "referred" pain in my gut. That nurse tried about five times and she never could find the vein in the back of my hand or above my wrist. I was ready to cry when she finally said she was going to get the one nurse who can put in the IV or it can't be done. She came in and seconds later without any pain the IV was in. I could have kissed her, but I didn't even try!

I woke up in my room after surgery and felt no pain (why should I?). I had a good bandage on the five inch incision (unlike the one inch cut left by laser surgery today) and after the doctor came by to see how I was doing, he said I could get out of bed later that night and roll up and down the hall for some exercise. I told the doctor that to get into the chair I would have to reach across to the right armrest and it would put a strain on the incision. He said it was stapled together good and that should not hurt it. So, later that night I got up in my chair (no pain, can't feel as his cut was below the last rib on the right side) and got some good exercise going up and down the hall about three times. The next day I was discharged and only had to go back to get staples removed. I healed up fine. No more sweats from the gall bladder, but it does change one's digestion of certain foods—especially oily foods, when it's gone. Forty-one years old and my gall bladder was gone.

Chapter Thirty-Nine

Lou Reed, R.N., introduced herself to me at the time when I was having my gall bladder removed at Malone Hogan Hospital in Big Spring, Texas. One day when she brought my medicine in to me she said, "Do you like to fish?" "I sure do," I said with the look on my face as though I was about to hear some good news. "Well, my husband, Sam, and I have a farm south of town and have a catfish pond out in back a ways from the house," she went on, "and you are welcome to come down and fish there any time you wish as long as you call first." "Great," was all I could say at first, but later I thanked her for the opportunity. "We'd prefer that you come with someone and not fish there alone, just for your safety," she added.

One summer day that was not so hot I called to get permission to fish there at "Sam's Pond" after work. I got the OK and arranged for Nat Hart to go with me, which he did. I had previously caught a couple five pound catfish in that body of water that was about thirty yards wide and sixty yards long. Lou asked me in a slightly upset manner, "How come you catch five pounders and all I can catch is the one to two pound fish?" I said, "The bigger the bait, the bigger the fish!" Mostly she and her friends and relatives used chicken liver that they dried in the sun a little and got it to stay hooked on the hook in a glob about the size of a half-dollar. I went to a bait shop and got minnows that were usually three to four inches long and used them. Maybe, just maybe, that's why I caught bigger fish.

Anyway, Nat and I were fishing and I was in my usual spot on the north end of the "tank" (all farm ponds are called tanks in west Texas, I think) which was the slightly deeper end. I had my six gallon bucket beside my right caster and my rod and reel was resting across the top of it. For some reason that time I had turned the crank after casting and forgot to push the release button before I lay it down. I was not too concerned as I fished with a float so my first indication of a bite would be the float moving and going down. I must have looked away for a minute or less and when I glanced back my rod jerked toward the water, I leaned to catch it and suddenly it jerked again out of my reach. I hollered at Nat who was fishing on the west side forty yards away, but he could not get to me before the reel went totally out of sight. We both casted a little with my other rod and him with one of his, but no luck catching the line.

The next day at work Nat came in to see me at my office and held up a piece of welding rod bent into the shape of a large treble hook. The hooks were about two inches from the center "post" and stuck up about two inches also. "Do you think this will work to catch your line and retrieve your rod and reel?" He had the "hook" attached to about one hundred feet of nylon rope that was very thin (maybe less than one-eighth inch). "Looks like a plan to me," I said with some renewed enthusiasm. "Are you free to go out and try to get my equipment tonight?" I asked with anticipation. "Sure, let's do it," he said equally excited about his newly developed tool.

Lou gave me the OK to come on down after I told her my "fish" story from the night before. Since it stayed light until about nine o'clock that time of year, we would have ample time to try to complete our mission. After grabbing a bite of supper, Nat and I went to the "tank." Like a cowboy with a lariat, Nat swung the treble hook around and around letting loose of it at the right time to have it go out into the water some twenty yards or so from us. About the fourth "cast" (toss) he felt a little resistance and said, "Jim, I think I hooked the line!" He was as excited as a kid with a new toy! He pulled slowly and kept feeling the slight jerking on the line. Finally, the treble hook came out of the water with the line draped over it. Then the excitement really started. He pulled on one side of the line and felt the dead weight of the rod and reel. He pulled on the other side of the line and he felt a tugging resistance. Then, he focused on the dead weight and hand over hand he pulled in the rod and reel. Next, he tugged on the other line and felt some tugging back, but it was not a snag. He jerked a couple times on the line and suddenly the line came tight in his hands and he, realizing what was happening, exclaimed, "That fish is still on the line!" "It's a nice one too," he added and realizing that he got the landing net and gave it to me so I could hand it to him when he got the fish close to the bank. He landed it and it was another five pound catfish like some others I had caught in the past.

The biggest catfish that I ever caught there at "Sam's Pond" was an eight pounder, but it was not near the excitement I had with Nat or with David Keyes one night. David and I went to "Sam's Pond" on a night after work when I should have stayed home. It was HOT and I mean HOT. David and I got to the pond and as usual I parked the car about fifteen feet from my fishing spot. We were fishing and not having much luck when I began to get overheated—fortunately my air conditioner was working on my car. I called David, who was fishing about where Nat had been the night I "lost" my rod to the catfish, to come and help me get into the A/C to get cool. He was always concerned and at times almost over concerned, so he left his lines and came running to help. I got into the car and David, who usually would rather talk than fish, started up a conversation about something. He glanced over toward where his floats had been located and yelled, "Hey, my float is gone!" A fish had bit on his minnow and dragged the float about twenty yards toward me and it was near the bank. David couldn't simply walk along the bank and reel up his slack line before trying to catch the fish due to four or five willow trees that grew right at the edge of the water or slightly above it. So he leaned out over the water with the rod tip and tightened the line which caused the fish to move out toward the middle of the pond.

Then the battle was on and David fought and fought that fish before he finally landed it. It must have been close to thirty inches long and weighed ten pounds!! Biggest one any of us ever caught there! Thanks to Sam and Lou my friends and I had some really fun fishing times at their tank.

It must have been in the spring of the year when my brother, Don, and I went out to the catfish pond to fish. It could not have been summer 'cause Don would not go from Wisconsin to Texas heat unless he had lost his mind—his comfort zone is around sixty degrees! Lou and some of her kinfolk were fishing, but she allowed us to fish since Don had come all the way from Wisconsin and he could fish there without getting a Texas license. In Texas you can use four "poles" for fishing and I had four so Don used two and I used two. We did not have much luck and the only positive thing was that it didn't get too hot and we had a chance to visit without much interruption of biting fish!

We had some bites as we were running low on minnows so I took a big dead one and put it on my hook. Lou and her group were gone to the house so we had the whole "tank" to ourselves. I casted way out—about a hundred feet—and the float landed a couple feet from the east shoreline with the minnow on the bottom of the pond. I told Don, "I'm just going to sit back and leave that dead minnow lay there until a "cat" finds it." Don replied, "Might as well, everything else has not worked very well." The float lay there tipped on its side and motionless until, suddenly, it slowly moved a foot or so away from the shoreline. Then BANG, like a gun going off, it shot out and down. "Hey, Don, something found my dead minnow," I yelled out. I picked up my rod and reel, pulled in some slack line and gave it a big heave when I thought I had enough tension to set the hook. I did and the fight was on. After about a ten minute battle filled with me trying every fishing skill I had to keep it out of any trees, brush or weeds, Don scooped up the six pound catfish in our net. That was about 2 p.m. and shortly after that we went "to the house" as they say in west Texas when they go home.

Don cleaned the big fish that afternoon and put it in saltwater in the refrigerator for overnight. We always did that with fish 'cause mom always did it and mom always did it 'cause grandma always did it—you know the story about the bread. Anyway, the next day Micki baked the whole fish in the oven basting it with lemon juice periodically. That night for dinner we ate catfish and more catfish along with other things. The next day or two we ate leftover catfish and it was better than after just baked!

Chapter Forty

Summer was still the season when I was looking through some magazines about needs of disabled persons and I ran across something that might make my mobility more enjoyable and less strain on my body. It was a Surry, made by American Tricycloped Corp. of Boise, Idaho. It would replace the need for my car when weather was dry and with the limited amount of rainfall in west Texas (about thirteen inches a year) dry weather was common. It was a vehicle powered by a Honda scooter (50 cc.) engine and from the engine forward it was that Honda scooter. However the seat post was cut down to the top of the engine and framework was built on each side. A rear axle was mounted down from the side frames and two tires with about fifteen inch outside diameter were used on the back. A lever allowed for the (about) five foot aluminum ramp tracks to be lower and raised from outside or inside the vehicle. The gas tank and oil reservoir were made of some form of plastic and mounted in the walls of it. The gas tank held about a gallon of gas, good for about fifty miles, and two quarts of oil could be stored waiting to seep down and mix with the gas in the two-stroke engine. There was a fiberglass framework over the top of the engine extending forward and back making a three foot by four foot platform for the chair to ride on. It had a centrifugal clutch so it needed no shifting. Turn on the key, rev up the engine and "hold on to your hat." Well, with a top speed of thirty miles per hour down hill with a tail wind, I guess you won't need to hold on to your hat very hard! I bought the Surry.

The Surry

Nat Hart called me at my office one day at work and asked me to join him at the local shooting range. He and Jay Calvin were both into a group called Mountainmen and they did things like throw axes and shoot muzzle load rifles. I had about a half tank of gas in my Surry and I had driven it a few weeks, just enough to know what kind of gas mileage I could get. I told Nat that I would meet him at the range, which was out toward Andrews, Texas. He went home after work that night to get his rifle and he passed me on the way to the range. It was thirteen miles to the range so I hoped when I got there that I would have enough gas to get home.

Nat in Mountain Man Outfit

Nat taught me all the ins and outs of shooting a muzzle load rifle and after he shot a few times he handed it to me and told me to load it and shoot it. Since I have no trunk balance lifting a rifle to my shoulder and aiming it would cause me to roll out of my wheelchair head first, I definitely needed a "rest." I put a couple sand bags and a towel over the splintery wood of the gun rest and after loading put a cap in to fire it. The target was a bowling pin, all white with the red ring on the neck of it, and it was about ninety yards away. I took careful aim and hit it tipping it over.

Then, I shot three more times hitting two of them. Nat said, "Man, you sure beat me," after he hit only one out of four. Remember, he was shooting free hand and I used a rest! I think he was just trying to give me a little ego trip—helped my confidence! Then I drove home and got within a half-mile of the·house when I ran out of gas. A nice person came along and went three blocks to the gas station and brought back a gallon of gas for the Surry.

Shooting a muzzleload rifle was fun, but I was not going to be overly consumed by it in my leisure time. Around that time, David Keyes and I had been doing some fishing at Colorado City Lake and were tired of fishing from the shore and watching others come in to dock their boat having a stringer full of fish. So, we decided to get a boat and we found one for sale that seemed to fit my plans for stability after some medications. Getting me and the 'chair into a boat that is in the water and very unstable is nearly impossible—takes at least two people to do it and then it is a scary experience. I did it once with two guys and was never so glad to be back on land!!

On the sixteen foot V-hull boat that we bought I wanted to construct a swivel seat (like the ones on bass boats) that was mounted on a post that had a base as wide as the boat seat (ten inches) and could be slid on rails from side to side of the boat. That way I could transfer into the boat going to my strong side (right) and then transfer out of the boat on the opposite side still going to my strong side. How will I ever find a way to get this done?

Chuck Preston and I were good friends after he joined the Social Work staff as BSSH a year or so after I moved to Texas. He was a quadriplegic with a C-5 spinal cord injury from a diving accident. He was one of the people who had a strange ability that reinforces how each injury is different, even if at the same level of the spinal cord—he could stand up for a short time once someone helped him up to that position. He reminded me of Vince Falardeau who used to stand up on his leg spasms while holding onto the window behind his study desk at the dormitory at UI.

278

Anyway, Chuck had a good friend, Marv, who was skilled in welding and we got him to weld the trailer hitch to my car as well as weld the necessary things to mount the swivel seat I bought at a second hand store for only a few bucks. We went fishing in it once and it was OK, but somehow never got to go again. I sold the boat years later for half the price we paid for it (not including the costs of the modifications).

During the years of having the Surry I got a letter from Mason Shoe Company in Wisconsin and the invitation to become a salesman of their quality footwear. I thought about it and decided to do it after thinking of all the people I knew at church and work. Most of these people fall in the category of ones we say "Hi" to once or more times a week, but never take or have time the time to talk with them. I felt that by selling these shoes it would "force me" to get out and spend a little time with my many acquaintances; AND it would be so simple without having to get in and out of my car as I would have had to do before getting the Surry. I recall I sold about two or three hundred pair of shoes over the four of five years I was actively selling in my spare time, but my main focus was not the income from it—it was the socialization.

I rode that Surry to work, to church, to the stores and all around town with a couple short jogs out of town. I put fourteen thousand miles on that scooter during the four years until one day I went to a motorcycle rally at the local City Park. At the rally I met a man from over by Abilene who was riding a Goldwing with a sidecar equipped with all the controls in the front of the sidecar. He was paraplegic in a wheelchair who had a low back spinal cord injury. The sidecar had a three foot by four foot steel plate and a short, fold-up ramp made of steel grate. He rolled right in, lifted the ramp, turned the key to start it and drove it from the sidecar with the cycle only providing the power. He gave me the name and address of the man/company that made it and I rode off smiling in my scooter . . . more later.

1986 was the worst year of my thirty-six in a wheelchair. I got a superficial ulcer on my left glutial area (butt) and it progressively got worse. In October I had to have surgery at the local hospital and I had Dr. Crockett do it. He did a good job, but I could not get it all healed and then learned of a plastic surgeon who had had some good success with a procedure called a flap rotation. This doctor was at a major hospital in Lubbock and after looking at my problem he advised that the special surgery was necessary. I had already missed a month or more of work and knew that I could not get the ulcer healed without his help so I agreed to have it done.

In this procedure the doctor cuts out any bad tissue around the ulcer area and cuts a line down the back side of the thigh, allowing him to move part of the muscle tissue from the hamstring muscle area (back of thigh) up to fill in the area over and around the "sitting bone." After a couple weeks or so on a special floatation bed, I was allowed to go home with orders to stay in bed until it was all healed over. The good friends at church made the hundred mile trip to Lubbock possible. The Pastor was also a Chaplain at the Veteran's Hospital and he borrowed a stretcher from there. With help from church members, he put me on the stretcher on my bed and they carried me out to the church van. Since the rear rows of seats were removed I could ride on my side or belly the whole distance without putting any pressure on the buttocks. Once at the hospital in Lubbock they got me transferred to one of their carts and took me to my room. The trip home was a reversal of going up there.

The next weeks and months were no fun for me or for Micki, as I got irritable at times from the cabin fever syndrome. She continued to work her regular schedule which was good as her normal routine after getting home around 8 a.m. was to sleep a few hours, run errands, cook supper and then sleep from about 6 p.m. to 10 p.m. before getting ready to go back to work at 11 p.m. Sometimes my requests for something to meet my needs (or desire at the moment) were at a bad time and I am sorry for those times. Thank God I healed up and could go back to work in the middle of April of 1987. Cope with adversity, life goes on.

One thing that I never did while working was call in sick just to miss work or misuse my vacation time. Yes, Micki was working and we had an income, but the fact that I had accumulated an enormous amount of sick leave and vacation time in the ten years I had worked there, allowed me to get my paycheck during nearly all of the six months I was off from work. Those items are fringe benefits, but when you need them they are lifesavers. Don't abuse yours; you never know what tomorrow may bring!

Mr. Gatewood retired and I had a new boss in 1986. She gained my respect early after she arrived on the scene. She was the late Dr. Ann Mann who was a psychologist with a PhD in some form of psychology. Our new Director of the Department was well organized, provided instruction when needed, used discipline as necessary and was upfront with me on all occasions. She was extremely intelligent yet did not flaunt it and seemed to have a very good understanding of my disability. She showed concern for me throughout my time of surgeries.

Later on during her four year term as our Director a new program was being implemented in some areas of mental illness treatment. It was called Psycho-Social Rehabilitation and a team of experts in mental health (some from Texas Dept. of Mental Health Mental Retardation Headquarters in Austin, TX) came to survey our hospital in relation to our readiness for the new program. For two hours each morning I was teaching classes in SLACS, the class I referred to previously. The surveyors came into my class with the intent to (as they told me later) stay a few minutes.

They were not in my class for more than thirty seconds until they realized that they could not be in my classroom just as spectators. The second question that I asked, after a brief explanation of the subject of the discussion for their benefit, was directed to one of the surveyors. Without excluding either my patient students or my visiting "students," within fifteen minutes I had directed at least one question to each of the visitors interspersed with questions to the patients. We had a great discussion and they did not leave until I looked at my watch and said, "Wow, it's 10:50, time to stop, any questions for me?" The surveyors left class saying, "Thanks, but we really stayed too long, we have other places to go, it was very interesting."

At the Summation Conference in the Chapel a couple days later I was "Proud as a Peacock" as the old saying goes! The head of the survey team was the Superintendent of a highly respected mental hospital in the middle of the United States. I was most proud because he was personal with me and suddenly I was somebody. He said, "Oh, Jim, I'm glad you are here," as he looked out to see me sitting fifty feet away in the isle directly in front of him, "Jim Potter is the best teacher I have ever seen in a mental health setting!!" One of the workers in Staff Development had his whole speech on the cassette she recorded and she made a copy for me to keep. Another thing I can listen to if and when I am "down" and need an ego boost!

Amy went to high school in Big Spring graduating in 1984 and then went on to a four-year college in Abilene, Texas. She was under some form of ROTC program studying to be a nurse and near the end of her training she had to have a session of "military" training; you know, out in the woods and weeds somewhere up in Oregon. Her commitment to the Government was to spend four years in the Army after her graduation from college, so she was eager to get into some of the things that would lie ahead of her. She went to the training session and after a few weeks came back home early as she had become extremely ill while out on maneuvers. It turned out that she had a severe allergy to many different grasses and weeds. She had claimed that she was allergic to grass when it came to mowing the lawn, but I was not so sure that she wasn't allergic to the lawn mower handle!! Sorry, Amy, now I know!

Chapter Forty-One

Early in 1988 I had been fishing a few times with either David Keyes or Jay Colvin or Nat Hart and had some good times. It was about the middle of May and I asked each of my friends if they wanted to go fishing with me on the Saturday just ahead. I had a real strong desire to go up to Lake Thomas near Snyder, Texas and none of my buddies were available to go with me. From previous trips I knew of a place where I could go and be able to get close enough to the water safely to fish by myself, and, be able to get back to my car without a winch.

It was fairly cool that morning when I got into my car about 7:30 a.m. to make the forty mile trip up to Lake Thomas, but the weather forecast was for a "high" of 105-110 degrees that day. I was actively fishing by 8:30 a.m. and caught a few doing the catch-and-release system. It didn't seem like I had been there long when I noticed I was starting to get warm. From previous experiences, except when I was sweating from the gall bladder attacks, once I started to get hot it wasn't long before I was too hot and had better get some way to cool down. I gathered up my poles and bait, put them in the trunk and got into the car. Just as I put the key in the ignition I remembered that I had recently had some trouble with the engine cutting out at times when I accelerated, but it just lurched ahead and kept on running. I prayed, Oh God, please make this car start.

The engine started without a hitch and I was on my way home.

My air conditioner was not working at that time and the temperature must have been in the upper nineties when I left the lake. I went out to the "Snyder Highway" and headed home. About halfway to Big Spring there is a huge valley with about a half mile forty-five degree hill on each side like a perfect "V". I went down the east side and was near eighty miles per hour when I hit the bottom giving me good momentum for the other side up hill. I got about three-fourth of the way up the west side when my car cut out and lurched and cut out and stalled! I coasted briefly but enough to get off the highway. At that time I was still fairly cool from using the "two-seventy" air conditioner (two windows down and seventy miles per hour)!

I don't know how many cars normally travel that road from noon to 1:00 p.m. on any given Saturday, but there seemed to be a real shortage that day. When I did see a car coming up behind me, I waved my white handkerchief frantically and just as they passed me I hollered out. As my body temperature went higher and higher about a dozen cars passed during the first half hour. Then a woman stopped, came over to the car and I told her my dilemma. She said she didn't think she could do much for me, but she told me she would go to Big Spring and get someone to come out and help me. I thanked her very much and felt that maybe, just maybe, I would not die out there with the sun blazing down on my car and temperatures in the sun must have been over one hundred twenty. In the car it had to be one hundred five. Not so sure that the woman would actually find someone to help me that Saturday, I continued to try to "flag down" anyone who would stop to help. Six or eight more cars came by in the next half hour and then the "Good Samaritans" stopped to help. I never did get their names, but they were four men who had been golfing at Snyder and they were on their way home to Odessa, Texas. My energy level was near zero by that time and I was burning up with fever. They helped me get my wheelchair out of the car, helped me into it and pushed me over to their caddy, that's Cadillac, not the one on the golf course. Air Conditioning NEVER felt so good, unless you remember the last time I was overheated! Just then a wrecker arrived on the scene (the nice woman had found someone after all) and they towed my car down to the shop of my regular mechanic. The men took me home as the wrecker followed with my car until he got to the mechanic's shop. Diagnosis was rust from the gas tank getting into the gas line and blocking it. I got a new gas tank a few days later and was thankful I had my Surry to drive to and from work. Good people help me overcome another adversity.

I only had about a quarter mile of highway to travel on my way to work, but at times it was dangerous with my Surry only going twenty-some miles per hour. It seemed that the cars wanted to be going faster—why not, it was in a fifty-five mph zone from Rip Griffin's Truck Stop to BSSH. That fact made me more eager to get a cycle like the one I saw at the rally back in April. Time to call the builder of it!

I called information to get the number for Tom Turning, Turning Enterprises, Valley Center, Kansas and then called him. After some discussion about my extent of disability, he suggested, "It would be a lot safer for you if you could get a cycle with an automatic transmission." "Automatic transmission," I said, "Didn't know they made such a thing!" "Sure, Honda made one back in 1978," he went on, "See if you can find one of them and buy it, then call me back." "Ok," I added. He then went on about the cost of having it made and about how long it would take him and his son (who was being groomed to take over the business when Tom retired) to make the sidecar and mount it on the cycle.

I knew a few people who had cycles in town and they sent me to a man I had seen before, but never met. The man said he had one that his wife rode some—10,700 miles to be exact—and it was for sale for thirteen hundred dollars. That was the price he came down to after I told him he could keep the fairing as I would not need it or want it on the bike—just be something else Tom Turning would have to take off. I bought the cycle and the man rode it to my house, then I took him home in my car.

June of 1988 was "right around the corner" so I called Tom

Turning and made plans with him to put on the sidecar while I was on vacation in Wisconsin. I had accumulated at least two weeks vacation time by then so I took off for two weeks to "kill two birds with one stone." I borrowed a trailer from my friend, Maurice Smith, and Smitty helped load the cycle along with technical assistance and some good muscles provided by my Surry mechanic from the local Honda Dealership, Cory Beevers. They secured the cycle on the trailer with chains and straps so it would not move in transit.

My brother, Don, had made plans to take off some vacation time while I was in Wisconsin so we could do some fishing and I could stay with them while up there. I also made arrangements to stay with Dennis Degner in a suburb of Kansas City the second night of the trip. The Thursday morning arrived and I took off from Big Spring headed for a familiar place to spend that night—Holiday Inn in Lawton, Oklahoma. After a restful night I headed on to Valley Center, KS on Friday getting there about noon or so. Tom had some other cycle that he was preparing with sidecars so I rolled on one of them so they could see better what my needs were in terms of space. Once that was completed I left and arrived at Degner's place around 6 p.m. He helped me, pulled me up the steps to get into his home and ordered a pizza for our supper. We ate the delicious Italian dish and I glanced around his abode keeping quiet about my observations. It appeared that some of the corners to get to a bedroom were a little sharp for my 'chair and the hallway looked a little narrow, like they all were in homes built during a certain period of time.

"Dennis, ol' buddy, Thank you for the good supper and the opportunity to stay at your house, but I am not the least bit tired and I think I will head up the road toward Hillsboro. If I get sleepy I guarantee I will pull over to the side of the road or find a rest area to get some sleep." "Well, since you said it that way, I guess I will let you go on, but you be sure you don't fall asleep again while driving." "OK, I won't, just help me back down these steps and I'll be on my way." It was about 7:30 p.m. when I rolled onto Interstate 35 North. Next stop, Des Moines, Iowa for gas and then I should be able to go all the way to Don's house outside of Hillsboro without stopping except for sleep.

From the Interstate I saw a sign on top of a service station and the name matched my credit card. Getting off the interstate and going only a few blocks put me at the station where I got a nice person to fill the tank, paid for it with the credit card and went back on the road again. I was somewhere north of Ames, Iowa when I began to feel sleepy and looked for the rest area sign. Shortly, the sign read "Rest Area One Mile" and I whispered to myself, "Thank God." After pulling into the rest area and shutting off the engine, I lay over in the front seat with my head on the passenger side and using a jacket for a pillow I soon fell fast asleep. My watch said 2 a.m. just before I lay down. Suddenly I woke up to the sound of a huge semi going behind me, sat up and looked at my watch—2:15 a.m. Power nap? I guess that's what they call it; I felt refreshed!

After sitting up and adjusting my feet and legs so I did not have my left foot under the brake pedal or my right foot on the gas pedal, I started the car and got back on the Interstate. I was well into Minnesota before it started to get light and my attention focused as much on the sides of the road as the road itself due to the strong possibility of deer crossing in front of me or, God forbid, me hitting a deer. I hadn't traveled far in semi-lighted conditions when I saw, laying on the side of the road, the results of some unfortunate motorist who had hit a deer. My eyes seemed to take a sharper look for deer after that, but I didn't see any live ones that night/morning.

Don and Mary had no idea I would be arriving so soon as they expected me to be there sometime around 7 p.m., so I really did surprise them when I rang their doorbell about 7:15 a.m., nearly twelve hours earlier than anticipated. "What's for breakfast?" I asked a half-asleep Mary when she opened the door. "Nothing yet," she said jokingly and followed with "Come on in." "Take your time, I got all day," I added, "Go back to bed if you want to, just show me the coffee first!!" Soon she and Don came down and we had a nice visit during breakfast—well, I was so wound up I did most of the talking about the trip, the excitement of the cycle and the value of my "power nap." After the meal I was ready to sleep a few hours and I did without any trouble.

The visit went too fast as I was able to see most of my relatives that live near Hillsboro and some friends from the past plus do a little fishing with Don. Mary, Don and I did get in some card games during the evenings. Soon it was time for me to go back to Texas. Tom Turning had told me that he had planned a fishing trip in Canada so he was not sure that he would have my sidecar on the bike by the time I went home. He instructed me to call him before I left Hillsboro, which I did and discovered the job was not done yet. I told him that since he had told me it would be done in our original agreement, he should bring the bike partway to Texas when he did have it done. A few weeks later Tom Greiner went with me to Lawton, OK to meet Mr. Turning and get the new machine. I wanted Tom with me to help me stay awake as it was going to be a long day. I used the Honda a few weeks and noted some minor problems that Cory Beevers corrected quite easily, but in September I was having some electrical problems with it. Once Cory identified that I needed a new stater put in and he did it for me, the bike ran smooth as a top for a long time with normal maintenance like oil changes.

Honda 750 Cycle—all controls in sidecar

That fall I developed a superficial ulcer on my buttocks and I was VERY scared that I might be in for more problems like I had two years earlier. Fortunately, there was a new Chaplain at BSSH and he was a paraplegic in a wheelchair. After discussion he showed me a cushion that he was using called a RoHo cushion. He said he had an extra used one that I could try to see if I liked it. It was a "low profile" cushion with air filled cells that were about three inches high up from the base. I liked the cushion, but due to my extremely pointed ischial bones I needed about another inch of protection. Thus, I got a "high profile" RoHo that gave me the cushioning that my tender buttocks needed. I have been using that cushion type for the past fifteen years without any problems of decubitus ulcers. The cushions are expensive (about three hundred dollars each) and insurance does not pay for them. It bewilders me that insurance won't pay that price to prevent ulcers, but they often do pay for most of the expenses for ulcer surgery—sometimes twenty to thirty thousand dollars. Doesn't make sense to me!!

By 1990 the Psycho Social Rehabilitation Program was being developed and our department was losing Dr. Mann as she became the Head of that Program Hospital-wide.

That meant that her job was open and I applied for it along with two psychologists who worked at the Hospital. After fourteen years in the Department I thought I was fairly well groomed for the Director job, but I didn't get the promotion. In a couple months I saw the direction that the Rehabilitation Program was going with all the new concepts, meetings off campus and other things; it was then that I realized that I could not physically or emotionally or mentally handle the job and I was VERY glad that Marilyn Clark had the job and not me. She did a hell of a lot better job in the position than I could have ever done! I commend her for her fortitude.

In the summer of 1990 Micki was having all kinds of troubles with her allergies and the air conditioning caused her arthritis to flare up severely, so when the chance came up for her to go to Colorado to house-sit for an old friend, I told her to go ahead. So she spent the summer in Colorado and was very happy doing it. Our marriage seemed to be slipping apart and we did not have the caring for each other and loving relationship that we once had. I feel that it probably was mostly my fault. She had also joined the Civitan Club but often did not go to the meetings due to it being during her sleep time. I was also a member of the local Association for Retarded Citizens (ARC) a group that promotes independence and provides help when possible for persons with retardation. It was about this same time that ARC decided to sponsor weekly bingo games as a means of making some money for our projects. Then, I began playing bingo one night a week, then two nights a week and nearly got addicted to it. It also was costing me about twenty dollars a night and I rarely won more than an occasional fifteen or twenty dollar game.

In natural progression I started doing something at which I thought I would be very good—calling bingo for pay. What a tradeoff! If I called bingo, I could make some money and would not be spending money by playing; sounds like a win-win situation to me. I started calling by substituting for a man named Bill and I did a good job, so when a new bingo establishment was starting up in Big Spring, the Director asked me to work for him, which I did. Eventually I was working Thursday night, Friday night, Saturday afternoon and Sunday afternoon. I developed a number of friendships through the bingo and unfortunately, for my marriage sake, I was unconsciously making distance between Micki and me. In September of 1991 she moved to Colorado and I stayed in Texas. In 1993 we came to an equitable agreement and I filed for a divorce, which was final in December of that year. She is happier, I am happier and we are still friends. I come to the conclusion that some people (me included) should never get married. Never again, that's for sure!

Chapter Forty-Two

Nat Hart and I had been fishing at Colorado City Lake a few times with only fair success when he had an idea for something different and possibly more fishing success. He introduced me to Stan Partee, son-in-law of Dorothy Garrett and the man who made all the decisions about the operations on the Garrett Ranch. Stan and Nat had gone to high school together and were still good friends about a dozen years later. The Ranch covered twenty-six sections; yes I said sections, which is over sixteen thousand acres. It had three or four small manmade lakes on it and some were stocked with largemouth bass. Nat acquired permission for us to go out there fishing. The first day we drove out through the pastureland to a lake and we saw a deer run freely over the meadows. At times the fishing was quite good and other times just fair or poor. The lake was fairly narrow, about a city block wide, and was a good quarter mile long. We caught a few twelve, fourteen and fifteen inch bass. After a few times going there with Nat, Stan said I could fish there any time I wanted and with any of my fishing buddies as long as I always asked permission so I would not interfere with other things that might be going on at the Ranch on the weekend.

One weekend I got the permission to fish at the Ranch and I took David Keyes with me. We fished just above a dam and David helped me get down to the water and back up to the car. The fishing was slow early in the morning (we always had to go early due to the temperature getting too hot by 11 a.m.), but about 10:30 a.m. I had a good hit and it went over to a log and unhooked itself as only bass can do so well! Surprised was the look on my face when I casted out another nice minnow and the hungry bass hit that one also. I set the hook and the battle was on. David was more excited than I was as he nearly fell into the water trying to net my fish. It was a nice one—biggest one I had ever caught at that stage in my life, nineteen and a half inches long and four and a half pounds. We had to go to one of the local grocery stores, put the fish in a plastic bag and weigh it there, as we could not get an accurate weight on my rusty old hand scale. That was my personal best bass, until the summer of 2002 when Don and I went to a cranberry farm lake near Tomah, Wisconsin. We fished in an area where they said mostly big northern pike were being caught and I hooked and battled a twenty-one inch, five pound bass. I have it mounted on my wall.

My biggest Bass

I met Gary Wollenzien, his wife, Bonnie, and their two boys at church one Sunday. They had moved to Big Spring where he was the new YMCA Director. With my background in physical education and recreation we had a good many common interests.

It was some time later when I found out that he also enjoyed fishing. By that time he had met Stan Partee through business ties and Stan being active at the YMCA. Gary said that Stan had given him the same permission as I had to fish at the Ranch.

I think it was the second time Gary and I went fishing at my favorite lake that we got run out by the man renting the land to graze his cattle. We don't know where the man had his tractor or truck parked, but he came tromping down through the brush like he intended to throw us in the water. He was just intent on getting over to give Gary a piece of his mind—and he did! Unfortunately, Gary and I did not know what to do, but due to the man's anger, we had better leave before the guy gets a gun!! When we told Stan the situation he said, "No, that man has no control over you fishing there, I will set him straight and don't let this keep you from going fishing again out there."

The last time I fished at the Ranch was the real gem of all. Gary and I went out there, did some good fishing and caught a few that were keepers. When it began to get hot we decided to get out of there before I was overheated. We rolled up our lines and Gary loaded the trunk of my car while I got in and slid over to the driving position. I pulled my coin purse from my shirt pocket (always carry keys and coins in that leather pouch in shirt pocket due to the difficulty of getting my hand into any pants pockets) opened it and got the car keys. I stuck the key in the ignition, turned it and—NOTHING! It was like the battery was totally dead, but the interior lights were on when the door opened, so it was not that. After discussion Gary said, "I'll just have to walk to the house to get some help." I wished him God's speed and suggested that, if possible, could he please "hurry back."

In spite of what Gary had ahead of him, he was still concerned about me. He asked, "Are you going to be alright here in the heat?" A bit sarcastically yet somewhat realistically I said, "Well, if I'm dead when you get back, you'll know I wasn't OK." At my direction Gary wet the towel I had in the trunk and put me in the shade where I could try to stay cool as long as possible and

293

hopefully until he returned. It was "only" about two miles or so to the house and home of the caretaker that lived there, so Gary would get to the house in about a half hour and be back to me in less than an hour—wishful thinking on my part.

Gary never told me but I believe he was a city boy growing up. As he walked along the same path that we had traveled by car out to the fishing spot he ran into a herd of the cattle that grazed in the area. They were congregated by the gate that he wanted to climb over and, as Gary related to me later, he was very scared of the chance that a Brahma bull would attack him. Needless to say, he was not very comfortable around cattle!!

Gary got to the caretaker's house unscathed, but no one was home. He looked around and saw a "cowboy" who was a hired hand working for the cattle owner, that same cattle owner that had chased Gary and I off the land previously. The cowboy was fixing a tire and when Gary told him of our plight, he bawked and told Gary how he could get fired if he didn't keep working. Gary was VERY aware of the guy's boss's temper, but finally convinced the cowboy to take his pickup and Gary out to get me. All the way to the fishing hole the cowboy constantly reminded Gary about how he could get fired for "doing this," but he drove on.

The cowboy stopped the pickup where Gary suggested and Gary jumped out to see me smile at his arrival. The cowboy sat in the truck and did not lift a finger as Gary struggled with my help to get me up that extra two feet higher than a car seat into the truck seat. Gary could not believe it—the non-help from the cowboy! Gary put my 'chair in the back of the truck and we went to the ranch house.

With the cowboy complaining all the way we made it to the ranch house and he went happily back to work on his tasks. It was about one hundred five or one hundred ten degrees in the shade by this time and after unloading from the truck I was able to get to sit under a big shade tree while Gary went to look for a towel to hold more water and aid in cooling me down. The Ranch had a swimming pool and bathhouse, which Gary found open.

He borrowed two towels from there and wet them before he brought them to me. There was no access to a phone, the cowboy went off driving something other than the pickup and there we sat hoping that the caretaker and his wife would come home. After a few minutes, Gary said, "This is ridiculous, I better do something." I said, somewhat jokingly, "It's only two or three miles to Forsan, you need to take another hike?" Suddenly, Gary got up and walked to the pickup, looked in and saw the keys were still in the ignition. "Do I dare steal this truck?" he asked with the 'I've never stole anything in my life' tone in his voice! "You'll only be borrowing it," I reassured him and squelched his guilt somewhat.

Gary took the pickup and drove to the little store in Forsan where he called the church in Big Spring. The Vicar answered the phone and in a few minutes he was on his way to meet Gary in Forsan. From Forsan he followed Gary out to the Ranch. While Gary was gone the towels kept me cool enough that I did not get overheated, but I was sure glad to see them drive in to get me. Once in the Vicar's car and on our way to Big Spring, I said to Gary, "See, I told you that you were only borrowing that pickup!" With concern again Gary asked, "What are you going to do about your car?" I replied, "Well, if we are still friends after all this, I hope that you can drive out to the car on Monday morning with the wrecker following you so they can find the car and tow it back to get it fixed." He said, "Sure I can do that." "Great," I added.

If I had consulted with one of my mechanic friends before calling the wrecker, I probably could have avoided that bother and expense. When my mechanic checked out the car he found that the reason it was "dead" was that the starter relay was shot and in a few minutes he replaced it with a new one and zoom, zoom, zoom the car was running again. Saved from another adversity!

Chapter Forty-Three

Work was going along at a regular pace as I was teaching SLACS classes and supervising Recreation Therapy in 1992. I found that living alone gave me the privilege of cooking anything I wanted for my suppers. I don't know how my boss and other working women with husbands and families can work hard for eight or nine hours and when home prepare a meal for the family. When I got home after work I had no desire to fix a meal—even a can of soup and a hamburger sandwich seemed like too much work!! "Hello restaurants. I am in your business for you to serve me. Thank you." I ate most of my meals in restaurants while living alone in Big Spring.

In June of that year a female friend was at my house delivering some food for me to eat as I was in bed having some physical problems of unknown origin. I had missed a couple days of work and she had been so kind to me by going out to get food those days and on the weekend. On Saturday I had some more problems sweating and thought it was more urinary bladder problems like I have often had over the years. At least I knew it wasn't my gall bladder since I no longer had it! I wasn't very hungry lying in bed all the time, but when Sunday arrived my friend called to see what I would like for food to eat. She insisted that I should eat something, so she made some soup and brought it to me around four o'clock. I ate the meal and we visited for a while until she said, "You really should call the hospital and go into the emergency room to get checked out—you are sweating like an old work horse." I finally agreed and called them to say I was soon to be on my way to the hospital. My friend wanted me to ride with her due to me being weak, but it would be too hard to get into her little car, so I rode my cycle. More adversity at age 49!

Soon after arriving in the ER the doctor checked me as they normally do and then sent me up to a room. In the room I was soon greeted with the X-ray man and the Electro-Cardiogram machine. The next thing I knew was that three men were pushing my bed down the hall and they didn't stop until I was in ICU, Intensive Cardiology Unit! "You have had a mild heart attack," was the doctor's message when he came to my bedside. "We are going to keep you here a couple days to get you on some medication and run more tests." Soon I was regulated on heart medicine and they had made an appointment for me to see a cardiologist in Midland, Texas a couple of weeks later. Just like the gall bladder problem, the sweats were trying to tell me something bad!

The first visit with the cardiologist in Midland led to arrangements for me to have an angiogram done at Midland Memorial Hospital, Midland, Texas. I did the necessary fasting and arrived (drove my car) at the 7:00 a.m. appointment with a nurse. The IV was inserted with ease and I lay on a bed waiting for them to take me down to the cardiology procedure room for testing. I was highly impressed with the IV monitor that I could watch while the dye was showing me and the doctor how my heart arteries/veins looked. To my untrained eye it was hard to see the abnormality, but the doctor pointed to a spot that was about ninety-eight percent blocked. "Oh, yes, I see it," I told the doctor. "Now," he said, "Do you want me to do the angioplasty to open up that blood line now or should I schedule you to have it done next week?" "No time like the present, no need to come here another day as long as you can do it now, go to it," I said eager to have it done and not have to come back again to go through the preparatory procedures. On the monitor I could see the thin catheter moving through the blood tubes until it got to the joint where the doctor began to pack the plaque against the walls.

After the angioplasty I was taken to a bed in the cardio-care area where I rested for four or five hours allowing the hole where the catheter was inserted (in the groin area) to heal over so I could drive home. In normal situations someone else has to drive the car as an able-bodied person would have to move the right leg often from brake to accelerator; however, since I use hand—controls I was allowed to drive home by myself. The next day I went to work just like nothing had happened, but I knew my blood was running better in my heart. About a year or so later a test showed that I needed another angioplasty but the good news was that it was not in the same spot as the first one; it was about one inch away and the first angioplasty was holding very well.

During a check-up with my cardiologist in 1994 we discussed my job working with mental patients and stress involved. He recommended that, if it was possible for me to live financially with Social Security Disability and Disability Retirement income, it would be best for my health to retire from all jobs. I checked into what I had paid into both retirement and Social Security and discovered I could make it financially.

Chapter Forty-Four

August 31, 1994 arrived before I knew it and the Department had planned a party to honor me for my eighteen-plus years working there at BSSH and to wish me well. Tears came to my eyes as I realized the finality of it all when the Superintendent handed me the paper showing my time of employment there, shook my hand and thanked me for my contributions to the patients. Then, the tears really flowed steadily when one of the patients who had been in my classes came up to me and presented a plaque that said, THANKS FOR THE MANY VALUABLE LESSONS. I treasure that even more than the letter of Commendation from the Vice President at the University of Iowa. I also received a little booklet with notes on each page from the fellow employees that knew me giving me encouragement for the days ahead.

It was over! Nearly twenty-four years had passed since I took that first job as a disabled worker in the Rehabilitation Hospital in Chicago. Bad and good times were weaved together throughout those years, but mainly the GOOD ones stand out! Without a POSITIVE ATTITUDE I could not have done many of the things— as a matter of fact, without my POSITIVE ATTITUDE I probably would have been DEAD a long time ago! I went home to an empty house and in a couple months my thoughts were directed to the value of family and I began to make plans to return to the old "stomping grounds."

In the spring of 1995 I contacted a realtor and put my house up for sale. When May arrived there was some talk of a man (disabled from war and in a wheelchair) and his family being interested in buying my accessible home. Many things had to be ironed out and when dealing with the Government we all know that takes a long time. The potential buyer was a Disabled Veteran and applied for some Government help in the purchase. In view of some delay in selling the house I made plans to go to Wisconsin and spend the summer near my relatives. Don had checked on a place where I could live independently, but after further discussion with me about the place we discovered it would not work for me. Then, Don and Mary invited me to live with them while I was in Wisconsin waiting for word on the sale of my house.

I contacted Smitty to see if I could borrow his trailer again to haul my cycle to Wisconsin. I figured that if my house sold before I needed to return to Texas in the fall, I would need to haul some of my belongings in a rental trailer and I could not pull two trailers with my car. Cory Beevers helped load the cycle and secure it with nylon straps so it would not get "away" from me on the trip. Then I headed for Wisconsin with stops at a Motel 6 near Oklahoma City the first night and one near Kansas City the second night. With about five hundred miles to go the last day, I decided to stop off at Iowa City to see my old friends Tom and Berth Ann Werderitsch. I had not called ahead, just hoped to find them when I got there. Less than fifty miles before Iowa City I noticed in the rear view mirror that one of the straps had come loose or broken. I was on Interstate 80 so I put on my flashers and slowed down to about fifty miles per hour hoping that nothing worse would happen and I could get some help in Iowa City. It was about 4:30 p.m. and I was three and a half hours from Hillsboro, so I decided to get a room in a motel and called Berth Ann from my room explaining my dilemma with the trailer and cycle.

"Why don't you get a good night's sleep and Tom and I will come over in the morning with some chains and/or ropes to secure the cycle for you," Berth Ann told me and set my mind at ease. What nice people they are; they called me in the morning and told me their plans and time frame for doing it in connection with his business responsibilities. They soon arrived and I went out to the trailer to provide moral support as there wasn't much else that I could do to help—Tom had it all in control. Then, to my delight, they invited me to join them in the nearby restaurant for breakfast—their treat! Boy, you CAN'T BEAT friends like that!!

With about two hundred miles left of the trip, I was on my way and it was nearly uneventful. I was quite surprised at one event. I was about twenty miles north of Dubuque, Iowa when a deer ran across the road forty yards in front of my car. Surprise!! When I was young and in school most of the deer population was in northern Wisconsin. Those we hunted were about thirty miles north of Hillsboro.

The summer was quite enjoyable and the facilities at Don and Mary's home were adequate for my needs. Don and I had some fun fishing and I had multiple chances to see relatives and old friends. In September the realtor called and stated that it did not appear that the buyers were going to make the deal on the house, so I planned to return to Big Spring in October for the winter in warmer weather. Some said that I had the best of both worlds and I could continue as a "snowbird" if my house did not sell. So, we loaded my cycle on the trailer and went back to Big Spring, Texas.

In the month before it got too cold I gathered pecans from under my pecan tree and gave them away, ate a few and sent some to Don and Mary. I also spent some time using my ONLY cooking skill—making peanut butter fudge!! I gave some of it away and a good friend told me I should sell that good stuff. So, I sold some and at least got back the cost of the ingredients plus a little profit. I still had my friends at church and developed a good relationship with people who own my favorite restaurant.

Suddenly it was May 1996 and I was preparing to go back to Wisconsin and the realtor did have some possible buyers for my house. By that time my Oldsmobile had way over a hundred thousand miles on it, but Cory had just put on a new alternator so I did feel fairly secure with it. Cory loaded my cycle on Smitty's trailer and, since I had told him of the strap breaking on the last trip, he chained the cycle to the trailer and said, "If that thing comes loose this time, I'll eat my hat" coining an old saying. I felt sure of his work being good like it always was when he worked on my cycle. I seemed hopeful that at my house would sell this time and I sure was not going to leave my cycle behind. No way!

This time the trip went smoothly and in three days I was again at Don and Mary's house enjoying a cooler summer (I thought). Many people in the Hillsboro area told me that the over one hundred degree heat in west Texas was not bad because it was/is a dry heat—I don't care if it is dry, hot is hot!! However, in June that year I was reminded of my youth when it got hot in Wisconsin—back when I sweat "like a horse" and could cool down when the temperature was hot and humidity was high. Well, that summer I was reminded of my youth as, unlike years earlier, they now have heat/humidity indexes that show effects of high humidity. The temperature got up around ninety-five or so and the humidity was ninety percent or higher causing the index to be around one hundred twenty, some places higher. It was hot and stuffy, but not any worse than when it's between one hundred five and one hundred fifteen in west Texas. The major problem with that sultry condition was that some cows and calves were dying on the dairy farms as well as some people, primarily elderly, in some places that did not have any air conditioning or a cooling mechanism (not even a fan).

Don and Mary taught me some things about their small business that they operated at home and I learned to take orders, call in orders, inventory products, disburse products and handle the paperwork for it. I enjoyed it, was fairly good at it and it gave me purpose; yes purpose, one of the main things that some retired people lose and the result of it is often *nothing to look forward to* which can be fatal! I felt important, was complimented by them and met some new friends through it all. It was like I had a new hobby. However, I did not forget my favorite summer pastime when the weather cooled off and Don and I went fishing a few times.

It was late August or early September when the call came in from my realtor. I had to return to Texas and take care of the business of selling my home. The same people who wanted to buy it the previous year were ready to make the deal now. I got a lot more money for the house than I paid for it, but no where near the total amount I had invested in it with all the improvements over the years. But, I was proud to be able to have a Veteran who was disabled in the war get to enjoy the accessibility of the home. I took care of business, had a sale of things I was not taking in the small trailer I needed to rent, gave what didn't sell to the church and moved the end of October. (Incidentally, I did return Smitty's trailer when I went back to Texas.)

Chapter Forty-Five

I rented a closed trailer from the same company that had a dealership in Hillsboro, Wisconsin so it would be easy to drop it off when I had it unloaded. Don, Mary and I worked out an agreement whereby I was not freeloading there and I went back to helping some with my newly acquired hobby (the business). Off and on we talked about the possibility of building on to the house where I could have my own place and they tried hard to make things good for me. The winter slipped by—time flies when you are busy and having fun—and during it I had opportunity to see my great-niece, Jenni, play basketball in high school. She was a good athlete in volleyball, basketball and track. In the spring she set a school record in the two hundred meters race. That was really neat because at that time there were three generations of Potters who held records in track and field. Don and Mary's son, Jeff, held and still holds the school record in the high hurdles. He participated in the State Meet also and did quite well. So, Jenni, Jeff and old uncle Jim all had school records, at the same time! Currently (2003), only two Potters have the records as a couple years ago my discus record was broken by a student who just happened to be State Champion in wrestling at the heavyweight level for the Division III school size. He was six foot, four inches and weighed about two hundred sixty pounds—nearly all muscle. I worked with him some that spring at school trying to get him to master the spin move that had added some twenty feet on to my throws back in high school. He tried it many times but never got comfortable with it, so I went to the meet to watch him throw the discus. He tried the spin the first throw and did not do so well; then he just pulled back and threw it about six feet farther than my best throw—and he did it almost flat-footed!! I was proud for him and congratulated him on taking over the record. I told him, "Well, that record has only been there for thirty-nine years, it's about time someone broke it—records are made to be broken!!"

Shortly after moving back to Hillsboro I had a strange experience that was actually quite ironic. I went to the local Piggly Wiggly store to buy a few things and the owner, a man I hadn't seen in about thirty years, came up to me and spoke to me. What he said was not "Hi, Jim" or "Hello" or "Is there something I can find, for you?" What he said was, "Damn good basketball player, sure got screwed at La Crosse." You never know how different people with whom you have an acquaintance over the years will remember you, but he remembered me mainly from the previously detailed "bad call by the referees" in the basketball game HHS lost to Reedsburg in the 1961 Sectional Tournament. I guess it is logical that he would remember me that way as I am sure he saw me more times on the basketball court than anywhere else; he was a good fan and attended often.

One important thing I had to do within a few months after my return to Wisconsin was arrange for a new cardiologist and urologist. I met my new cardiologist at the Gundersen Lutheran Clinic in La Crosse, Wisconsin after calling and getting an appointment. We discussed my medications and my situation regarding the lack of feeling and he scheduled some tests. He made a change in my medicines and each year I have tests to check on my condition since I have no normal feeling. A few years ago an angio-gram showed some partial blockage and he did the angioplasty to clear it up. The last couple years my tests have shown the heart condition staying the same.

I was "spoiled" by my urologist and his examination room in Texas. I was always scheduled for treatment in the same room at the clinic—the room with the low and well padded examination/ treatment table/bench with electric adjustments. This was the very same table used to examine women in their latter months of pregnancy and it had the stirrups to prove it. It was excellent for me as I could get on and off it independently, it was also wide enough that I could comfortably take my pants down and dress myself after treatment. Unfortunately I didn't have the same experience with the urologist at Gundersen Clinic.

After making an appointment with a urologist at Gundersen Clinic I had expectations similar to the ones I had in Texas. As I waited in the waiting room I told the receptionist that I might need some help getting onto the treatment table if it was too high. I don't know if that message was transferred to the doctor assigned to me, but when I got into the room the need for "muscles" was obvious to me. I "love" their first question and believe me I have heard it way too many times in doctors' offices or treatment rooms. That proverbial question is, "Mr. Potter, can you stand up at all?" to which I usually reply, "No, I haven't done that in thirty-six years," and, "You are going to have to get a couple husky fellows to get me up on that high table safely." Soon two men arrive and, feeling totally helpless, I start to pray: "God, please help them get me on the table without bruising my buttocks area." Then, once on the thinly padded table I have the feeling that I am going to fall off any minute. The table is so narrow that, as I lay on my back, there isn't any room beside me to rest my arms! Usually, I feel like an able-bodied person would feel lying on a four inch wide balance beam and sometime during the treatment session the doctor's assistant says, "Will you be all right there while I go to that cabinet to get something?" Fear of an untimely muscle spasm overcomes me and once again my life is in God's hands. Many broken bones would I have if a spasm caused me to fall off the table and meet the floor about forty inches below!!

When I saw the doctor I told him that I thought I needed a bladder neck dilation based on my past years of treatment, symptoms of inadequate bladder drainage and the fact that I had taken antibiotics for a while to clear up, at least temporarily, an infection therein. So he did a systoscope, which is an insertion of a piece of equipment, with which the doctor can see the inside of the bladder to check for stones or other problems. I guess he was also dilating the bladder neck (some) at the same time. When he was done my focus was on how I would get my new condom on and would I be embarrassed if I had to get help from one of the two young beautiful gals that assisted him. Thus, I forgot to tell the doctor to give me a shot of an antibiotic since I had just had a "foreign object" inside my bladder, which always results in infection and DID that time. Actually it took a day or two to develop into a full blown bladder infection, but once it got going it was a real doozy. It took two weeks of antibiotics to get over it.

It's terrible to be afraid to go to a doctor because of the chance that I might fall off the treatment table and break bones or kill myself. After over two years of ignoring the problem as though I erroneously thought it would go away by itself, I finally called the Services Representative at Gundersen Clinic to see about getting a low examination table put in the Urology Department. The woman said she would relay my message to the Adult Disability Coordinator with whom I plan to speak soon.

I had a related experience with regard to the afore mentioned time when I burned my right thigh with hot coffee. The exam table at the Hillsboro Clinic was too high for me to transfer onto without help and when I transferred with help, one of those helpers injured their back. That clinic has since gotten two lower tables which will make me happy when needed and save their backs from pain or injury.

Because I had smoked cigarettes since the summer of 1962 except for the short period from my accident until I went to Rehabilitation (about four months), I asked the Urologist caring for me at the time if he thought I should quit smoking. I told him that I have had to give up a lot of things I enjoy and I would like to keep smoking since I did enjoy that. I told the doctor that I was concerned about getting cancer and he said, "You'll die of kidney infection long before you'll die of cancer." So, my bladder and kidney functions should be given a high priority—equal or more important than my heart care. Thus, I should be regularly checked by a Urologist and not be fearful of injury.

Yes, I guess kidney infection is the thing that will kill me and I am reminded of it almost daily. You see, the urinary system is very prone to infection due to the poor drainage of the bladder. In the spinal cord injured person with an indwelling catheter, there is constant infection and they take medication for it on a regular basis. In my situation there seems to be a constant "low-grade" infection that flares its ugly head more often that I like to admit: probably due to me not drinking enough water, AND the lack of complete bladder drainage as an able-bodied person would have or a person with an indwelling catheter would have. Consequently, I wake up quite often in the night due to what is usually severe sweating that is my body telling me that the bladder is not draining. My first question is, Why not? And, I start to go through my list of possible causes. Is it a bladder stone lodged in the urethra, is it cloudy urine that does not flow easily, or is it a kink in the urethra from the position in which I was lying? Then as I turn to my back and stimulate the bladder to drain it, the flow begins and I am relieved of the concern and the sweating. Therefore, the obvious cause was a kink in the urethra and I am grateful that it was not something more serious.

Muscle spasms are usually called cramps for an able-bodied person and we often see them in athletic events where the participants are expending a great amount of energy in a warm and humid environment. They usually become dehydrated and one big result is cramping legs. My cramps are different. On the bright side, they could be beneficial in that they grip the vessels and force blood back up toward the heart and provide some increase in circulation—something lacking in a paraplegic. However, spasms can be a real pain like the times when I do wheelchair pushups for arm exercise and to relieve pressure from my butt—sometimes they are triggered by my change in position and nearly throw me out of the wheelchair. These are solid gripping spasms.

Sometimes spasms are the rapid jerking type causing the legs to shake like the arms of a man running a jackhammer or (I imagine) shooting a machine gun. Sometimes the spasms work like the sweating and are indicative of something wrong. For example, a few times I had a fever and when I went to bed at night the spasms just jerked and jerked keeping me awake for more than an hour. Sometimes after having the spasms I have learned that the reason was that my bowels were somewhat constipated or over loaded—I was "full of it" literally. Sometimes I have discovered that the spasms are an indication that I have a bladder infection as the spasms are triggered when I stimulate the bladder to drain it in the morning before changing the condom. When the spasms are jerking the bladder won't drain and at times it takes an extra half hour to drain the bladder causing me to be late for work or some other appointment, in the past.

Spasms can also have a detrimental affect on skin care of the feet. Nearly every morning when I awaken and turn over to my side, one leg or the other starts to jerk causing the feet to rub together. I try to keep the toe nails clipped quite short, but there is still the possibility of the nails scratching the skin of the other foot. That can easily result in breakdown and a sore that is not easily healed. In my older age, recently, I have been wearing my socks at night to hopefully solve this problem—doesn't keep them from rubbing, but does protect against the nails.

Now, I bet you are thinking, "Boy, that guy must have stinky feet wearing his socks twenty-four hours a day like he does!!" Well, remember me telling you about *not* sweating when the temperature is ninety or a hundred degrees, that also applies to my feet with socks on them. They don't sweat!! Thus, my feet do not stink!

It was fairly cool in June 1997 and I started actively looking for an apartment that would fit my needs. I wanted to be independent again and after nearly nine months living with Don and Mary it was time for me to move out—just need to find that RIGHT place. "God works in mysterious ways, His wonders to perform," and that's how I found my new and current home. I went down to visit with a lady that I knew was in the housing business with her husband. They own a few homes in Hillsboro and I asked her about any that might be accessible enough to meet my needs. She did not have any then, but thought she might have a suitable one open up in the next month or so. I wasn't satisfied and was going to pursue some other avenues after lunch that day. We barely finished our noon meal when the phone rang and it was the lady I had just seen. She said, "Mike Helbing was in here (the office where she worked) this morning and he told me that he had an opening in his fairly new apartments in Union Center, would you be interested?" "Yes, how can I contact him?" I asked. "He's in the phone book under the Elroy numbers," she said. "Thank you very much, I'll let you know what I find out," I responded.

Without too much effort I was able to locate Mike and set up an appointment to see the empty apartment for rent. I took my folding wooden six-foot ruler and went to check it out. The apartment had one neat feature for me—a garage inside the structure. My heart thumped with anticipation when I measured the width of the garage, as I needed width to be able to get my long door open on the passenger side to get my wheelchair in and out—eleven feet was the tally. Now, I have to measure my car width with the door all the way open. On the way to the kitchen a built in washer/dryer also caught my fancy. Next I loved the open space of the kitchen, dining and living areas all connected and wide open—no walls inside, no doors, just open—a wheelchair users dream come true! As with previous homes in Big Spring I found that the hallway was too narrow for my 'chair to make the turn into the bathroom—the bathroom door was thirty-two inches, wide enough to go through straight, but not by making a sharp corner. I questioned Mike about it and he said they would make it usable by changing the door to a thirty-six inch door. "Will you be able to use it, if I make that change?" "Yes, it may be a little tight, but I surely believe I will be able to negotiate it," I added, "Then later we will have to see about some bars to put up along the back wall of the tub/shower." "OK, we can do that," he said. Then I said, "Let me measure my car and get back to you, if it measures good for a fit in the garage I want to rent this place; could I move in the first of July or near then?" He agreed and I went home to find the car narrow enough to fit, so I rented it.

Chapter Forty-Six

I moved into the apartment on July 3, 1997 and it is still my home. It is quite conveniently located being just a half block from the Kwik Trip convenience store and one and a half blocks from Dave and Jerita's Center Tap—both easily within rolling distance in my wheelchair when I feel energetic and it's not too hot or cold. I buy a few things at the convenience store every week and, since I don't drink, I mostly go to the Center Tap to see people, eat lunches and other meals. My new home is also nicely located about halfway in between my brother's home and my sister's home. Being the youngest of siblings it seems only proper to me, maybe ironic, that the "little brother" lives in the same proximity to them as I was as a child in the back seat of the car going fishing or somewhere else: stuck in the middle!

Since moving out of Don and Mary's house my relationship with them has not changed. I still went there to help with the business until the system changed and my services were not needed—once again progress has taken away another 'job". I am still considered by them to be part of the "family" as I am included in all Christmas and birthday parties, invited often for meals or table games, Don and I continue fishing together and they (Don and Jeff) have gotten me back into doing some hunting. More on that later.

When the spring of 1998 rolled around my brother and nephew were very concerned about the longevity of my '79

Oldsmobile! I guess I was a little leary of its dependability as it now had over 145,000 miles on the odometer. I always have to look for specific types of cars so they will fit my needs and my nephew had seen one for sale that was an '85 Buick LeSabre he thought would work for me. It had bucket seats which I hate, but I liked it and got a foam pad covered to put across the whole front making it more functional for my movement from the passenger side to driver's side and vice-versa. It had a modest 74,000 miles on it and I drove it for three years averaging about ten thousand miles per year. I then sold the Olds for about thirty percent of the cost of the Buick.

The Buick had nearly 110,000 miles on it and the rust (it had a lot when I got it) was really taking a toll on the doors and the bottom in general. So, in 2001 my niece's husband found a nice clean, rust-free Cadillac, 1989 model with 111,000 miles on it and it ran like a top (as they old saying goes). I put the front seat pad in it from the Buick and the bucket seats are not so bad to cope with. I hope it will last another few years and be near the age of many other cars I have had to "retire".

It was in 1999 when Don and I were fishing in our favorite fishing spot—a place where we usually caught fish in the past and sometimes eight or ten different species. It was in a section of the old main channel of the Yellow River. There was a high bank above the water on which I parked after Don wheeled me down a slope from the car. About four o'clock that day I had a hit on a minnow and the float went down rapidly with the fish taking it away from the bank. As the line became tight I jerked to set the hook and it felt like I was hooked for a second on a post—it felt that heavy, but as soon as I felt it, it was gone and so was my minnow. I put on another minnow and threw it in the same original spot.

I waited, and waited. Then, as if lightening had struck, the float disappeared just as it did before and I repeated my hook-setting technique with a little more energy applied. This time I hooked him good and the battle was on. He went east, west, north and south at will and after about five minutes of keeping a tight line on him he began to tire. By that time Don had responded to my "fish on" call and was standing beside me patiently waiting with the landing net to net the fish. He had to get down on his knee to reach the water with the net and then had difficulty getting the fish to cooperate and swim into the net. After seeing the fish he realized that the usual "let the fish swim over the net and lift up" was not going to work as the fish was way too long to go into the net that way. He knew he had to scoop him head first and hope he got the bulk of the heavy body in the net before he lifted. As the fish tired some more, he finally was able to land it. It was the thirty-five inch, approximately ten pound northern pike shown in the picture below!

My biggest Northern

The fishing hole where I caught that nice northern pike was and is fondly called our "honey hole" by Don and I. The next spring we went across the Buckhorn Bridge and north toward the honey hole. When we got to the entry area beside a boat dock, we discovered that the trail back nearly a quarter mile to the honey hole was blocked with dirt mounds a big gate with a padlock on it and a sign that read, "No Trespassing, Hunting or Fishing past this point" and it was signed by the Landowners

Association who owned the property. Needless to say, we were very upset. So, we fished in another place with very little success that day.

The next day I called the number that was on the sign and a couple days later I drove about eighty miles round trip trying to talk to the Landowner—no luck. That property stayed blocked off for two years and then the Dept. of Natural Resources, State of Wisconsin received ownership of the land. Now the trail is still blocked off, but we could walk in and fish in our honey hole. The aggravation is not worth it. Don would have to make at least two trips, one to carry in all the equipment and another to push me down that quarter mile road which many times would be impossible due to large dips in the road that have often contained water at least a foot deep.

I decided to "take the bull by the horn" and went to talk with the Manager of Buckhorn State Park of which the honey hole was now a part. I had no success and the best he could do is suggest that I use the Handicapped Peer which was farther down in the park and easily accessible for wheelchair travelers. The Peer is at the end of a fairly long walkway over water and sits out in the direct sun. Therefore, it is no good to me on a sunny day even if the shade temperature is only in the seventies—I got too hot both times we tried using that peer. And, we only caught a couple striped bass when we did fish there. So much for special fishing spots. Also, whoever constructed the fishing peers with a railing to lean against having a sloped board with holes to stick the end of your rod into, must have never had a rod and reel in their hand much less ever done any fishing. Whoever heard of fishing with the rod tip about twelve feet above the water—even a slight breeze could blow the slack line into the next township!!

In late 1999, Jerita Brandfort and I gathered together a few of the concerned citizens of Union Center and developed a group with the focus on improving the little park in the Village. We called the group the Union Center Betterment Club since that was really what we have tried to do—make it a better place to live. We have named the park, Eagle Parkway, with suggestions coming from children of the Wonewoc-Center Grade School. We have financed some improvements in the Parkway through the efforts of many people helping with our annual Party in the Parkway held each September. We have also conducted bake sales before Thanksgiving annually and a Chili Cookoff and Euchre Tournament in February. Our biggest event was combined with the Chili Cookoff a couple years ago when we had a benefit for a local woman fighting cancer. The outpouring of LOVE at that event brought tears to my eyes and greatly helped the woman.

Chapter Forty-Seven

My nephew, Jeff Potter, has been extremely helpful in getting me back into some hunting—an activity that I enjoyed some in my able-bodied years. I had heard about a Disabled Permit that allows a person with severe disability in terms of mobility to shoot a gun from a vehicle parked along a country road (not main highway) or in a field off the road. The first couple years after I got the permit I went deer hunting during rifle season with no success. When you have no ability to swing a rifle around to fire at a moving target, you have to be lucky and have the deer come into range and stop in order to get a realistic shot at it. Those first years I had some deer run by bobbing and weaving at their usual speed of thirty miles per hour or faster—no chance. Then my third year hunting I was thrilled when a deer stopped about two hundred yards away, I took aim and was able to drop it with one shot. It was a big doe and that year the Department of Natural Resources was encouraging a large deer kill by giving out many doe permits to hunters. Two days later I had another chance at about one hundred forty yards and had the same result—renewed my confidence in accuracy with a rifle.

In connection with the Disabled Hunter Permit is the right to use a crossbow for hunting deer. After discussion with Jeff and Don I bought one with a fair amount of power but not a real good one. I wanted to limit my investment in case I could not use it well or, since I had to get a strong person to draw the string back to cock it, I might not find someone to cock it for me and Jeff and Don were both working at most of the times I wanted to use it. After using it for a couple years with some success, I decided to get a bigger one, Quad 300, with a crank on it for cocking it. Then, in the year 2000, Jeff shared a beautiful idea with me.

Jeff had talked about hunting wild turkey and how much of a rush it was to call them in close enough to shoot with a shotgun. He showed me his twenty gauge shotgun, a single shotgun without much weight—easily handled by me in spite of my limited balance, but I still needed a rest in order to shoot it with accuracy. Jeff's idea and his enthusiasm led me to some experiences that are detailed in the seven articles that I wrote in the third person and were printed in the Hillsboro Sentry Enterprise newspaper in 2000, 2001, and 2002. They are reprinted here:

More than one way to call in a turkey

By "Fine as a Frog Hair"

"I wish there was some way I could go out in the woods and hunt deer and turkeys like able-bodied hunters." Jim Potter made this statement periodically the past few years since he moved back to this area to be near relatives. He did not hunt at all for 30 years after his disabling accident in 1966, but did go to graduate school and work in the recreation therapy field for 24 years while living outside of Wisconsin.

"Why not?" said Jeff Potter, Jim's nephew, a few months ago, "Why don't we build a hunting shack on wheels so we can move it where we want it?" Jim replied,

"I'll go for that! Even though I've had successful hunting from my car and appreciate the Disabled Hunters Permit, I'd just like to do it more like 'normal' people."

At the beginning, as with most projects, there were more questions than answers. Where can you find a small trailer you can adapt to your needs? Would a modified fishing shack work'? How high will it be off the ground? How will it be ramped? How many and what size shooting holes (windows) are needed? What kind of roof? What material to use for a light weight, yet sturdy, shack? Where to put the door? How to make it stable (on two wheels) and level—on uneven ground?

Well, these and a few more questions have been answered and the proof is in the picture printed with this article.

Jim wishes to express his sincere thanks to his brother, Don Potter, and nephew, Jeff Potter, for their ideas, hours of work, and financial help. Thank you to his brother-in-law Ray Manguilli, for his carpenter skills, some materials, his work and use of his tools. Thank you to Lyle Janousek and Jim Johnson of Horstmann Industries for welding and fabrication supplies. Thank you to Dick Minett and Friske Farms for the use of their barns for storage. Thank you to Heding Trucking for the use of their truck wash bay during construction periods. Thank you to Rich Bell for shingles. Thank you to Dan Saunders for trailer wheels. Thank you to Doris Picha and Picha Furniture for the carpet. Last, but not least, thank you to God for the gift of life and the enjoyments that are possible.

Make a wish foundation? Jim thinks so!

The Hunting Shack

' . . . what a monster gobbler!

By "Fine as a Frog Hair"

Jim Potter slept a little later than desired on May 1, 2000 two days before his season for turkey hunting started. After driving past a few hunting spots where he had seen a jake, a tom and a hen in three separate locations, he arrived at his "observatory" at 9:30 am. This spot was some 400 yards from his new hunting shack now placed near the woods for wildlife to become comfortable with their new neighbor.

With binoculars he saw four crows feeding in the meadow near the "shack." Then, in the small visible grassy area to the right of the shack, a dark object appeared in view to the naked eye. "Could it be?" he said as he picked up the binoculars, "Oh my God, what a monster gobbler!" It walked slowly and sternly (out of view) past the front of the shack and into the clear area. It stopped—fanned out like it was King Kong—what a sight. Again it moved to the left giving a perfect profile and a beard nearly dragging on the ground. For the next 10-15 minutes it repeatedly fanned, then walked a few feet.

At about 10:10 Jim shifted his binocular view up the hill where the tom appeared to he heading. There, a hen had emerged from the woods and was only about 20 yards from the tom. The behaviors for the next 20 minutes seemed analogous to the timid ritual of a quiet mannered teenager (in the 1950's) in quest of his first date to go to the movie at the local theater. The hen played hard to get—the tom strutted and fanned, then moved closer. She'd move closer, then away some—keeping a teasing distance between them.

Through the whole ordeal, the tom and the hen gradually moved up the grassy hill to where it corners the woods to the north and the east. At the closest point these two appeared to get within 6 or 8 feet of each other. At 10:25 the hen slipped into the woods and some ten yards away the tom did likewise. He was last seen at 10:30 a.m. a few yards into the woods and all fanned out again.

This was probably better than any movie Jim has ever seen!

Early turkey hunting lesson

By "Fine as a Frog Hair"

With assistance from his brother Don, Jim Potter was settled in his hunting shack about 6:00 a.m. opening day of his 5-day season. He felt quite smug knowing he was very well hidden from the extremely keen eyesight of turkeys. Within fifteen minutes of his arrival, he knew for sure how well hidden he was as the pasture around him was peppered with crows showing no fear.

His hen turkey decoy was placed some 20 yards in front of the shack at the edge of the woods. Soon he wished to have his camera instead of the shotgun as (within about 10 minutes) a total of 4 gray squirrels and 2 fox squirrels were observed together playing and eating—all within 3 yards of the decoy. He thought of "Ring around the rosey," but this was "Squirrels around the decoy." What a neat sight!

At 6:35 a.m. a large dark object was seen in the woods heading toward the decoy. It emerged from the woods about a yard to the left of the decoy. It was a large jake. Strangely, it appeared to take one look at the decoy and realize its artificial nature. It walked off to Jim's left until it entered the 'blind spot"—the area between the end opening and side opening where the hunter can see nothing. Jim quietly rolled his wheelchair to a position where he could look out the side opening where the jake was headed. No jake! Where did he go? Jim shifted back to the end opening just in time to see the jake walk right in front of him just ten yards away. Buck fever? No, but Jim was too hidden!! The camouflage netting covered with artificial leaves was over the opening with only a two-inch gap at the bottom for his gun. "Jeff told me not to put the gun out the opening if the turkey is broadside to me as the turkey will see me and run," Jim thought. Hindsight says he could have rolled his wheelchair back a little and shot the jake right through the camouflage netting but he waited. The jake walked tall right past the front to the right side and then angled back toward and into the woods leaving nothing but his rear end as a target. "That's just one bird and there are hundreds, even thousands more," Jim said to himself as he poured a cup of coffee and calmed his nerves a bit.

The next three hours were nearly uneventful. The squirrels that scampered into the woods at the advent of the jake never returned to play by the decoy. Some sixty or seventy yards up the hill to Jim's left a hen, then a tom left the woods for a little period of feeding in the pasture. However, they never got close enough to Jim to get his blood flowing very fast.

The lesson for the day is you can have too much

camouflage—some of the leaf netting needs to be cut or folded to allow more room for shooting.

Adjustments for turkey hunter

By "Fine as a Frog Hair"

As with any facet of life, in the sporting events a continual process of adjustments is a major key to success. Pitchers make adjustments to hitters the second time they bat and batters make adjustments to pitchers the same way. Likewise the hunter, after an unsuccessful outing, needs to make adjustments. Sometimes they work, sometimes they don't.

Jim entered the shack at 5:00 a.m. (not 6:00) with brother Don placing not one, but two decoys—a hen and a jake near the woods and with scissors in hand clipped away a small part of the lower edge of the window camouflage. Jim figured that if the jake couldn't see him when he walked by just a watermelon seed spittin' distance from the window he must be too camouflaged. As daylight arrived, Jim took the scissors and began to increase his shooting area and his visibility, maybe not enough yet.

During the first hour a few crows mingled around feeding in the pasture grass by the shack. Ironically, there were no signs of squirrels as was the case previously.

Jim peered out the narrow left side opening—off on the knoll about a football field distance away stood a big tom, apparently eyeing the hen and jake decoys and he was all fanned out showing his majesty. Jim stole a peek at his watch, 6:35 a.m.

His heart was jump-started with anticipation. The bird was headed toward the decoys just as the hunter hoped. It advanced a few yards, then fanned, and repeated this behavior until it got within about thirty yards of the shack. Jim waited, thinking and hoping the gobbler would continue its path to get a close look at what that jake (decoy) was doing so close to "his" hen (decoy). Toms don't like jakes messing around with "their" women.

The front opening of the shack was taller (14 inches tall) and two feet wide with camouflage covering only the top half while the side openings were only 8 inches tall and 3 feet wide with only about a 3 inch clear opening below the camouflage.

As the turkey proceeded toward the decoys, Jim lost sight of it in the "blind spot" between the left opening and the front opening. He was ready—heart was thumping as he intently looked out the front hole. "When will that tom appear? Gee that's a nice big tom," he thought. It didn't show up.

"Where is he?" Jim waited. Seemed like an hour, but was only 5-10 minutes. Then he rolled his chair back to the left opening only to see the tom slowly heading back up the hill some 35 yards away angling toward Jim's left. Jim leaned forward and put the gun out the hole, he then wished he had cut out more of the opening as a dark area of the camouflage covered his gun sights.

He adjusted the gun and thought of the old saying, "you'll never get anything if you don't shoot," and drew a bead. POW!! Missed that small target at 40 yards and the tom ran over the hill.

That's why they call it "hunting" instead of "going to shoot a turkey!"

An hour or so later, two hens were seen out the right opening as they grazed in the meadow—no toms behind them.

'Success at last' on the 4th day

By "Fine as a Frog Hair"

Jim didn't go to the shack on Day 3. After shooting

at one on Day 2, he consulted his "guide" (nephew Jeff) who has 100 times more turkey hunting experience than Jim. Jeff said, "Give it a rest for one day and I'll call for you on Saturday." Great! Jim needs all the help he can get! More adjustments!

By 5:15 Saturday morning Jim and his guide were in the shack with no decoys, just one very good turkey caller. Jim was excited—as he thought—now this is the real deal, only thing that might make this better is if Jim knew how to call and could do it all himself. But, as previously stated, admit it Jim, you need all the help you can get!

Daylight is approaching and Jeff says, "I am going to step outside and give those toms a wake up call." He did. "Gobble, Gobble, Gobble, Gobble, Gobble, Gobble. "That should do it," he said as he got back inside of the shack and told Jim he could have a cup of coffee and move a little for a few minutes. Every slight (usually unnoticeable) noise of Jim shifting in his wheelchair was magnified in the shack like sounds amplified in an empty silo. It made Jeff nervous. "Be quiet," he whispered, "you sure are noisy." Soon Jeff began his series of hen calls. They waited. Jeff called. They waited. Jeff called. They waited.

Sometime after six o'clock a hen appeared on the same knoll that the tom arrived on Day 2. The guide told Jim to get ready as "things could happen fast now." The hen was moving at a fast walk/slow run pace and heading toward the area by the front of the shack. "Hear those blue jays?" Jeff whispered. "It's going down," he said sounding like he and Jim were stake out police officers about to interrupt a big heist. The blue jays screeched again "Hear those blue jays?" he repeated very quietly and Jim whispered. "Yes, I did!" He hardly had those words out when "There he is," came from his partner. The tom only stopped a couple times to fan out and covered about eighty yards fairly quickly as it pursued the hen now located somewhere in front of the shack or maybe in the woods already, but who cares? Four eyes were on the tom who slowed to a "one step at a time" pace leaving its head and neck continually going up and down as it moved inside of thirty yards away. It was out that same "window" that Jim had missed a longer shot on Day 2 and that surely went through his mind. Jeff whispered, "Get ready. I'll hold this camouflage up and you'll have a better chance." "Wish he'd stop." Jim responded. "I better take him before he gets to the blind spot." POW! The bird took off running across the pasture but was obviously injured. In seconds Jeff had the fasteners pulled and the door open—he was gone—running like the track star he was in high school, after that bird. Somewhere over the hill two or three hundred yards away his long legs won the race and with his hands he finished off the twenty-one pound, 10 1/2 inch beard turkey. Success, at last!

Hindsight is always 20-20 as Jim and Jeff rehashed the experience. "If I would have just gave a "putt" when the tom was walking he would have stopped and gave you a better shot," Jeff told Jim. Jim thought here we have yet another lesson in the old adage. "Use your head and save your feet!"

Waiting for "Tom" pays off for a turkey hunter

By "Fine as a Frog Hair"

Some of you may remember reading a series of five articles by this writer about a homemade portable hunting "shack" and Jim Potter hunting turkeys last year. Well, that wasn't the end of it. He received permits to hunt the 4th and 6th seasons this year which came about on the first and third week of May, 2001.

Thus, early in April the shack was parked and leveled with sturdy steel levelers in about the same spot as previously—in the pasture about 20 yards from a fence row at the edge of the woods. The fence row has a frequented turkey route along it in the pasture. The turkeys had ample time to learn to accept this harmless object in their "frontyard" prior to hunting seasons.

Although the shack was conceived as a means for Jim to hunt "normally" from his wheelchair, it was a family project and brother Don, nephew Jeff and Jim all planned to use it at some time.

So, it was no surprise to Jim when Don and Jeff used it during heavy rains on a day in Don's season #1. Jeff called and Don waited with excited anticipation. Soon it happened—a line of 8-10 hens, one behind the other followed by a tom, came over the crest of a large knoll in the pasture straight (at half-running speed) toward the decoys. The parade passed about 25 yards from the shack and Don had a bead on the fast moving tom but desired a better shot for a cleaner kill. "Make that tom stop," he told Jeff. "Putt," came from Jeff s mouth. The 21# tom stopped "on a dime" and dropped "in his tracks." Don calmly (Ha-Ha!) ejected the spent shotgun shell and blew the smoke from the barrel. Another successful hunt.

Soon May arrived and Jim was in the shack on three of the five mornings. The first two times he saw many hens, once ten at a time, and toms "talked" to him and the hens. One tom sounded like he was about 30 yards in the woods (50 yards away) and he gobbled periodically, but Jim only heard 2 different hens call to him, one time each. The hens ate bugs and worms within 40 yards of the shack for about an hour. Occasionally one hen slipped into the woods for about 10 minutes or so and then returned to the pasture, but tom never came out in the open.

On the last day in the shack for the season only three hens were seen, but one tom was out in the pasture. One hen picked at food about 20 yards away along the woods edge. The tom arrived from the right on a knoll some 100 yards away. Two hens were in an area near the tom. One of them went behind the knoll and was not seen again. One slowly worked its way towards the area in front of the shack and the tom followed part way. Then the hen eased back up the knoll and with the tom disappeared out of sight. Time passed. Finally, with the one hen still eating rear the woods edge in front of the shack, the tom slowly came down the slope near the woods. Jim thought, "If he just comes down by that hen, I'll get a good shot." Suddenly, about 60 yards away he began a straight line perpendicularly away from the woods. This finally put him about 35-40 yards from Jim's gun barrel. He appeared frightened by something and was very cautious with his moves. He stopped and seemed to puff his chest. Jim figured this *35* yard shot was the best he was going to get, so he took a solid aim at those red waddles and squeezed the trigger. Feathers flew and so did the bird showing no sign of harm. The end of that day's hunt had arrived.

Brother Don had been observing with binoculars some 400 yards away and told Jim later that the bird flew about a quarter mile landing somewhere at the edge of a neighbor's woods. He also observed (just after Jim's shot) a big dominant tom running down the valley behind the shack. It probably had been up there close enough to intimidate the other tom and make it act so weird prior to Jim shooting at it. Oh, Jim hit the bird, probably in the chest that is multi-layered with feathers, as many feathers were found at the spot of the shot. Lesson: A 20-guage single shot with 3 inch #5 Turkey-Load shells kills a big tom much better at 20-25 yards. Lesson 2: Maybe Jim needs to learn to use a "call" him-self. Maybe he would have had that big dominate tom up by the shack—if he could call it—maybe!

With two unsuccessful hunts during the last Spring turkey hunting season behind him, Jim Potter met his "guide", "caller" and nephew Jeff at 4:45 a.m. on May 19 to head for the shack. By 5 a.m. they were settled in the shack and Jeff had made some preliminary calls. They waited until about 6 a.m. when a tom's gobble was sounded over the big knoll on the left side of the shack and about 200 yards away out of sight. Jeff called once—they waited—6:10 a.m. He called again—they waited.

Then at about 6:20 a.m. Jeff began with a startle, "There he is at the top of the knoll by the woods—100 yards—get ready Jim—he's comin'—cock that gun—get your balance and a good rest on the window."

The bird was coming down the fence row toward the decoys at a fast walk. Jim peered out the end window opening waiting for the bird to come into sight from the left. The tom stopped to fan a couple times and finally was in view at about "10 o'clock." Jim's gun was ready and he was still and the gun aimed at "12 o'clock". The tom stopped at about "11 o'clock" for (what seemed like) an eternity.

"I hope he keeps coming," said Jeff. He whispered, "Can you move the gun if you need to?" "Not very slowly with my lousy trunk balance," Jim answered.

Then, as if scripted for a play, the tom walked slowly and steadily with waddles as red as a fire engine and head blue as the sky straight to "12 o'clock."

Jim squeezed the trigger. The slightly less than 20 pounder (probably lost 5 pounds or more in mating season) had three beards totaling 26" in length. One spur was broken off probably from fighting. Maybe he was a lover and a fighter?!!

Until next time, I am . . ."Fine as a Frog Hair."

Three beards!

Turkeys learn once again: Beware of the shack! Potter team meets Toms in successful Spring hunt

By "Fine as a Frog Hair"

Before the biggest snowfall of the year (April 1st) Jim Potter's brother Don and nephew Jeff put the wheelchair ramped hunting shack in location for the spring hunts. It was letting the birds get adapted to it being there with no one in it and ready to be used by Jim and the others if rain made their hunting too miserable.

"I got my turkey permit—First week," Don told Jim in mid-March. "Did you get yours?" he asked. "Two," Jim replied. "How do you rate?" Don retorted with a slight hint of envy in his voice. "Good clean livin', ha-ha," said Jim "Jeff get his?" he asked. "Yes, finally did— got the second week, when are yours?" "The third and sixth weeks, just what I asked for," Jim said. (Later Jim thought, if you ask for a prime rib and a hamburger you are less likely to get it than if you ask for two hamburgers!) Don got his "tom" on his opening day and Jeff did the same so their seasons were over.

The evening before Jim's April 24th opening day, Jeff went near the shack to "put the birds to bed" as he calls it. "Two toms went to roost on that point to the north and another on a point to the south," he told them at 4:55 the next morning as Don prepared to help Jim into the shack. Jim got out of his car into his "old" wheelchair—the heavy duty chair that now has a portable little table that mounts to the front of the chair for a "rest" making it possible for Jim to shoot without sticking the gun barrel out of the window which might (would) scare away the turkeys if they saw him move it. He was in the shack and ready with a walky-talky—Don had the other one when he took Jim's car and went some four hundred yards away to observe and notify Jim if anything was coming around him that he could not see. There were four hen decoys placed between the shack and the woods (25 yards away).

5:36 a.m., first time to legally shoot, soon arrived but it was overcast and way too dark to shoot anything. Fifteen minutes later Don notified Jim that there was a hen in the pasture left of the shack going toward the woods. Jim didn't see it at first, it was too far behind him, but it later went by him about 70 yards away, then veered left and went on over a knoll and out of sight.

Jim decided it was time to "yelp" with the new call he had purchased the day before. "Yelp, yelp, yelp, yelp, yelp," squawked the little plastic box with a plunger in it. About 6:30 a.m., a hen emerged from the woods in front of Jim. It was a big hen and it fed a little until another hen came out of the same spot. Jim thought— bet there is a tom behind them—he was close to right as he spotted a jake coming toward the edge of the woods and out of it moving toward the second hen with haste like a teenage boy going to ask the "prettiest girl in school" to dance with him.

The jake got up real close behind the second hen and Jim thought—I better not look, might see something I shouldn't! But they just milled around between the decoys and slowly moved to the left side of the shack, temporarily out of sight. Then they slowly worked their way back in front of the shack and off to the right feeding on worms and bugs. Jim could have shot that jake on three of four occasions, but he wanted a tom.

As the three birds went over the knoll to the right he gave another series of four "yelps". Soon Don's voice came over their "P.A. system," "See that tom by the woods by your left?" "No," Jim said and then quickly. "Yes, it just walked into sight in front of me," he whispered and lay down the "phone."

It walked right between a decoy and the woods until it stopped—the result of a 20 gauge #5 shot turkey load. It flapped its wings a bit, but Jim knew it wasn't going anywhere because its head was in the dirt all the while. So he "got on the horn" and said, "Don, it's a done deal! Come and get me." It was 7:15 am. when he squeezed the trigger— 99 minutes into the season. That's better than having to wait until the 4th or 5th day as he has in the past!

Incidentally, there was another tom some five yards into the woods behind the one Jim shot. It appeared to be a little bigger than the 22.5 pounder Jim got, but he sure wasn't going to pass up the opportunity he had. Jeff surely was right—the two toms he "put to bed" the night before on the point off to the left were probably the same two that came onto the scene at 7:15!

2002 Turkey

P.S. The sixth season was worse than a "hamburger"—it was more like pieces of gristle in between two old moldy dry crusts. After three mornings in the shack, Jim saw no turkeys—not even a hen! But, he was very satisfied with his one bird for the spring hunts.

Chapter Forty-Eight

The preceding stories were written under the pen name of "Fine as a Frog Hair" a name that came from a saying I often used over the years when people asked me, "How are you?" and I replied with, "Fine, fine as a frog hair."

Now in my sixtieth year on this earth and my thirty-seventh year of living with my disability I am proud to be alive and still able to do a few things. Most mornings for the last ten years I thought and felt like I had a case of premature rigormortis setting into my body parts that I can feel; namely my neck, arms and shoulders. But fortunately, after getting up and moving about some, the stiffness and pain seems to gradually go away throughout the day's limited activities. My right arm is getting weaker and it has been my most valuable set of muscle for transfers to and from my wheelchair. I pray for an early spring so I can get out and get some more exercise than is offered me in the limited space of the apartment. That's no excuse though; I do have enough room to exercise if I would get the energy to do more of it. Once again it comes to ATTITUDE, because our actions usually follow our attitude.

It has been said by people smarter than I am that when we compare ourselves with others we may become vane and/or bitter. A comparison with someone who is very obviously "better off" than we are may make us bitter toward them; such as the feelings poor people have when around rich people. Likewise, when comparing to someone "worse off" than us we could have the tendency to get a "big head." However, I believe that comparing ourselves with others can be beneficial as it was with me when I was in Rehabilitation and when I was at the University of Illinois. In both situations I did not have to look very far to see a human being with a more disabling condition than my own. My response in these situations was simple: COUNT MY BLESSINGS! And I did. IF we learn to count our blessings, we can avoid the "pity pot" that many sit on all day long!

I cannot end this writing without including a few thoughts and beliefs that I have acquired and taught over the years. Personal adjustment refers to development of a positive self-image; it does not come to us automatically. Your interpretation of your own experiences is vital in the formation of your self-concept or, simply stated, your attitude about yourself. It is cyclical and spirals upward or downward depending on YOU! The cycle goes like this: Positive experiences *lead* to feelings of some success, *which lead to* a positive attitude, *which leads to* doing more things, *which leads to* more success, *which leads to* a more positive attitude, etc., etc. Failure to recognize successes and appreciate them for their true value usually is the cause of the spiral to go downward and the person doing less with less chance for success, less success, decreased self-image, more negative attitude, etc., etc. If a person is down and has hit "rock bottom" the only way to come out of it is by DOING SOMETHING!! There is no way a person can come up by sitting or lying around feeling sorry for yourself and, worse yet, having others around you feeling sorry for you!!

Worry is a waste of mental energy burned up regarding a situation that you have no control over, or a situation in which you have control over but are doing nothing about it! I believe that definition fits all forms of worry that all people experience. The Alcoholics Anonymous groups recite a prayer at each meeting that relates to this topic—God grant me the serenity to accept the things I cannot change, the courage to change the things I can and the wisdom to know the difference. To not worry is to have Faith and accept the things you cannot change. In every form of adjustment there is always change and in the case of accepting the things we cannot change we MUST change our attitude toward it and not let it have a detrimental effect on us. For those things we have control over, we need to make the necessary changes and not just procrastinate and hope the problem or situation will simply go away.

I have often heard, "I'm just worried sick about . . ."—all I say is "keep on worrying and you soon will be sick!!" Sometimes it's Faith in God, whatever you conceive Him to be; or Faith in yourself or Faith in your fellow human. However you look at it, when you quit *trusting* you have a heap of worries. What are you worried about today? QUIT IT!!

Since it is my nature to do so, I must finish on a positive note. Remember that Adult Disabilities Coordinator with whom I said I hoped to speak soon, the one from Gundersen Clinic in La Crosse; she called me the other day and told me that her research found "high-low" examination tables in many areas of the clinic with none found in Urology. She assured me that she would call me as soon as one is acquired and in place in the Urology Department; in July 2003 she confirmed it was done.

You, the reader, may have gleaned from the preceding pages that all of the results of a spinal cord injury are very negative. Contrary to common belief, there are a few exceptions that are positive. Some of these are:

1) Not having to "stand" in lines of over a hundred students waiting to register for specific classes in college—or not "standing" in any line while feet begin to hurt.
2) Not sweating under my arms—I have not had to buy and use underarm deodorant for many years.
3) Not having to get up to go to the bathroom in the middle of the night when the floor is ice cold in the winter.
4) Not stubbing my toes on various objects in the dark if I had to get up at night.

5) ALWAYS have a RESERVED SEAT no matter how large the crowd at an event!!
6) Feeling smug when at a long meeting my able-bodied peers begin to squirm and complain of having to sit for so long!!

"Today is the first day of the rest of your life." Make it a good one!

To Request Additional Copies or Comment on What You've Read:

Jim Potter
S1503
County Highway WW
Hillsboro, WI 54634

BVG